THE
VITAL LIE

THE

VITAL

LIE

REALITY
AND
ILLUSION
IN
MODERN
DRAMA

Anthony S. Abbott

The University of Alabama Press
Tuscaloosa • London

Library of Congress Cataloging-in-Publication Data

Abbott, Anthony S.

    The vital lie : reality and illusion in modern drama /
Anthony S. Abbott.
      p. cm.
    Bibliography: p.
    Includes index.
    ISBN 0-8173-0396-0 (alk. paper)
    1. Drama—20th century—History and criticism.
2. Drama—19th century—History and criticism.
3. Reality in literature. 4. Illusion in literature. I. Title.
PN1851.A23 1989
809.2′04—dc19   87-26286
                                    CIP

British Library Cataloguing-in-Publication Data is
available.

To the Memory of My Father

Howard Johnson Abbott

(1904–1982)

Contents

Contents

Preface:
The Vital Lie

Deprive the average man of his vital lie and you've robbed him of happiness as well.

—Dr. Relling in Ibsen's *The Wild Duck*

Shortly after his seventy-fifth birthday, my father suffered a slight stroke. His sister, with whom he lived, deduced that he was also suffering from drug withdrawal. He had been in a great deal of pain during the months preceding his collapse and was taking heavy doses of pain-killing drugs to numb himself. The trembling, the disorientation, the fantasies that dominated his life during the first two weeks of his recuperation must have been caused by withdrawal, she reasoned.

It so happened that I was in Princeton, New Jersey, working on this book during the period immediately after his attack and was able to visit him in the hospital and talk with him during these periods of disorientation. He was seized with the idea that he had committed some crime and had been sentenced to thirty days in jail. He knew that he was in the hospital, he knew who I was, and he knew that I was trying to arrange for my sisters to come and visit him. But he insisted for several days, without variation in the story, that the girls could not come and visit him because he would have to serve his sentence as soon as he was well enough. Nothing that I could say would convince him otherwise. He also believed that there was, at the hospital, a Russian plot in which some of the doctors were involved and that he was being watched and his behavior studied by certain unidentified men writing on clipboards. White hair waving, pale, thin, joints gnarled with arthritis, the old man fought his giants—tilted at windmills, Sancho Panza would say—for nearly a week before peace finally came to him.

And here I was in Princeton, some thirty miles away, trying to write something about the reality-illusion theme in modern drama. I had begun teaching the modern drama course in the mid-sixties, after having studied the discipline at Princeton and Harvard with Alan Downer, Robert Chapman, and Louis Kronenberger. I had become increasingly convinced that the reality-illusion theme was the dominant theme in modern drama, and I wanted to look at its beginnings in Ibsen and then trace its development over the hundred years or so to the present time. No one had really done that. I had read some marvelous books on modern drama—classic studies like Eric Bentley's *The Playwright as Thinker*, Robert Brustein's *Theatre of Revolt*, Richard Gilman's *The Making of Modern Drama*, and Arthur Ganz's *Realms of the Self*. I looked at important studies of more recent drama, books like Ruby Cohn's *Currents in Contemporary Drama*, and June Schlueter's *Metafictional Characters in Modern Drama*. Though I found them all enormously valuable, none of them did quite what I wanted to do; and so I set out on what has proved to be a long and complex journey, using these studies and my own teaching experience as guides and at the same time trying to incorporate the insights of studies that became available as I was working, studies like C. W. E. Bigsby's remarkable two-volume analysis of modern American playwrights and Keith May's excellent new book *Ibsen and Shaw*.

I did not want to write just another critical study. Rather, I wanted to write something that was critically competent but also personal, a book written by a human being for other human beings to read. I wanted to ask some questions in a tongue that any intelligent playgoer or reader of modern drama could understand.

First, I wanted to place the question—why? Why should the reality-illusion theme be so preeminent at this time? Secondly, I wanted to see if I could establish whether the way in which that theme is treated by playwrights has changed significantly during the last hundred years and whether the vision of reality presented by Albee, Pinter, and Genet is fundamentally different from that of Ibsen, Strindberg, and Shaw. Finally, I wanted to explore the relationship between art and life, between the dilemmas faced by the heroes of a number of modern plays and the problems of real human beings. Still, I did not know how to pose the central questions. My father's illness had some connection with all this. What was it?

We had often in the past read books together, and one book that had made a powerful impression on both of us was Ernest Becker's monumental study *The Denial of Death*. "The main thesis of this book," says Becker, "is that . . . the idea of death, the fear of it, haunts the human animal like nothing else; it is a mainspring of human activity—activity designed largely to avoid the fatality of death, to overcome it by denying in some way that it is the final destiny of man."[1]

I took the book from the shelf at the Princeton library and began rereading it. After I had read for a hundred pages or so, things began to fall into place. *Something or someone had led me to that book.* "Chapter Four: Human Character as a Vital Lie." It was a kind of literary and psychological detective story. If I could put it all together, I could find some explanation for my father's illness and at the same time find a central thesis for my book on reality and illusion. I began with the term *the vital lie.* In modern drama we first encounter it in Ibsen's *The Wild Duck* where Dr. Relling, who lives in the apartment below the Ekdal household, employs it to describe his treatment for the "demonic" Molvik and for the play's central figure, the photographer and would-be inventor, Hjalmar Ekdal. By "vital lie" Relling means an illusion created by a physician (himself in this case) to give the patient the idea that he is special or important. To transfer the idiom to Becker's terms, a vital lie enables a man to feel that he is a hero, a somebody, "an object of primary value in the universe."[2]

Becker elaborates on the concept in a way that goes far beyond anything the good Dr. Relling had in mind. Relling sees Hjalmar and Molvik as failures, "average" men who would not be able to continue living without this boost to their egos. Becker sees *all* men as subject to vital lies. "The hostility to psychoanalysis in the past, today, and in the future, will always be a hostility against admitting that man lives by lying to himself about himself and about his world, and that character . . . is a vital lie."[3] The term itself he defines a few pages later as "a necessary and basic dishonesty about oneself and one's whole situation."[4]

Becker's contention may be summed up as follows: man fears death, he understands intuitively that he is a paradox, a dualism half divine, half perishable, "a god who shits," says Becker. He cannot face the full reality of his position. He sees himself as small, physically and morally inadequate to face the decisions of adult society; he is overpowered by the awesomeness of the external world. If he had to face all that continually, he would go mad or die. So he creates structures, conventions, games, pastimes to help him forget. He becomes immersed in the roles that he learns from the time he is a small child. All these structures are part of the vital lie, the lie, says Becker, "that we have fashioned in order to live securely and serenely."[5]

When these patterns are broken, we suffer. If we are strong, exceptionally strong, we may grow through this suffering. More often than not we may be so hurt by the breakdown of these patterns that we either create new ones as quickly as possible or fall into despair at the thought of having to face life naked. What had happened to my father, I conjectured, was that his structures had broken down. He had sat in his room, weakened by age, brooding on death, on the inevitable decay of the body that was taking place. He had lost the desire to live. Then a new set of defenses took over: in his fantasies he was a hero fighting battles against evil—against the Russians and the PLO, against imaginary disasters in the hospital. He had created in his fantasy world structures that were temporarily replacing the old ones. This saved him from despair. And underneath that he gradually regained the will to live. When he was ready, he came back.

In his madness he reminded me of Lear and Quixote, especially of Quixote, who believed he could fit the world to his image of it, and he enabled me to begin thinking about the heroes of modern drama, that remarkable group of men and women so seized by their personal visions of life that many of them do in fact die or stay mad rather than face the emptiness and the meaninglessness of a life in which they are nobodies.

Another step is necessary before my thesis forms clearly. I am studying modern plays at Princeton with Michael Goldman in a National Endowment for the Humanities Summer Seminar, and I read Goldman's essay: "The Ghost of Joy: Reflections on Romanticism and the Forms of Modern Drama." It is perfect for my purposes, and I quote his central assertion:

> Here is the paradigm: First we are caught up in the campaign of the individual soul to break through to reality in what the soul perceives to be an unreal world, a campaign on the side of joy, of an inner flowering, a campaign that seems to be leading to a breakthrough. And then comes the moment of breakthrough, in which the campaigning soul plunges into— an absence of some sort. In the nineteenth century this is usually represented as an absence of joy, of fulfilled life. Later dramatists tend to treat it as an absence of reality. But whether it be Mrs. Alving discovering that the joy of life is impossible, or the revolutionaries in *The Balcony* learning that their war against illusion can only be sustained by illusion, or Brecht's Shen Te finding that she can only be a good woman by masquerading as a bad man, the final revelation opens a fissure between the individual drive that makes for the play's action—that "haunts" the main actor—and the world in which he tries to act.[6]

My task now is to get Becker and Goldman together and then apply their combined insights to create a paradigm that I can use for the analysis of the role of the vital lie in modern drama, and that is the subject of my opening chapter, "Reality, Illusion, and the More Abundant Life."

In the meantime I must finish the story of how this book came to be written. During that fateful summer at Princeton, I completed five or six chapters, my father recovered from his illness, and I returned to Davidson to resume my normal teaching load. During the next two summers, I worked on a novel, and in the summer of 1982, I received an NEH grant to participate in Tom Bishop's seminar on avant-garde theater at New York University. It was a perfect opportunity to finish my book, since the chapters that needed the most work were those on the more recent playwrights. My father was still in Lambertville, New Jersey, but now his condition was much worse, and as I visited him during the closing months of his life, he seemed to me less a Don Quixote and much more a character from one of Beckett's recent plays. Three days before his actual death, he appeared to my sister in a dream. In the dream he was young, thirty or thirty-five, and he carried two suitcases, one in each hand. "What do you have in the suitcases?" she asked him. "My pain," he answered. "It's too heavy for me," he went on. "May I put it down?" "Yes," she answered. A strangely different scene from the one played three years before—clean, honest, dignified, with no wasted words. On January 1, 1983, my sister and I and her children scattered his ashes through the waters of the Pacific Ocean off the coast of California, where he had lived so much of his life. This book, which is associated so much in my memory with him, is dedicated to my father.

It is now 1987, and the book has been finished after an extensive journey through the hands of many readers. The most telling criticism during that journey was that the manuscript did not reflect the best recent criticism; thus it has been my main task during 1985 and 1986, to read and to integrate into the argument the criticism of the eighties. I have also reordered the chapters and reshaped my argument into three main divisions. "Part One: The Hegelians" concerns the work of Ibsen, Strindberg, Chekhov, Shaw, and Synge, all of whom (except Shaw) died before World War I. Their vision of reality is shaped by the Hegelian hope for human progress born out of the nineteenth-century belief that human beings can change and that the Spirit will manifest itself more and more fully in human life with the passing of time. "Part Two: Lost and Found" concerns a generation of playwrights influenced by the First World War, the twenties, and the depression: Pirandello and Brecht on the Continent; O'Neill, Miller, and Williams in America; and T. S. Eliot in England. All of them deal with smaller heroes than their predecessors, and all explore the trauma of the ordinary man in the face of the growing mechanization, urbanization, and competition of the twentieth century. "Part Three: Absurdism and After" deals with the last thirty years. We could almost call it, as Ruby Cohn does in her tribute to Beckett on his eightieth birthday, "Growing (Up?) with *Godot*."[7] Beckett, Ionesco, Albee,

Pinter, Weiss, and Genet form the focus of this section, which explores the meaning of reality and illusion in a world without given values, a world in which role playing and theatrical self-consciousness have replaced the notion that drama is a representation of life. In my closing chapter I return to Becker to explore both the meaning and the value of vital lies in light of the previous chapters.

I am aware of the dangers inherent in my study. In the words of Austin Quigley, from his fascinating 1985 study *The Modern Stage and Other Worlds*, "I have wished to avoid writing two kinds of book . . . the kind that addresses itself accurately to the field but deals with only a cross-section of it, and the kind that determinedly seeks to deal with the whole field but addresses only a few lines to each of several hundred plays."[8] If I have erred, it may be on the side of the latter, but I feel that it is essential to demonstrate both the pervasiveness and the continuity of the reality-illusion theme throughout the history of modern drama. At the same time I have given considerable attention to a number of historically important plays.

Finally, I must address the question of who I think the readers of this book will be. My first answer is, "Students and teachers of modern drama." I have written the book largely out of my experience of teaching modern drama for twenty years. I hope that playgoers will also find the book interesting as a way to think about modern plays, and I hope that scholars will find the book a useful starting point for further research and study. I have sought to combine an easy, somewhat colloquial style with adequate scholarly documentation in order to create a book that is both accessible to a popular audience and useful to a scholarly one.

I have incurred many debts during the course of this book's composition, the greatest of which are to Michael Goldman and Tom Bishop, who read the manuscript in its early stages, suggested useful criticism, and encouraged me to keep going. My work with them was made possible by Summer Seminar grants from the NEH in 1979 and 1982. I would like to thank Judith Knight and Ellen Stein of The University of Alabama Press for their faith in the book and the students in my modern drama classes for listening to my ideas and stimulating me in turn with theirs. They will find many familiar things here, and some new ones. I wish them, and all others who may encounter this book, enjoyable reading.

Davidson, North Carolina

THE
VITAL LIE

1

Reality, Illusion, and the More Abundant Life

> . . . *the action of most, if not all great modern plays*
> *regularly defines itself as a struggle between vitality*
> *and deadness.* Characters in modern drama are
> typically driven to act by a feeling of being cut off from
> the joy of life or indeed from life itself, a feeling that
> they are dead.
>
> —Michael Goldman,
> "Vitality and Deadness in Beckett's Plays"[1]

The question is: How can we have life and have it more abundantly? It's what Ibsen's heroes are after, and Chekhov's and Shaw's and Pirandello's and everyone else's. That's really all Willy Loman and Blanche Dubois are asking for. On the one side is the individual soul, on the other side the world. The soul wants joy; it also wants purpose. We could argue that the soul has two ways of fulfilling itself—the Christian (through duty, self-sacrifice, commitment to service) and the pagan or Dionysian (through dance, music, celebration, what Ibsen calls *livsglœden*, or the "joy in life"). It is conceivable that *both* of these ways are structures that Becker would call means of evading the issue of death; as long as we work, we are happy because it puts the thought of death at a distance. In the dance we also lose ourselves. These two elements in harmony may be sufficient to keep the human being at peace, the one satisfying the need to serve and the other fulfilling the desire for joy. Perhaps this is exactly what the Roman Catholic Church was able to do until the Reformation—incorporate the Dionysian and Apollonian elements into the structure of the church to give human beings a sense of joy and a sense of purpose simultaneously, while at the same time telling people that they didn't need to worry about those rotten corpses they were carrying their souls around in. It was a perfect solution to Becker's problem.

Something went wrong during the sixteenth century, and Western civilization has never quite recovered from it. The Reformation banished joy, throwing it into the corner of some dark fjord, where Ibsen and Strindberg's characters eventually went searching for it, and by the time of the playwrights themselves, not only had joy been banished, but God himself had been thrown out by Darwin and Marx, and the corpse would be given a few more swift kicks by Freud for good measure. So where was the more abundant life to come from? If you had no joy and you had only duty without God and there was no heavenly reward after all, you were in a desperate state. This is the condition that necessitates the romantic quest—an attempt to break through to reality, to get beyond the structures of what, in Goldman's words, the soul perceives to be an unreal world. The challenge is to develop the self in a universe that offers the self no fixed or meaningful identity.

The danger, of course, is that, if you look too deep into the self, you move below the structures of the real world right into the arms of death. At the root of the self is nothing—at least that is the fear. The new and almost unbearable task of the hero in this contest is to create, like God, ex nihilo, to act as if there *is* something, to create meaning for the self in the face of what seems like a conspiracy between the external world and society to make life meaningless. The task of the hero, finally, is to stare down death. This is what Solness is doing in *The Master Builder*, it is Shotover's mission in *Heartbreak House*, Henry's in *Henry IV*, and it is what Willy Loman, Blanche Dubois, Vladimir, Berenger, Shen Te, and a host of others are all about.

The fact is that they all fail. This is the thrust of Goldman's argument—"the failure of romantic desire to make contact with reality."[2] But the plays in which they appear are all, paradoxically (this is my point, not Goldman's), *celebrations of their failures*. This is finally the source of their greatness and the reason that we love them. If they fail to outstare death, at least they have tried, and there are other ways of dying. These, our playwrights most eloquently remind us, are worse. Human beings can achieve greatness only by discarding the illusions that society has enjoined upon them to protect them from the truths about their condition . . . but the very process of discarding those illusions, like peeling away the skin of an onion, is so dangerous that it leaves the hero at the end of the process either dead or more vulnerable than he was at the beginning of the play. In order to go on living at all, the protagonist may have to adopt another set of illusions, less stifling perhaps than those that society accepts, but illusions nonetheless. In some cases we may call that second set of illusions madness, or the strategy of the truly sane for living in an insane world. We see this process first in Pirandello and later in Genet, Weiss, and Pinter.

What suggests itself is a three-part process, which Goldman outlines in *The Actor's Freedom*:

2

A familiar pattern in twentieth century theatre shows the hero, the source of free energy, moving up to attack the borders of the real and being thrown back in some climactic explosion—and then, if he survives, the hero falls back to his position outside the system.[3]

In more detail the process may look like this:

1. The hero senses that he is out of step with society. He wants a kind of freedom that the world does not permit, "half-allowed, blasphemous, and sacred," Goldman calls it. He senses the basic unreality of that which the world calls real. He wants to explore the means within himself of achieving deeper fulfillment than has been permitted him.

2. The hero and the world engage in battle. The antagonists of the play, usually representing the harder, more practical "adaptive" elements of society, try to demonstrate the folly of the hero. He is soft, idealistic, unfit to survive in the tough, realistic, "modern" world.

3. At the point of climax the hero *almost* wins. In tragedy, says Arthur Miller, "the possibility of victory must be there."[4] As audience we must believe that the hero can make the breakthrough, can convert society to his views, can at least find an acceptable way of life apart from society (the Thoreauvian ideal). But he doesn't, and the reason, finally, that he doesn't is not only that society is stronger (that is too simple a view) but that *death* will not be stared down. It is not society that finally wins; it is death.

Robert Brustein's view in *The Theatre of Revolt* that the hero's quest manifests itself in three stages may be helpful here. In the first stage, the messianic, the hero tries to replace God. He tries to create within himself a substitute religion or vision that will enable him to live life at its deepest and most intense. In the second stage, the social, he battles with society for the freedom to enact, to put into practice, the vision he has had. In the third stage, the existential, he confronts the ultimate reality of life itself, which means, of course, death itself—the total reality of his being. It may be argued that not only does this three-part process exist as a historical movement from the mid-nineteenth century to the present, and as a developmental tendency within the work of individual writers (this is Brustein's thesis), but that it also exists as a pattern within individual plays.

At this point I can now offer some tentative definitions of the terms *reality* and *illusion* as they will be used in this book. If the notion of the three-part quest of the hero has any validity, then we may argue that the terms have at least two separate and seemingly contradictory meanings as applied to the quest. The term *illusion* may mean that set of structures—games, rituals, masks, disguises, diversions, roles—that human beings use to keep themselves from facing reality, which, if viewed nakedly, would destroy them. On a deeper level, an illusion may be a special strategy—a dream, ideal, fantasy, a created vision—which the individual devises to give life meaning. Such a strategy may allow the hero to face reality in a way that the more superficial games do not. It may, for example, allow him to see through the pretense of the world and preserve for him at the same time a sense of the heroic, a sense of his own specialness, his godlike quality.

The term *reality* would also have two basic meanings. On the more superficial level, it would imply what college students familiarly call "the real world." It would imply that set of social, political, and economic structures that adult society uses to transact the business of everyday living. It would imply certainly what Freud means by the word *civilization*. On a deeper level, reality has the implication of "truth," the truth about the human condition. In this sense it means Becker's "god who shits" or, to put it more paradoxically, "the god who dies" and, in Christian terms, "the god who dies and is born again."

What we have here, finally, is a spiritual question. If reality is ultimately physical, if life ends with the death of the body, if Darwin and Marx and Freud are right, if religion is the opiate of the people or our most basic illusion, then the word *god* itself is the final illusion, humankind's most absolute and fundamental vital lie about the nature of reality. If, on the other hand, God really *is*, if reality is ultimately spiritual, then the life of the body itself is the final illusion, the final mask to be removed, the final layer to be stripped away before reality is confronted. Disagreement over that particular subject separates many of the playwrights in this study.

Lastly there is the fact of the theater itself, the illusion, if you like, that while watching an actor perform a role in a playhouse you are watching something real, perhaps something even more real than your own life. Pirandello was the first to confront this type of question fully, but in our own time playwrights like Genet, Beckett, Pinter, Shepard, and Weiss remind us almost obsessively that the theater itself must be incorporated into our understanding of what is real in the plays we are watching.

Again Goldman is very helpful, especially in *The Actor's Freedom*, and I would like to quote an especially pertinent passage:

... the leading role or roles of any play act out some version of a half-allowed, blasphemous, and sacred freedom characteristic of the era in which the play was written. In the enactment, by the very nature of the freedom pursued, the hero risks destruction.[5]

This is wonderful, because it reminds us simultaneously that the theater is *not* life, that the theater is larger than life, and that we go to the theater precisely for those two reasons. We go to the theater that we might live more abundantly. We crave, as individuals, the freedom that these heroes possess, the joy of life, the capacity to grow, to face reality, to be driven by some deeper power. Seated in the theater, as Goldman suggests, we may have the satisfaction of emotional identification with these characters (we become them for three hours) without feeling the anxiety or frustration of being personally responsible for them. What would you do if you had to take care of Henry IV or Master Builder Solness or Willy Loman or Blanche? It is the actor's freedom to enlarge his life by the playing of the role. Is that in fact the actor's final illusion? Is the playing of the role the performer's protection from reality? Perhaps. It is the audience's freedom to identify with the acting out of its own deepest and darkest dreams, wishes, terrors, and aspirations. We will look at this phenomenon more closely when we examine the theories of Artaud at the end of the book.

For now it is enough for the reader to be aware that I do not approach the question of reality and illusion academically. I sustain the position that what is going on before us on the stage is more deeply a part of our real lives than we are consciously aware of. Those who avoid modern plays in performance do so frequently because such performances make them uncomfortable, make them aware of the littleness of their own daily lives. It is precisely the function of the theater of revolt, as Brustein has stated, to shock us into greater awareness of our true condition. The theatrical method is part of the therapy. So is our own humanness.

In the epigraph for this chapter, Michael Goldman reminds us that what the major protagonists of modern drama want is life, and, I would add, they want it more abundantly. Fear of the unlived life is not only a central motif in modern drama, but in all of modern literature. Maybe it is the endemic disease of modern life. Whatever the causes, the heroes of modern drama want desperately to live, from Nora to Vladimir, from Solness to Guildenstern. And they will adopt stratagems necessary for their purposes—call them "vital lies" or "illusions" or "dreams." At the heart of the matter what we call them is less important than our acknowledgment of their necessity both as dramatic devices in stage

5

plays and as stratagems real human beings use to cope with real life. If we do not bring our humanness to the theater, we deny the stage one of its most powerful aspects and reduce it to the sort of escapist entertainment that Ibsen and Chekhov and Shaw were rebelling against in the first place. It is my hope that the following chapters will contribute both to our understanding of modern life and of the modern stage. Perhaps that is my vital lie.

Part One
The Hegelians

2

Henrik Ibsen

*The old beauty is no longer beautiful,
and the old truth is no longer true.*

—Julian in *Emperor and Galilean*

We think of Ibsen first of all as the seer, not in the sense of prophet or mystic, but in its literal meaning as "one who sees." Those who knew him well talk about his eyes, his hawk's stare that could look right through a man, his capacity for penetration, for seeing *through* things. He loved to look at the sea, into the sea, as if he could stare through its depths into some deeper reality. Ibsen, for all his vaunted realism, no more believed in those solid chairs and tables, walls and doors than Nora Helmer believed in her husband. As Brian Johnston puts it in his introduction to *The Ibsen Cycle*,

> I believe that Ibsen saw the world of everyday reality in the way that Plato saw it in his allegory of the cave: as a world of massive falsehood and illusion behind and beyond which essential and universal reality lay; I also believe that in each of the plays in the Cycle he removes one veil of illusion, infiltrates some of the essential reality into the stifling realm of falsehood until, by the end of the cycle the whole illusory fabric has dissolved and we come close to looking at the naked spirit.[1]

While Johnston's thesis is a little too neat, too systematic, I believe that his approach to Ibsen is the right one, and to understand what Johnston means by terms such as "reality," "illusion," and "naked spirit," we need to begin with *Emperor and Galilean* (1873), the work Ibsen considered his masterpiece, a play which set forth "the positive Weltanshauung which the critics have long demanded of me."[2]

In the third act of Part One, the following conversation takes place between Julian and his teacher, Maximus:

MAXIMUS: There are three empires.
JULIAN: Three?
MAXIMUS: First, that empire which was founded on the tree of knowledge; then that empire which was founded on the tree of the cross.
JULIAN: And the third?

9

MAXIMUS: The third is the empire of the great mystery, the empire which shall be founded on the tree of knowledge and the tree of the cross together.[3]

This passage and others like it that appear in the second part point clearly to Ibsen's Hegelianism—a reception on the playwright's part of ideas current in European intellectual circles—which would form a backdrop for the twelve plays to be written between 1877 and 1899 and a commentary on the plays just completed.

In *Emperor and Galilean* the empire of the tree of knowledge stands for the pagan tradition and will be associated in Ibsen's plays both with the spirit of Dionysus and the joy of life I referred to in the opening chapter. The empire of the tree of the cross represents the Judeo-Christian tradition with its emphasis on high ethical standards, nobility, self-sacrifice, and commitment to duty. These two kingdoms will conflict throughout Ibsen's plays. What Julian comes to recognize in *Emperor and Galilean* is that progress to a deeper reality can be made not through a choice between the two but through a synthesis of them, which would allow human beings richer lives, denying neither the need for beauty nor the quest for truth. But as Arthur Ganz has noted in his fine study *Realms of the Self*, "the Hegelian synthesis that is to result from the conflict of pagan and Christian lies inevitably outside the limits of the text."[4] None of Ibsen's heroes is able to reach "the empire of the great mystery," although, as Johnston suggests, it may be that the heroes of the last plays, especially Solness, Allmers, and Rubek, come closer than anyone else. But to answer that question, we need to look more closely at the heroes themselves, from Brand to Rubek.

We may see Brand, Peer Gynt, and Julian as a kind of Hegelian thesis, antithesis, and synthesis, with Brand representing the Christian pole (Galilean) and Peer the pagan pole (Emperor).

Ibsen was clearly fond of the title character of *Brand* (1866). In an often-quoted statement, he said in a letter to Peter Hanson, "Brand is myself in my best moments."[5] This is a statement that is bound to make us uneasy; after all, Brand is one of the most inhuman of Ibsen's heroes, and his excesses lead to the deaths of his mother, his wife, and his child. Ibsen might have said, "Brand is my Christian self in its most extreme moments." What he admired about Brand was the minister's total devotion to his cause, his willingness to give everything to his calling:

Be wholly what you are, not half and half
Everyone now is a little of everything. . . .

A little sin, a little virtue;
A little good, a little evil; the one
Destroys the other, and every man is nothing.

Brand's position then is "all or nothing": we must serve God totally or serve Him not at all. There can be no compromise. It is not necessary that Brand be a priest. Ibsen writes, "That Brand is a priest is really immaterial; the demand of all or nothing is valid for all aspects of life, in love, in art, etc."[6] So Brand becomes Ibsen's symbol of the individual who gives himself totally to his cause and who is willing to pay the supreme price, that of his own life, to make real his dream. Brand tells us:

What I must do.
Live what until now was only *dreamt* . . .
Make *true* all that is still *illusion*.

In terms of the scheme laid out in the opening chapter, Brand has already reached the third level. He has rejected the games and pastimes of the world, he has moved beyond the realities that the Mayor and the Provost support (political, social, and economic institutions) to a faith in his own *ideal*. Brand almost succeeds in establishing his church, overcoming great odds to get it built, only to find at the crucial point in the play that the state will take it over (like institutional Christianity) to use it for its own purposes. He calls upon the people to destroy the church and follow him, the new Moses, into the wilderness. But the people ask:

First, how long shall we have to fight?
Secondly, how much will it cost us?
Thirdly, what will be our reward?

These are the questions of the practical realist, questions that Brand has transcended, but that very transcendence finally isolates him and leads him to his death. Brand never realizes what Agnes had tried to teach him earlier. "Your church is too small for me," she says to him. Brand loses for two reasons. First, human beings cannot bear the kind of reality that Brand forces upon them. Secondly, and more importantly, Brand's church lacks love. He has banished the joy of life from his church, and the Christian element is doomed to its own destruction without the saving warmth of the pagan. The deeper reality, Ibsen implies, must come from the saving synthesis, and this Brand will never be able to understand.

11

The title character of *Peer Gynt* (1867) presents the opposite problem. If Brand is duty without warmth, Peer is the old beauty that is no longer beautiful because it has deteriorated into hedonism and self-indulgence. Peer is likable, but useless, the other side of the self that needs to be redeemed by Brand's ascetic discipline. It is Ibsen's habit to work by contraries and then show the limits of both. In *Emperor and Galilean* he finally shows what Peer and Brand are lacking, but Julian only knows what must be done; he can't do it, and it will take Ibsen over twenty years to get back to the point he had reached thematically in this play. It is as if he has said, "I have outlined the process by which humans must grow. Now I will show you in my plays, step-by-step, how that process will take place." Thus the cycle from *Pillars of Society* to *When We Dead Awaken*.

Ibsen's last twelve plays are written, consciously it seems, in three groups of four: (1) *Pillars of Society* (1877), *A Doll House* (1879), *Ghosts* (1881), and *An Enemy of the People* (1882); (2) *The Wild Duck* (1884), *Rosmersholm* (1886), *The Lady from the Sea* (1888), and *Hedda Gabler* (1890); and (3) *The Master Builder* (1892), *Little Eyolf* (1894), *John Gabriel Borkman* (1896), and *When We Dead Awaken* (1899). The plays may be viewed as both a unity and a progression, with the last play, subtitled *A Dramatic Epilogue*, clearly marking what Ibsen felt to be at least the end of this cycle. With a lesser playwright than Ibsen we could select two or three plays from the group and use them to illustrate a central thesis, but with Ibsen it is not possible, because he never repeats himself. Thus each stage of the cycle must be examined and a thesis developed, which takes into account the evolution of Ibsen's dramatic position from one stage to the next. Only by looking at the entire group can we reach some reasonable conjecture about Ibsen's views.

In the first group the reality-illusion conflict exists on the material level. The heroes of these plays—Karstin Bernick, Nora Helmer, Helene Alving, and Dr. Thomas Stockmann—are individuals who are both strong enough and courageous enough to face the truth of who they are and to act (at least eventually) on the knowledge of that truth. In *A Doll House* and *An Enemy of the People* the issue is simplest. Nora and Dr. Stockmann are at odds with society, because of acts that they have committed or perceptions that they have. Both hope to reconcile themselves to society by getting society (her husband, Torvald, the "compact majority") to accept their criticisms. When they cannot get that acceptance, they are forced into exile, much as Synge's heroes will be in Ireland two decades later. As characters they expose the hypocrisy of institutions; they peel off the illusions of society. For their behavior they must pay with banishment. Bernick in *Pillars of Society* is not banished, probably because his confession of his crimes does nothing to threaten the status quo. The real point of *A Doll House* is that Torvald must change if Nora is to come back to him. That is "the greatest miracle" to which Nora refers as she departs. Ibsen never tired, during this period, of pointing out that the farsighted individual is always ahead of society, and that even if someone like Torvald does change, Nora will always be ahead of him, unless he can break loose from convention, which seems as likely as a brick turning into a butterfly. So at the end of both *A Doll House* and *An Enemy of the People* we are left with a certain sadness. Stockmann's "the strongest man is he who stands alone" is really a kind of whistling in the dark. Whatever either he or Nora will achieve as human beings during their exile will be paid for again and again in the shame that society will make them feel and in their inevitable disappointment over society's lack of progress. Like Brand, they may eventually pay the full price for their honesty.

Ghosts makes that clear. In *Ghosts* you pay the price no matter what you do. The title refers to those institutions and ideas from the past, including our own past actions, which prevent us from taking positive action in the present; Helene Alving's dilemma is that neither her knowledge of the truth nor her desire to act upon the truth can prevent the tragedy from taking place. Helene pays twice. Having failed to make the break with Captain Alving, she pays for it by watching the destruction of both his life and her own. Then, at the end of the play, she pays again by watching the orphanage and the life of her son go up in flames. In this play Ibsen is more pessimistic than he had been in *A Doll House* or would be in *An Enemy of the People*. And like Helene Alving, he was made to pay for it by the press notices the play received, especially in London. *Ghosts* seems to come back, at least indirectly, to the pagan-Christian conflict of *Emperor and Galilean*, with Captain Alving and Pastor Manders, respectively, representing corruptions of the pagan and Christian ways of life. Alving's æsthetics have turned to decadence, and Manders's faith to pious institutional moralizing. Helene, rather than becoming the instrument of regeneration for either her husband or Manders, has contributed to the destruction of both by choosing to do nothing. As Ganz observes, "Whereas Nora may well succeed because she is able to reject her husband, Mrs. Alving may have failed because she could not accept hers."[7]

We can see then that by 1883 Ibsen had not got very far with the Hegelian pattern. The conflict between the individual and society becomes the form for the reality-illusion theme, but it doesn't get much beyond the surface level. The heroes give up the games, illusions, pretenses of society and are forced to pay the price—but we never see what happens to them inside, afterward. Ibsen has, as he realized, repressed too much. So he wrote *The Wild Duck*.

The Wild Duck, for the purposes of this study, is the most important play Ibsen wrote, not only because it is the play in which he introduces the concept of the vital lie, but because it is the play in which he finds for the first time the dramatic method that will be his primary technique for the remainder of his career, a method that allows him to treat the human psyche with greater complexity than he had in the first four plays of the cycle.

Viewed from the point of view of those earlier plays, Gregers Werle, during the first act at least, looks like the protagonist of the piece. Returning home after a long absence at his father's works, he discovers that his friend Hjalmar Ekdal has been married to his parents' former housekeeper, Gina Hansen; that Hjalmar's father, old Lieutenant Ekdal, has been forced to take the blame for some of Werle Senior's business irregularities; and that Hjalmar's pride and joy, his daughter, Hedvig, is quite likely Werle's illegitimate child. What it all adds up to, reasons Gregers, is that the old man has set up the entire Ekdal household on a lie. His mission, he concludes, will be to inform Hjalmar of this tissue of deceit and enable the family to begin life anew on the basis of "truth." This sounds very much like *Brand* or *Enemy of the People*. But when Gregers puts his plan into operation, the results are disastrous. Hjalmar, rather than welcoming the opportunity to begin life anew, sulks and carries on like a spoiled child, so much so that Gregers suggests to Hedvig that she kill her pet wild duck in order to convince her father of her love for him. In that way, Gregers surmises, the father's faith in the child will be restored. But the child loves the duck too much to kill it and sacrifices herself instead. Thus we in the audience are confronted with the fact that Gregers's "claim of the ideal" has served only to destroy the most sympathetic character in the play.

So where are we? Has Ibsen paradoxically turned round on himself and denied the value of facing the truth without illusions? Not at all, if we read the play carefully. Dr. Relling, whom we met in the preface, serves as a foil to Gregers. If Gregers says that people *always* ought to be forced to face the truth, Relling says, "Rob the average man of his vital lie and you rob him of his happiness." Hjalmar is the archetypal average man, and he can no more live with the truth than fly to the moon. But that does not mean that all men must have vital lies. In his preliminary notes for the play, Ibsen wrote, "Liberation consists in securing for individuals the right to free themselves, each according to his particular need."[8] When individuals, such as Nora Helmer, are ready to free themselves, they must be given both the opportunity and the encouragement; but freedom cannot be forced on people. Neither Gregers nor Dr. Relling speaks for Ibsen, but because neither cares genuinely about individual human beings. Each, ironically, is obsessed with running other people's lives rather than doing anything about his own. Neither considers what his own vital lie might be.

But the title of the play is not *The Vital Lie*, it is *The Wild Duck*; and with the creation of the wild duck itself as the play's central symbol, Ibsen is able to dramatize Hegelian themes that have lain dormant since *Emperor and Galilean*. Rolf Fjelde and others have pointed out that the word for wild duck (*wild and*) and the word for spirit (*wildand*) in Norwegian are almost identical. This parallelism suggests the play's central theme. The Ekdal family has created the world of the loft out of some inner necessity to transcend the materialism of their environment. They have been confined to a small area, a photographer's studio where realistic photographs are developed and retouched. Old Ekdal is no longer permitted to wear his uniform or to hunt. Life has been reduced to mean and petty terms. Within this environment Gina fares best, because she is able to live happily within these limits. If the reality-illusion theme existed only on the surface level in this play, she would be the heroine. She is the pragmatic realist who knows the truth and lives by it without hurting anyone else. But she cannot think figuratively. She cannot understand symbols. Her *imagination* is dead, and that is precisely what worries Ibsen about this kind of world. Man's spirit, like the wild duck, has been wounded, and it is in danger of dying out altogether unless it is nurtured through the wildness of nature, poetry, music, and the active use of the imagination. In the loft the Ekdal family nurtures its imagination; Hedvig, Hjalmar, and Lieutenant Ekdal keep their spirits alive by tending the wild duck and hunting. In this light we can argue that Hedvig's death symbolizes the death of the spirit, the destruction of the poetic or imaginative element in life. She *is* the wild duck, and if she is not yet the creative artist, she is certainly the potential artist in all of us, whose death leaves our world smaller, grayer, and more barren.

In *Rosmersholm* and *Hedda Gabler* Ibsen continues to develop this theme, but in a different key. Fjelde hits the right note in his introduction when he says, "Rebecca has come to Rosmersholm, in Maurice Valency's phrase, like a secret agent of the Third Empire, the next great era of cultural historical evolution into which Western civilization is moving."[9] Or to put it in different terms, Rebecca is, in *Rosmersholm*, the agent of

15

transcendence. The projected union of Rebecca and Rosmer is the union of the pagan and the Christian, Emperor and Galilean, the Pan-Logos to which Julian refers in the earlier play. Rebecca is not merely an adventuress, coming to Rosmersholm to take John Rosmer for herself. It is essential that the audience believe she and Rosmer could succeed in some measure to ennoble themselves and others if they could overcome their sense of guilt. Between them they have the intelligence, the moral fiber, the vitality to transcend the cheap liberalism of Mortensgaard and the stifling conservatism of Kroll. Ironically it is the deceased wife Beata (the blessed one?) who destroys them, for if Beata sacrificed her own life that they might live, that sacrifice has made Rosmer and Rebecca, first separately, and at the end together, too weighted by guilt, the Rosmer tradition, to put their plan into action. Their mutual suicide seems the only way that they can be true to their love for one another and to the Rosmer heritage, which, like the ghosts of an earlier play, draws them into the millrace. The key to the play is that we believe in their suicide, that we, as audiences, find it both surprising and at the same time inevitable. Ibsen will use the same pattern in *Hedda Gabler*, *The Master Builder*, and *When We Dead Awaken*; the ending of *Rosmersholm* seems particularly strange to us mainly because it is the first. If the plays are read in reverse order, the ending seems perfectly natural. I will comment more fully on this pattern at the end of the chapter.

In *Hedda Gabler* the theme of transcendence centers around the figure of the artist-philosopher, Eilert Lovborg. It is important to understand that in all the major plays from *Rosmersholm* to the end the idea of transcendence is tied to union between male and female. Where the unions fail, no growth can take place. Where the unions succeed, the results may be harmonious (*The Lady from the Sea, Little Eyolf*) or tragic (*Rosmersholm, The Master Builder, When We Dead Awaken*), but the unions always suggest growth in character and perception, growth in *vision*. In *Hedda Gabler* the only growth that takes place is the growth based on the union of Thea Elvsted and Eilert Lovborg. That union has produced a child, the manuscript that Hedda burns in the third act; and that child is significantly a study of the future, a project which the plodding scholar-husband, Jorgen Tesman, cannot even imagine. "Fancy that, Hedda," he says, unable to imagine how anyone can write about something that hasn't happened yet.

More and more we sense Ibsen's exasperation with the merely earthly. With Lovborg he is moving toward Solness and Rubek, but Lovborg falls short of the stature of the two later heroes because neither Thea nor Hedda can serve as his Hilde or Irene. Thea is a helper, but she is not an

16

inspiration. Hedda has the power that Thea lacks, and one senses clearly in the magnificent scene between Hedda and Lovborg in the second act that a union between these two would have been stormy, but rich and vital. It might have served both Hedda's and Lovborg's Dionysian needs and prevented Hedda's powerful drive for freedom from turning into such destructive channels. Hedda's equally strong sense of the conventional, inherited from her father, forces her to dismiss Lovborg, finally marry Tesman, and create for herself a life of boredom and frustration, which in turn she can only relieve by playing with pistols and the lives of others. Hedda's cruelty to others is not natural. It is the result of her having been afraid to act on her instincts with Lovborg. It is, Freud would argue, the inevitable result of repression. Hedda's sterility, like her cruelty, is the result of her cowardice. Her death is a cry for freedom and a final protest against the cowardice that has held her back from everything she has wanted. "Not free. Not free, then!" she cries to Judge Brack a page before the end. "No—I can't bear the thought of it—never." As Keith May observes in his excellent new study *Ibsen and Shaw*, Ibsen's later heroes and heroines "go voluntarily to their deaths because they would rather be dead than wanly alive."[10]

Throughout the plays of this period there is that terrible desire by the heroines to break through into a larger world. Hedvig has the wild duck, Rebecca has Rosmer, Hedda has Lovborg, and Ellida Wangel in *The Lady from the Sea* has the Stranger. Significantly, the only play that ends happily does so because the heroine is finally content to accept the limitations of her life on land:

> ELLIDA: . . . Once you've really become a land animal, then there's no going back again into the sea. Or the life that belongs to the sea, either.

If the sea in this play suggests, as it does in *The Wild Duck*, the mysterious, the strange, the wonderful, then Ellida Wangel has freely chosen to reject that aspect of her life in order to live happily on land. She becomes a kind of Gina or Thea Elvsted. "Human beings," says Ballested, "can acclimatize themselves." True. Or is the sea, in evolutionary terms, a step backward? Is Ibsen implying that a step forward must come through the sea to Dr. Wangel and then on to something else? In the last plays Ibsen will abandon the sea as his central image and turn to a symbol perhaps less ambiguous—that of *height*, the tower and the mountain peak. Here, he seems to be saying, is the proper direction for human evolution.

Ibsen never repeats himself. Each play is unique, but there are patterns, structural and imagistic, that dominate within each of the periods. During the last period the pattern centers around a titanic male artist—in contrast to the female protagonists of the period from 1879 to 1890—who long before the play opens has married a woman who does not enable him to fulfill his highest potential. There are Halvard and Aline Solness in *The Master Builder*, Alfred and Rita Allmers in *Little Eyolf*, John Gabriel and Gunhild Borkman in *John Gabriel Borkman*, and Arnold and Maja Rubek in *When We Dead Awaken*. The pattern is archetypal in all four plays, with subtle variations on the central theme.

There is always another woman: Hilda Wangel in the first play, Asta Allmers in the second, Ella Rentheim in the third, and Irene in the fourth. Whatever else Ibsen is doing, he is clearly using the triangle and the man's necessary choice between the two women as the structural means of developing his theme. Through that choice and the means by which the man handles the choice, we are able to see whether or not he is able to make that almost evolutionary leap forward to a deeper creative vision and more abundant life. Ibsen develops the pattern most clearly in the cases of Solness and Rubek, the most important characters in these plays.

At the opening of the play which bears his name, Master Builder Solness is, as Bernard Shaw notes in *The Quintessence of Ibsenism*, a dead man. He is not so much physically as spiritually and emotionally dead. He has reached an impasse in his life where it is no longer clear to him what it is he wants to do. The result is a kind of paralysis. Toward the end of the first act he tells Hilda:

SOLNESS: It's really so good that you've come to me now.
HILDA: (*with a probing look*) Is it?
SOLNESS: I've been so alone here—and felt so utterly helpless watching it all.

The play is filled with words like "willed," "wished," "desired," "called." Hilda's arrival is surely no coincidence. Out of the depths of his fear, his failure, his paralysis, his terror of the young, his inability to continue growing, he has called for help, and help has arrived in the form of Hilda. In Jungian terms Hilda is the anima, the female principle in the soul, repressed and ignored in men until the crisis of middle age, when they have the opportunity to reach down deep into the self and call it up. It is only through the nurturing of the anima that the psyche can continue to grow.

"You're the one person I've needed most," Solness cries out to Hilda at the end of Act I, and he is right. It is only through integrating Hilda into his own personality that he can revitalize himself enough to begin a new phase of his life. The rest of the play dramatizes that struggle. Hilda is dangerous. She will take him into places he has never been and make him do things that have always terrified him. She will challenge him to overcome old fears and cross into dark and forbidden territory. She is, to use the play's imagery, both "bird of prey" and "dawning day." And Solness rightly and simultaneously fears her talons and yearns for the new life she offers him. She is love itself, available at a price he is afraid to pay. To love her he will have to follow the "troll" in him, but his conscience is too sickly. Like Rebecca and Rosmer, Hilda and Solness are temporarily paralyzed by the great wound of conscience. Hilda feels guilty and threatens to leave, but the terror of her leaving is worse for Solness than the terror of her staying:

SOLNESS: And what'll become of me when you're gone? What'll I have to live for then? Afterwards?
HILDA: There's no real problem for you. You have your duties to her. Live for those duties.
SOLNESS: Too late. These powers—these—these—
HILDA: Devils—
SOLNESS: Yes, devils! And the troll inside me too—they've sucked all the lifeblood out of her. They did it to make me happy! Successful! And now she's dead—thanks to me. And I'm alive chained to the dead. (*In anguish*) I—I, who can't go on living without joy in life!

Everything we have been talking about in this chapter comes to a head here: the tension between Christian and pagan, between material and spiritual, the need to make the commitment to the richer life, "the castle in the air, with solid foundations," the fear that the step forward will bring disaster. For Solness, the only possible solution is to climb the tower and die. He must climb it to prove that he is worthy of Hilda's love, that he is truly the master builder, the man that she has dreamed of. He must climb it, and he must succeed, standing at the top, waving and talking to God. But he must also die, because he could not bear coming down again—down to what?—to Aline? He can neither go back to Aline nor go off with Hilda. Literally, death is the only answer. On another level, maybe death is the final reality. Solness has gone as far as a person may go alone. A statement by the great British psychiatrist, R. D. Laing, is useful here:

True sanity entails in one way or another the dissolution of the normal ego, that false self competently adjusted to our alienated social reality; the emergence of the "inner" archetypal mediators of divine power, and through this death a rebirth, and the establishment of a new kind of ego functioning, the ego now being the servant of the divine, no longer its betrayer.[11]

This is a pretty accurate description of what happens in *The Master Builder.* The play is so compressed that we hardly realize that Hilda has, in a way, engineered a kind of death and rebirth in Solness, in which the new ego, instead of using all its energies to keep youth down, is the servant of the God within, symbolized by Solness's love for Hilda and his need to serve her by climbing the tower. Though his fall marks his physical death, he is Hilda's master builder forever, because he has been true to the deepest instincts within himself and in that sense made his death a triumph rather than a defeat. In Keith May's words, "Ibsen saw death as heroic whenever it is the result of maximum endeavor."[12]

The Master Builder can end nowhere else but on the tower, just as *When We Dead Awaken* can end only in the high mountains, for Solness and Rubek are twins almost, and their fates are virtually the same. Both are artists, both have had moments of great triumph early in their careers, and each has succeeded through a kind of selfishness that is both necessary in the pursuit of art and destructive to the human personality—that of the self and others. Rubek, Irene reminds us, is "the artist who so casually and unfeelingly took a warm-blooded body, a young human life, and slit the soul out of it—because you could use it to create a work of art." Like Solness, Rubek is in a state of paralysis at the opening of his play, and in both plays there is the implication of growth through death and rebirth. The resurrection imagery in the last play is dominant through Rubek's extended description of his famous masterpiece, through the emphasis on climbing and mountains, and through conversation between Rubek and Irene:

> **Rubek:** You have the key! You alone have it! (*Beseeching her*) Help me— so I can try to live my life over again!
> **Irene:** (*Impassively as before*) Empty dreams. Aimless—dead dreams. *Our* life together can never be resurrected.
> **Rubek:** (*Brusquely, dropping the matter*) Then let's just keep playing our game!
> **Irene:** Yes, playing, playing—only playing!

Ibsen makes explicit in this play what was only suggested in *The Master*

Builder. Solness and Rubek want *life*, and they want it more abundantly. Rubek says to Maja in the second act, "All the talk about the artist's high calling and the artist's mission, and so on, began to strike me as basically empty and hollow and meaningless." "What would you put in its place?" asks Maja. "Life," answers the sculptor. That is the central point of both plays: Hilda comes to bring Solness the more abundant life, and Irene comes back to give both Rubek and herself the chance to live. Irene must overcome the Nun (the spirit of Rosmersholm, or perhaps the Christian tendency to renounce life), and Rubek must overcome the selfishness that caused him merely to *use* Irene rather than to love her. Both these plays are love stories, and both heroes risk death for love, for a higher definition of the self that incorporates not only the artistic calling but also the joy of life shared with another human being who is, in Rubek's words, able to "reach my innermost self." In the evolutionary scale Maja finds her counterpart in Ulfhejm, the Bear Hunter. They, like Irene and Rubek, must be free to fulfill their needs at their own level of development. Nowhere is Ibsen's Hegelianism so clear as in this play. Suggested in the love of Solness and Hilda, and perhaps even more clearly intimated in the final position of Allmers and Rita at the end of *Little Eyolf*, the evolutionary synthesis born of the union of Dionysus and Christ is forcefully symbolized by the final union of Rubek and Irene, who have awakened from one death of the spirit and may well awaken to another.

But death still has the last word here, as in *Rosmersholm*, *Hedda Gabler*, and *The Master Builder*. Of the eight central characters in these four plays, Hilda is the only one to survive. One could write an essay on that subject, but it would be another chapter. In a way, Hilda can't die. She is the muse, the spirit of life and creative activity itself. Her spirit, like that of the wild duck, transcends the deaths of the characters in Ibsen's last plays. The characters who live live because they give up something. The characters who die die because they risk too much. There is no in-between, except in fantasy, and the characters of the last plays are too honest for that. The key word is *risk*. Rebecca and Rosmer dare each other to risk everything. Hilda dares Solness. Irene dares Rubek: "Do you love me enough to do the right thing even if it costs you your life?" "Do you love me enough to do the joyful thing even if it costs you your life?" One must imagine them happy.

3

August Strindberg

> *Thesis: affirmation; Antithesis: negation; Synthesis: comprehension . . .*
>
> *You began life by accepting everything, and then went on to denying everything on principle. Now end your life by comprehending everything. Be exclusive no longer. Do not say: either-or, but: not only—but also! In a word, or two words, rather, Humanity and Resignation.*
>
> —*To Damascus,* Part III

Strindberg is, in one sense, the most purely Hegelian of the playwrights we will study in this book: he quite consciously sees life in triadic terms. Where Strindberg is misunderstood, it is most often because readers are familiar with only his famous naturalistic phase and fail to see it as part of a pattern of development in his work, or because readers of the late fantasies and chamber plays tend to overlook elements of the earlier Strindberg that remain in the last years. Ironically, the person who seems to have understood Strindberg best was Harriet Bosse, the great actress who became his third wife and the mother of his favorite child, Anne-Marie. She sums up the nature of her husband most perceptively in this statement, written for the publication in 1932 of the first volume of her correspondence with Strindberg:

> Strindberg was kind and warmhearted. He was never ill-natured and fierce as he sometimes depicts himself in his writings. Only when he took pen in hand did a demon take possession of him . . . I think that he in his youth stretched out his arms toward all the fair and beautiful things that life holds in promise for the young. Later, having discovered that things did not go according to his expectations . . . he imagined that he alone had been cheated. It was for this reason he raged in righteous indignation and fury against the world's deceit and its betrayal of him. His personal feeling of resignation was merely momentary. He lacked the balance for it.[1]

Thus, to connect Harriet Bosse's statement with the passage from *To Damascus,* Part III, written in 1901, the year he married her, one might divide Strindberg's life and career into three phases: affirmation—the period of youthful hope and idealism, culminating in his marriage to Siri von Essen in 1877; negation—associated with the breakdown of his marriage in the 1880s and the adoption of a naturalistic philosophy and aesthetic from 1886 to 1892; and comprehension—the period from his Inferno crisis to the end of his life, in which he struggles desperately to find both a philosophy of life and a dramatic form that will embody both his inner conflicts and the more spiritual view of life that has emerged as a result of those conflicts. Strindberg's treatment of the reality-illusion theme must be seen in terms of these stages of development, especially the second and third.

The most decisive event in Strindberg's life was his marriage on the 31st of December, 1877, to Siri von Essen, the former wife of Baron Carl Gustaf Wrangel, a captain in the Swedish Guards. Strindberg had courted Siri for two years, and her desire to become an actress, so critical to Baron Wrangel's decision to give her a divorce, was to play an equally critical role in her second marriage. Strindberg and Siri, who was just a year younger than he, set up a household in which the husband and wife were equals or "comrades," as she liked to think. In the play *Comrades* (1888), the painter, Axel Alberg, says concerning his relationship with his wife, Bertha: "Well, you see, we have made an arrangement between ourselves to be as two comrades; and friendship is both finer and more enduring than love." As Michael Myer notes in his definitive new biography, both Siri and Strindberg hoped that their marriage could be built on the idea of friendship between two working artists.[2] They envisioned a relationship of mutual support in which both could invite friends to the house to share in artistic endeavors and social life. The lesson marriage taught Strindberg was that equality was impossible. Two talented people could live together in harmony as friends only if both were of the same sex, because there was between man and woman a natural, even unconscious, rivalry that would never be still as long as the weaker party had the strength to fight. Nearly all the major plays of Strindberg's naturalistic period deal with this struggle—with the shattering of the illusion that men and women could be "comrades."

The Father, written in 1887 and the first of these plays to be produced, is a classic statement of the conflict. Conceived and rapidly completed when Strindberg's marriage was fast deteriorating, the play tells the story of how Laura gradually destroys the sanity of her husband, a captain in the Swedish Cavalry, through a combination of unscrupulous lies and a careful use of his own weaker qualities against him. The Captain is a "modern" man, an archetype of the sort of man Strindberg admired at the time—sexually virile, a freethinker in religion, interested in science, intellectually brilliant, yet with a military toughness. He is likened, mythologically, to Agamemnon and Hercules, both strong men destroyed by women. Laura admits in the second act that she is after power: "Power, that's it. What's this whole life and death struggle for if not power."[3] But near the end of the third act she denies that she has developed any premeditated plan for the gaining of power:

> But I didn't mean this to happen. I never really thought it out. I may have had some vague desire to get rid of you—you were in my way—and perhaps, if you see some plan in my actions, there was one, but I was unconscious of it. I have never given a thought to my actions—they simply ran along the rails you laid down.

What she says here is true in one sense: like Iago, she has no plan of action, she merely makes use of things as they come along. It is the Captain himself, in relation to the soldier, Nojd, who brings up the crucial point that a father can never be certain his child is really his own. The doctor brings up the question of certification for insanity. Laura *uses* what she learns from them. At the same time, she is an unscrupulous liar, calling a spectroscope a microscope to deliberately mislead the doctor and intercepting the Captain's book orders, thereby making his scientific work impossible. She carefully surrounds herself with men she can manipulate—her brother; the pastor, who knows what kind of woman she is but is helpless to stop her; and a new doctor whom she can win to her cause.

The Captain is unable to combat this formidable array of foes because his willpower has been broken. Torn by suspicion, his nerves worn ragged by years of infighting, he explodes at the end of the second act, hurling the lamp at Laura. By the end of the play we understand that the supposedly strong figure of Act I is really a complex human being undone by the duality of his own character. Laura is not to be exonerated, but as a character she lacks depth, as do nearly all Strindberg's characters except for the ones in each play who suggest Strindberg himself. Laura acts on instinct, and so we cannot analyze her motives. The Captain explains himself at many points, one of the most important of which is this third-act speech to Bertha:

> You have two souls. You love me with one and hate me with the other. You must love me and only me. You must have only one soul or you'll have no peace—neither shall I. You must have only one mind, fruit of my mind. You must have only one will—mine!

He might well be talking to himself. For the Strindberg hero has two souls, one the masculine, aggressive character the Captain tries to be, and the other, as Brustein has shown, a feminine, childlike soul. This is the little boy who wants to be mothered, to be nursed and protected from the terrors of the world. This is the captain who first married Laura, who took her as his second mother. This is the captain who allows the nurse to put the straitjacket on him in the final act. The last sequence of action, a symbolic desexing of the Captain, reduces him to infancy, something a part of him really wants; but the other soul revolts against the tyranny of woman, and his stroke occurs as a final protest against his defeat. Thus, what makes *The Father* work dramatically is not so much the conflict between Laura and the Captain as the conflict within the Captain himself.

Viewed from the perspective of the reality-illusion theme, *The Father* stands, on the surface, as a strong statement against Ibsen's hope that the deeper reality may be reached through a union of male and female. It seems to say that reality is conflict, conflict between male and female, and that survival is all that matters. On a deeper level the play denies its own surface assertions. Strindberg, during this period, was full of talk about Darwin, and he sent *The Father*, as an example of his Darwinian worldview, to both Zola and Nietzsche. For a while he espoused, with great enthusiasm, Nietzsche's view of woman.[4] But for all this, as both Brustein and Bentley remind us, we never quite believe him. Maybe the real illusion is that the male can eliminate the feminine element in his soul or that he ought to. Within the naturalistic view of reality that Strindberg is trying so hard to propagate, there is no room for kindness, gentleness, or spirituality, and Strindberg will have to go through ten years of hell before he will successfully rebuild his vision to incorporate these elements.

In the meantime, naturalism comes even more strongly to the fore in *Miss Julie* (1888). The play, with its deservedly famous preface, is the most objective play Strindberg wrote. Strindberg himself is not at all like Jean; Siri is not at all like Julie. The playwright wrote better than he knew, when he completed this play, because the preface indicates that he wanted the play to exist as a completely scientific picture of a struggle for dominance between two people. He wanted Jean to appear as essentially without guilt, simply the stronger in a battle which was inevitable, given the conditions of his ambition and Julie's noble heritage. In essence, says Strindberg in the preface, Julie's feelings of guilt and her need to make some atonement for her act are signs of weakness and degeneration, while Jean's calmness is a sign of strength. Yet the play

25

works dramatically in quite a different manner. We admire Jean's restraint, his coolness, his adept handling of Julie's strange and reckless manner in the first half of the play. But as the play progresses, Jean's hardness becomes increasingly repulsive, culminating in the scene where he kills the bird. Julie is broken at the end, but she is not without dignity:

> Push the responsibility on to Jesus, like Kristin does? No, I'm too proud and—thanks to my father's teaching—too intelligent. . . . Whose fault is it? What does it matter whose fault it is? In any case I must take the blame and bear the consequences.

Jean, transformed into the cringing valet by the return of the count, loses what little strength he had and can only hope that Julie's inherent nobility will rescue him from an ugly situation. It is Julie who "walks firmly out through the door" at the end. The point I wish to make is that though the situation is almost totally reversed from that in *The Father*, it is still the weaker character to whom our sympathy is drawn. Strindberg is still not a pure naturalist. Normally he will pit a sympathetic male figure against an emancipated woman as in *The Father, Comrades*, and *There Are Crimes and Crimes*. What makes *Miss Julie* unique is that the female is for once both the weaker character of the two and the more sympathetic. Strindberg's objectivity is particularly noteworthy when we realize that Julie is the type of woman whom Strindberg describes in the preface with clear disgust as the modern "half-woman . . . who thrusts herself forward, selling herself nowadays for power, decorations, distinctions, diplomas, as formerly for money." When we compare the skillful psychological portrait of Julie with the playwright's caricature of the half-women, Bertha and Abel, in *Comrades*, we can see what happens when an artist allows his passion to overcome his self-discipline.

What both the plays and the events of this period of Strindberg's life tend to confirm is that the playwright was attempting to support himself during the last seven years of his marriage (1884–91) by imposing on reality a set of impossible conditions. He had convinced himself that the only happy relationship was that between a dominant male and a submissive, feminine wife. He adored his daughters and wanted to be able to think of himself as the proud father surrounded by his worshiping, happy family. When reality turned out to be tragically different, he struck out at "modern" thinkers like Ibsen, blaming them for ruining women. One might say that Strindberg's image of the happy family was his vital lie, a sustaining illusion that he both nurtured and struggled to outgrow throughout his life. What made this condition particularly tragic was

26

that he continued, despite their mutual recriminations, to love Siri until they died, within months of one another, in 1912. In the process, however, Strindberg discovered and put on the stage for the first time in modern form the love-hate relationship. He had seen that love could not stop the power struggle any more than the struggle for power could totally destroy love. The Captain and Laura, Jean and Julie, Axel and Bertha are all tied together in a dance of death (to use the title of one of Strindberg's most famous later plays) in which they make love by fighting. They are the antecedents of Shaw's Jack Tanner and Ann Whitefield, of Albee's George and Martha, and of a host of Eugene O'Neill couples. The Nietzschean male and the womanly woman might be illusions, but in his groping for some basis of hope and peace for himself, Strindberg created one of the central themes of modern drama—the notion that love was a state of war in which each party, like a vampire, sustained his own life by feeding on the other. Images of vampires will permeate Strindberg's later plays, as he comes to depict with increasing complexity and compassion the paradox of a love that destroys itself in its own growth.

During the 1890s, Strindberg's view of reality underwent a series of changes, changes literally forced upon him by events that denied him emphatically his customary roles as Prometheus or Faust; yet his change is not as complete as many critics have made out. It is rather a shift in emphasis. Gunnar Brandell, in a brilliant essay on *To Damascus*, Part I, catches the balance perfectly:

> When the Stranger is forced to his knees by the pangs of conscience in the Asylum scene in the center of the play, then occurs that searching of the soul that was also the central experience of Strindberg's Inferno crisis. But just as Strindberg's titanism carries within itself an awareness of a coming defeat, so his surrender contains a note of defiance and victory.[5]

The Stranger, who is in one sense the only real character in *To Damascus*, Part I, is a familiar character. He is the Herculean, Promethean rebel of the early plays, sullen, defiant, unconventional. But he is also the more humble, chastened, Christ-like male of the later plays. This is why *To Damascus* is so central to an understanding of both the "old" and the "new" Strindberg. The play is divided into seventeen scenes, as follows:

On the Street Corner
At the Doctor's House

At the Hotel Room
By the Sea
On the Road
In the Ravine
In the Kitchen
In the Rose Room
The Asylum
The Rose Room
The Kitchen
In the Ravine
On the Road
By the Sea
The Hotel Room
At the Doctor's Home
The Street Corner

What strikes us here is not only the perfect symmetry of the play's construction but the way Strindberg uses the symmetry to develop his theme. In the first scene the Stranger meets the Lady (modeled on Strindberg's second wife, Frida Uhl), and after an encounter with the Doctor, who is both the Lady's husband and an old school acquaintance the Stranger once wronged, he sets off with the Lady to meet her mother and grandfather. His attitude throughout these adventures is sullen, prideful, bitter. He resents both his poverty and the charity of others. He uses the Lady to gain strength. "When I'm alone," he tells her in the first scene, "I'm as weak as a paralytic. But as soon as I fasten onto someone, strength comes flowing back into me." He insists on viewing life from its darkest perspective, and he finally goes mad, when the Lady reads the book he has forbidden her to open. In the Asylum scene the Abbess tells him: "You were seen in the mountains above the ravine, with a cross you had torn down from a calvary, and you were using it to challenge someone you imagined you could see in the clouds." Here is the archetypal image of the defeated titan challenging the gods, the last gasp of Strindberg's Nietzschean phase burning itself out in the agony of the Inferno crisis. The Abbess sends him back to the Rose Room, where his recovery slowly begins. There the Mother tells him: "Don't you see that you've misunderstood everything by thinking of it as an affair just between you and the others, when it's really a matter between you and Him?"

The Stranger must come to understand that both he and others are under the control of powers rendering them unable to resist certain temptations and vices. People do not commit crimes because they want to. Maurice in *There Are Crimes and Crimes* meets Henriette because fate, in the form of Emile blocking the kitchen door, prevents his escape. The death of Marion in that same play seems the result of a weird act of fate that just happens to coincide with Maurice and Henriette's drunken wishes. Human beings must learn that they have little control over their destinies. Chastened by this new understanding, the Stranger must, in the second half of *To Damascus*, retrace his steps:

THE MOTHER: My son, you have left Jerusalem and you are on the way to Damascus. Go there. The same way you came here. And plant a cross at each station, but stop at the seventh. You don't have fourteen as He had.

THE STRANGER: You're talking in riddles.

THE MOTHER: Then let me put it this way. Travel. Look up those you have something to say to. And first of all, your wife.

And so he begins his journey, seeking to ask forgiveness of those he had formerly offended—especially the Beggar, the Lady, and the Doctor. But the Stranger is no Saint Paul. The road to Damascus contains no total conversion. Reality, the new Strindberg seems to say, is spiritual. Humans must suffer a series of penitential experiences; they must be tested again and again; they must be punished. But the Stranger will never find the peace of complete faith. The Lady invites him, in the closing scene, into the church; but he is skeptical. "Come, please," she asks, and he responds, "Oh well, I can always pass through. But as for staying there—definitely not." He follows her toward the church door, but the church will not be his final resting place. There is still too much of the worldly man.

In *Crimes and Crimes*, written in 1899, Maurice is invited by the Abbe to come to the church to do penance for the sin of wishing his daughter dead. Maurice is all ready to become a convert, when news comes to him that his play is to reopen and that the public has forgiven him. And so Maurice makes a compromise: "Tonight I meet you at the church to settle accounts with myself. But tomorrow—I go to the theater." The endings of *To Damascus*, Part I, and *Crimes and Crimes* are strikingly similar and, I agree with Eric Bentley, closer to revealing the true Strindberg than the more celebrated early naturalist plays or the more purely spiritual *Dream Play*. Bentley writes:

Strindberg, known as a dogmatist, was above all a skeptic. That is clear from *There Are Crimes and Crimes*. Perhaps all the Chamber Plays, intentionally or not, bear witness to it. In them we see his inability to believe

29

not only the materialism of his youth, which he now openly abhorred, but also the religion which he pretended to have discovered later and which he was to go on parading till the day when he asked that the Bible should solemnly be laid upon his corpse.[6]

But Bentley's statement, through words such as "pretended" and "paraded," goes too far in implying that the religion of Strindberg's later years was not genuine. The tone of Bentley's statement fails to convey the reality of Strindberg's struggle to believe, particularly during the period of his courtship of and marriage to Harriet Bosse in 1900 and 1901.

What happens during this phase is that the male-female conflict becomes integrated with religious themes, so that the acceptance of the female is almost equated with religious faith. Gunnar Ollen argues that the stages of love in Strindberg's work parallel the stages of religious faith. He indicates five phases: (1) love at first sight; (2) adoration or worship; (3) courtship; (4) suspicion accompanied by feelings of inferiority that prompt attack; and (5) struggle, conflict, and separation. Part of Strindberg wants to worship the woman or the divine, but the other part rebels against it. Thus Strindberg's position, Ollen concludes, is a "yearning for the protection of the Eternal One, conceived as father or divine mother, together with a pride that revolts against the lack of freedom implied in such protection."[7]

In this light it is foolish to call Strindberg either a misogynist or an atheist. The woman-hatred, like the atheism, is part of the cycle, part of the attempt to achieve comprehension, a comprehension that he never fully found because of the skepticism, because of the pride, but one that he genuinely and deeply wanted to achieve. This is most clearly seen in *Easter* (1900) and *A Dream Play* (1901).

In both plays a central female character, Eleanora in the first play and the Daughter of Indra in the second, achieves a direct communication with the divine that is impossible for the male characters. In a method of characterization that anticipates and parallels the Jungian division of the unconscious self into the anima (the feminine part of the male, which must be discovered and integrated before the personality can mature) and the animus (the masculine element within the female psyche), Strindberg creates in these two plays characters that represent both parts of the self.

In *Easter* the Heyst family has been nearly destroyed by a series of catastrophes—the death and disgrace of the father, the apparent mental instability of the daughter, and the failure of the play's protagonist, Elis, the son, to prepare his pupil, Benjamin, for the Student Examination. The play, which opens suitably on Maundy Thursday, is one about death and resurrection, suffering and renewal. The resurrection and renewal are brought about primarily by Eleanora, the Easter-child who returns from the sanatorium, bringing light and joy into this bleak atmosphere where spring cannot quite seem to overcome winter. "Poor Eleanora," remarks her brother, "she's so unhappy herself, and yet she can make others happy." And throughout the play she does, giving the young student, Benjamin, a reason for living, reviving the spirit of her mother, and even touching Elis, the most moody and brooding figure in the play. Her religion allows her to comprehend intuitively that the divine at the center of life overcomes human suffering, as Christ through his resurrection overcame the death of the cross. She sees—as Strindberg struggled to believe—that her mission in life is to bear the suffering of others, to take their pain upon herself, not because she has done wrong but because she is capable, through her faith, of bearing the pain.

In Eleanora we see the spirituality, the oneness with spirit, toward which Strindberg is striving. In Elis we see the moody, skeptical part of the self. In *A Dream Play* we see these dualities played out in much more complex and thorough fashion. The play, despite its title and its apparently formless structure, is a carefully wrought parable about human life, in which the Daughter of Indra, like Christ, comes to earth to study the human condition out of compassion for mankind. The play is divided into three major sections, each dominated by a different aspect of the male personality. In the first third the dominant figure is the Officer, who might be equated with the romantic idealism of Strindberg's youth. He waits eternally outside the stage door for Victoria. Time passes with the fragmentation and distortion of a dream. He grows old and then young again. Nothing changes. Victoria never comes, and even if she did, she would not be quite what he had in mind, any more than the green tackle box and fishnet is quite what the Billsticker had in mind. In the first phase of the play, romantic aspirations are presented, only to be shattered and disillusioned.

In the middle section of the play, the central male figure is the Lawyer. Just as the Daughter of Indra is forced to take on the suffering of humanity in the first part by wearing the shawl of the Doorkeeper outside the opera, so in the second part she participates fully in human life by marrying the Lawyer. The scene depicting their married life comes at the very center of *A Dream Play*, at the farthest remove from the world of spirit. This is important to understand. For just as the marriage between the Lawyer and the Daughter of Indra is the most realistic scene in the

31

play, it is at the same time the most nightmarish. There is no escape for them. Kristin gradually pastes up all the cracks in the room, destroying the air, and the Daughter of Indra, who is spirit, begins to die. Likewise, the Lawyer, who has devoted himself to the eradication of human suffering, begins to take on the likeness of the sufferers he has helped. His ugliness symbolizes the necessity of the innocent suffering of the good. In the material world, Strindberg suggests, everything is backward. To right matters, the individual must consciously purge the self of earthly concerns and return to the realm of spirit. Thus the structure of the play is one of descent and ascent: in the final movement the Daughter of Indra returns to the spiritual realm through a process of suffering and transcendence. "Deliverance," says Maurice Valency in *The Flower and the Castle*, "is a matter of freeing the spirit from its material involvements. This necessitates suffering."[8] Once we see this, the play's third movement becomes clear. The central male symbol in the third movement is the Poet—who has achieved the comprehension that the Officer and the Lawyer lack. The Daughter of Indra returns to heaven, moving back through the stages by which she descended, ending significantly at the Growing Castle. Here, as the play ends, the castle bursts into flames and "the flower-bud on the roof bursts into a giant chrysanthemum," symbolizing the blooming of the life of the spirit as it grows out of the muck and manure of the world of the flesh. It is the Poet who understands this, and the Daughter of Indra leaves earth, assuring him that she will carry his complaints to her father's throne:

> Farewell you child of man, dreamer,
> poet, who knows best the way to live.
> Above the earth on wings you hover,
> plunging at times to graze the dust
> But not to be submerged.

That Strindberg identified himself with the Poet is evident from a later statement to Harriet Bosse in a letter:

> I am striving toward the heights—but am sinking into the mire; I desire to do the right thing—yet act wrongly; my old self is at odds with my new-born personality: I yearn to discover beauty in life—but find beauty only in nature. . . . The only consolation given me, I receive from Buddha, who tells me quite frankly that life is a phantasm, an illusion, which we will only see in its right perspective in another life.[9]

This statement informs us very clearly of the deepest meaning of the title *A Dream Play*: it is this life that is the dream, and the dream may be pierced only by suffering. As the Daughter of Indra says, " . . . in order to be freed from the earthly element, the descendents of Brahma sought renunciation and suffering. And so you have suffering as the deliverer. But this yearning for suffering comes into conflict with the longing for joy, for love." And it is precisely this conflict that Strindberg is never able to resolve either in the plays or in his life. He can never renounce love, nor be happy in it. Love is still conflict; thus, despite all he had written about his desire to change, the marriage between the playwright and Harriet Bosse erupted into explosive quarrels that led finally to her need for a divorce. "Can't you understand why I went away?" she asks him in a letter. "I left in order to save at least the final remnant of what remains of womanly modesty and self respect."[10] Instead of acting out *A Dream Play*, Strindberg and Harriet end up playing *The Dance of Death*.

And so we might argue that Strindberg throughout his late phase as a playwright, from the end of the Inferno crisis in 1898 until his final play, *The Great Highway*, in 1909, is trying to make a breakthrough, which never quite happens, trying to find a faith, a peace within himself, which never comes. In *The Ghost Sonata*, the most famous of the chamber plays, that struggle toward peace is symbolized by the attempts of the old man, Hummel, to atone for his past sins by working off his own guilt and exposing the guilt of others. Just as in *The Dance of Death*, Part II (1900), hope emerges through the love of Allan, Kurt's son, and Judith, Edgar's daughter, so in *The Ghost Sonata* (1907), the love between Adele, Hummel's daughter, and the student, Arkenholtz, symbolizes a spiritual union that will transcend the evil of this world. But in both plays that union is too fragile to survive in this life. Adele's strength has been sapped by the struggle of "keeping the dirt of life at a distance," one of Strindberg's favorite images, and she dies at the end, leaving us with perhaps the most persistent thought to be generated by Strindberg's late plays—that only death can release us from this place of illusion called earth and that, if there is an answer behind the cloverleaf door, not even our most persistent inquiries will answer the riddle in this life. Austin Quigley's perceptive essay on *A Dream Play* summarizes the tone of Strindberg's final phase most effectively:

> At the end of the play, the on-stage characters, like the off-stage audience, adopt their recurrent stance of persistent inquiry; at the same time the burning castle and the flower bud on its roof recapitulate our recognition that transcendent inquiry consists of reaching towards what we cannot grasp, and that in so doing, we, like the flower, "bloom and die."[11]

33

4

Anton Chekhov

> VOINITSKY: *Age has nothing to do with it. When one has no real life, one lives on illusions. It's better than nothing.*
>
> SONYA: *The hay has all been mowed and with the rain every day, it's rotting, and you occupy yourself with illusions. You've completely neglected the estate . . .*
>
> —Uncle Vanya, Act III

For all his vaunted realism, Chekhov is a playwright of patterns—clear, indelible, almost archetypal patterns. His genius lies in how well he hides them: he is a master of disguise. In his important study *Chekhov the Dramatist*, David Magarshack calls Chekhov's last four dramas "plays of indirect action."[1] On the surface there is life, just as Chekhov says there should be:

> After all in real life people don't spend every minute shooting each other, hanging themselves and making confessions of love. They don't spend all the time saying clever things. They're more occupied with eating, drinking, flirting, and talking stupidities—and these are the things which ought to be shown on the stage. A play should be written in which people arrive, go away, have dinner, talk about the weather and play cards. Life must be exactly as it is, and people as they are—not on stilts. . . . Let everything on the stage be just as complicated, and at the same time just as simple as it is in life. People eat their dinner, just eat their dinner, and all the time their happiness is being established their lives are being broken up.[2]

Underneath that surface there is a strong pattern, and before we can understand what illusion and reality really are in Chekhov, we must understand that pattern. To me it looks like this.

The scene is a country estate—Sorin's in *The Sea Gull*; Vanya's sister's (the professor's first wife) in *Uncle Vanya*; the Prozorovs' in *The Three Sisters*; and Lyubov and Gayev's in *The Cherry Orchard*. On these estates there live (and sometimes work) characters with whom the audience is invited to sympathize: Treplev in *The Sea Gull*; Sonya and her uncle in *Uncle Vanya*; the three sisters and their brother, Andrei, in *The Three*

Sisters; and Lyubov, Gayev, Anya, and Varya in *The Cherry Orchard*. I call these people "soft" characters.

As Harvey Pitcher notes in *The Chekhov Play: A New Interpretation*, into the world of these soft characters a new group intrudes.[3] Often relatives or friends of the first group, they gain power as the play develops, and at the end of the play they either have control over the estate or over the lives of the central figures in the first group. They are "hard" characters, more practical and clearly more successful in dealing with the real world than the first group. Arthur Ganz calls them "the catalyst group."[4] They would include Trigorin and Arkadina in *The Sea Gull*; Serebryakov and his second wife, Elena, in *Uncle Vanya*; Natasha and Protopopov in *The Three Sisters*; and Lopakhin in *The Cherry Orchard*.

There is a third group of characters, outside the central action because they are not directly involved in the transfer of power but essential to the pattern and in some ways the most important part of it—these I will call the philosophizers, because they are great talkers—Nina in *The Sea Gull*, Astrov in *Uncle Vanya*, Vershinin and Tuzenbach in *The Three Sisters*, and Trofimov in *The Cherry Orchard*. If we except Tuzenbach, who is killed in a duel by Soliony, we may note that none of these characters is defeated. They all leave the worlds of their respective plays to go on talking somewhere else about their two favorite subjects—work and the future.

Their importance in the pattern cannot be stressed too much. We know from Chekhov's letters that their views about work and the future are often his own, and we must deal with them very carefully. Here, for example, is an important Chekhov statement to which we must make reference later:

> I simply wanted to say to people in all honesty: "Look at yourselves, see how badly and boringly you live." The important thing is that people should understand that; and if they do understand it, they will surely build different and better lives for themselves. I shall not live to see it, but I know it will be completely different, nothing like what we have today.[5]

A closer look at the four plays will reveal that the pattern is not nearly so clear in *The Sea Gull* as it is in the other three plays; therefore, I will examine the last three plays in some detail and then look at the ways in which *The Sea Gull* is different before proceeding to a conclusion.[6]

In *Uncle Vanya* (1897) the normal running of the estate has been ruined by the arrival of the professor and his twenty-seven-year-old wife,

Elena. He works on manuscripts that, according to Vanya, show no understanding of his field. He writes only what "intelligent people already know and stupid people aren't interested in" (somehow that line always makes me shudder). If this is so (it may be that Vanya's jealousy causes him to exaggerate, but I have never had any love for the professor and prefer to believe Vanya), then the life of the estate is built on a lie. As Vanya claims, he and his mother and Sonya have worked for twenty-five years to support a fool, in whom they had for a long time believed. "A soap bubble," says Vanya. So be it, but the professor has had enormous success with women, and more importantly, he has power over every character in the play. Elena chooses to stay with him, Sonya and Vanya continue to work for him, old Maria worships him, and if Vanya's outburst in the third act has saved the estate, it has so totally incapacitated him that the professor's power over him will, it seems, be even more firmly established in the future. One point of the play may well be that the world exists to serve people like the professor and Elena. He is a pompous ass, and she is beautiful and intelligent, but bored, idle, and utterly useless. The soft characters lack the will, the potency, the energy to change things. Chekhov's third-act climax, in which Vanya attempts to shoot the professor and misses, becomes the perfect symbol for the title character's frustrations. He can't even do *that* right. It's a bit like a Western where you have the incompetent good guys—bumbling Vanya and poor, plain Sonya—and the successful bad guys—the professor and Elena—and the bad guys ride off into the night with an income from the good guys, who rather pathetically turn to God (who isn't going to help) for some solace for their suffering.

At least Astrov has the consolation of the forests. Like Vanya and Sonya, he is worn out with work. "Life itself is boring, stupid, squalid. . . . It drags you down, this life," he tells the old nurse, Maria. Doctoring has killed his joy of life, destroyed his capacity to love, blunted his emotions. But he still has his dream. Vanya has given his life for an illusion, but Astrov's name points to something higher and more distant. "If a thousand years from now, mankind is happy, I shall be responsible for that too, in a small way," he says, tying together the two crucial themes of work and the future. If we work hard enough now, if we shed our illusions about reality and devote ourselves to change, then life will improve. Here is Chekhov's Hegelianism, similar to Ibsen's and even more similar to Shaw's, where reality, as it ought to be, stands before us like a beacon to the future. We will come back to this theme again.

In *The Three Sisters* (1901) the pattern is nearly the same. The play opens in a much happier mood, with the celebration of Irina's name day, but as the four acts progress, we see Natasha's gradual takeover of the house, with her husband, Andrei, at the end outside pushing a baby carriage, while the invisible Protopopov remains inside, master both of the house and of the town itself. He is not only Natasha's lover but chairman of the school board and thereby Andrei's superior. There is no avoiding his presence or that of Natasha, who grows from a timid, uncouth country girl into a proud and forceful manipulator of people. Of all Chekhov's characters she is the hardest. Andrei, her husband, admits, "A wife is a wife. She's honest, good . . . well, kind, but for all that, there's something in her that reduces her to the level of a small, blind sort of thick-skinned animal. In any case she's not a human being." She will move Andrei, as soon as the sisters leave, into Irina's room and cut down the fir trees. She even gets her revenge on Irina by complaining about the young girl's sash—she hasn't forgotten the first act.

Magarshack suggests in *Chekhov the Dramatist* that we may read *The Three Sisters* almost as a morality play, where life and death struggle for control. The "life" characters are those who possess warmth, personal charm, culture, intelligence, grace. In Ganz's words, they yearn "for a new state of being in a world beyond the life of pettiness, drudgery, and disappointment to which their selves are confined."[7] They want *more*. They would include the three sisters, Andrei, Vershinin, and Tuzenbach. The "death" figures have either given up on life, such as Chebutykin, who can no longer work as a doctor but writes down home cures from the local newspaper, or are sources of boredom and frustration for the "life" figures. They would include Natasha and Protopopov, Soliony, and Masha's husband, Kulygin. The life figures are soft; the death figures, hard. Natasha destroys Andrei; Soliony kills Tuzenbach; Kulygin continually oppresses Masha and is left in control when Vershinin, the most vibrant of the life figures, leaves at the end of the play. As in *Uncle Vanya*, the figures with whom we most identify are all but defeated. I say "all but" because the play ends with a remarkable dedication to life by Olga, Masha, and Irina:

> OLGA: . . . our sufferings will turn to joy for those who live after us, happiness and peace will come to this earth, and then they will remember kindly and bless those who are living now. Oh my dear sisters, our life is not over yet. We shall live! The music is so gay, so joyous, it seems as if a little more and we shall know why we live, why we suffer. . . . If only we knew, if only we knew.

Two things need to be said about this speech. First, Olga's emphasis on the future parallels the philosophy that Vershinin expresses several times earlier in the play:

VERSHININ: In two or three hundred years, let's say a thousand years—
the time doesn't matter—a new, happy life will dawn. We'll have no
part in that life, of course, but we are living for it now, working, yes,
suffering, and creating it—in that alone lies the purpose of our existence, and, if you like, our happiness.

Second, Vershinin's speech really does answer her question: we live and
suffer to create the better life. At another point in the play, Vershinin tells
the sisters that though there are only three of them in their town today,
there will be six someday, then twelve, and eventually a majority of
cultured people in the community. But is he right? Is the Astrov-Ver-
shinin-Tuzenbach dream of a better future merely another vital lie, an
illusion one must believe to give life meaning?

The Cherry Orchard (1904) pushes the question a little further. Again
we see the familiar transfer of power. Lyubov, Anya, and Gayev return
home to the estate after a long absence. They hope to save the cherry
orchard, but all their efforts are totally ineffectual, because they have no
capacity to face the real world. Gayev goes to borrow money from their
aunt, but the money is only a fraction of what it would cost to save the
orchard. Lyubov refuses to allow the land to be broken up into tracts,
because she finds summer cottages vulgar. In short, the aristocrats in
this play are sentimental, inefficient, disorganized, but generous to a
fault (Lyubov gives money to a beggar when she can't even buy her
servants food).

Enter Lopakhin, structurally the heir to Serebryakov and Natasha. The
first thing we notice about him is how much warmer he is, and I think it
possible to do a production of the play in which he becomes the central
character, the person through whom we experience the play. He is
devoted to the family. The son of a serf, he has grown up on the estate
and feels both a sense of loyalty to the family members as individuals
and a personal attachment to the estate, if not the orchard. His speech in
the third act, when he has bought the orchard, is not a vindictive one but
a cry of joy:

I bought the estate where my father and grandfather were slaves, where
they weren't even allowed in the kitchen. . . . Come on, everybody, and see
how Yermolai Lopakhin will lay the ax to the cherry orchard, how the trees
will fall to the ground! We're going to build summer cottages, and our
grandsons and great-grandsons will see a new life here. . . . Music! Strike
up!

He knows that his purchase of the orchard is painful for Lyubov, and he also knows that his step is not a final answer to anything. "Oh, if only all this could be over quickly, if somehow our discordant, unhappy life could be changed," he cries in the very next speech, balancing the joy of his ownership with a surprising show of sensitivity to the awkwardness of the situation for the others. Lopakhin is a bear in some ways, unable to talk to Varya when left alone with her and boorish enough to start cutting down the trees before the family has left, but he is not evil, only human, only the new middle class on the rise and anxious to get started.

Of all Chekhov's plays *The Cherry Orchard* is the most objective, the most perfect fulfillment of his dramatic theory. The pattern is still there, but our emotions are not guided, as in *Uncle Vanya* and *The Three Sisters*, to one side. In *The Cherry Orchard* the soft characters are a little too silly to be totally sympathetic, and the hard characters aren't nearly so hard (except, perhaps, for the callous young servant, Yasha). The balance is more even. Gayev's speeches to the bookcase and to nature are meant to be laughable. Lyubov, for all her tears, gets what she really wants: she goes back to her lover in Paris. There is a sense of appropriateness at the end that is missing in the other plays, and it helps to explain why Chekhov insisted so vehemently on this play being a comedy, even a farce in places.

Trofimov, the philosophizer of the play, is also different from his predecessors. He makes a marvelous speech about work and about the future in Act II:

> We are at least two hundred years behind the times, we have as yet absolutely nothing, we have no definite attitude toward the past, we only philosophize, complain of boredom, or drink vodka. Yet it's quite clear that to begin to live we must first atone for the past, be done with it, and we can atone for it only by suffering, only by extraordinary, unceasing labor.

Of course he is right, and words to this effect may be found in Chekhov's letters and notebooks. What Chekhov hopes is that we will not confuse the validity of Petya's ideas with a belief that he will do what he describes. As a character in the play, poor Petya is destined to be an eternal student, but that does not invalidate what he says. As Richard Peace points out in an excellent recent study,[8] one of Chekhov's great gifts in characterization is to balance the good and bad, appealing and unappealing characteristics in all his figures. That is one of the things that makes *The Cherry Orchard* his best play, but also the most elusive to analyze. Trofimov and Lopakhin, between them, represent the future, and neither character is idealized. The result is that the richer life envisioned by Astrov, Vershinin, and Trofimov himself is both postponed to a more distant future (Ganz's point in *Realms of the Self*) and called into question as a conceivable reality.

By contrast, Nina's idea of the richer life in *The Sea Gull* (1896) is neither postponed nor unduly idealized. The theme of the play is the nature of the artist: the four central figures are all artists—Treplev, an unsuccessful playwright and writer of fiction; Trigorin, a successful novelist and short-story writer; Arkadina (Treplev's mother), a successful actress; and Nina, the title figure, a potentially successful actress. Treplev's failure is the result not only of his softness, a sensitivity that makes him overreact to criticism, but of his lack of direction, of purpose. "You have found your way, you know where you are going," he says to Nina at the end, "but I'm still drifting in a chaos of images and dreams, without knowing why it is necessary, or for whom . . . I have no faith, and I don't know what my vocation is."

"There is a sort of stagnation in my soul," Chekhov had written to his friend and editor, Alexi Suvorin, just before his fateful trip to the island of Sakhalin off the coast of Siberia. For Chekhov the trip to Sakhalin and his study of the conditions in the penal colony there was a means of spiritual and emotional regeneration, and a rededication of his life as an artist to depicting not only "life as it is" but "life as it should be."[9] Treplev never finds that sense of purpose. He and his opposite, Trigorin, are both missing something essential. If Treplev creates worlds without living characters, forms without substance, then Trigorin is the totally successful realist, the Chekhov of the early stories, with marvelous "real" characters and subtle descriptive effects, but without depth and passion. And he knows it. In Act II he says to Nina, " . . . I feel that I only know how to paint landscapes, and in all the rest I am false—false to the very marrow of my bones."

Trigorin and Arkadina are the hard characters in this play, hard in the sense that they are sensible and reasonable practitioners of their crafts, successful because they are experts in working in the media they have chosen. There is a certain and inevitable callousness that comes with success. Trigorin is so used to being courted by women that he simply accepts Nina's advances because it is an exciting new experience for him; when he is through with her he casts her aside as Treplev destroys the original sea gull. He and Arkadina are not treated as villains, only as limited human beings.

Thus far the pattern of *The Sea Gull* is quite similar to that of the other plays: the destruction of the soft central figure (Treplev) and the success of the hard figures. Of course there is no transfer of power, as in the last two plays, because Treplev, like Vanya, never had the power to begin with. The important difference in the play is Nina. I know of no other character in Chekhov like her. She is not the philosophizer of the last three plays, although in some ways she has that function. The simple fact is that Nina does something almost no other Chekhov character does—she works first and talks afterward. Her growth from sea gull to actress represents the most hopeful and positive element in all of Chekhov's drama. Chekhov does not romanticize this hope but represents it in Nina's last speech in all its unglamorous detail:

> Tomorrow, early in the morning, I must go to Yelets, third class . . . travelling with peasants, and at Yelets the educated merchants will pester me with their attentions. It's a coarse life. . . . Now I'm a real actress, I act with delight, with rapture, I'm intoxicated when I'm on the stage, and I feel that I act beautifully. And since I have been here, I've been walking, continually walking and thinking . . . and I think and feel that my soul is growing stronger with each day. . . . I know now, I understand, that in our work, Kostya—whether it's acting or writing—what's important is not fame, not glory, not the things I used to dream about, but the ability to endure. To be able to bear one's cross and have faith, and it's not so painful now, and when I think of my vocation, I'm not afraid of life.

When *The Sea Gull* was so joyfully accepted by Moscow audiences in 1898 and became the means by which Chekhov's dramatic career and that of the Moscow Art Theater were successfully launched, Stanislavsky and Nemirovitch-Danchenko, in gratitude, had emblazoned on the curtain the image of a sea gull. "I'm a sea gull," says Nina. "No that's not it . . . I'm an actress." The sea gull itself is an ironic symbol for Chekhov, appropriate in some ways and not in others. The germ of the play is in Chekhov's letter to Suvorin on April 8, 1892, where he tells how Levitan, the painter, who was visiting Melikhovo, shot a snipe and then asked Chekhov to finish it off. "I had to obey Levitan and kill it. One more beautiful enamored creature gone, while two fools went home and sat down to supper."[10] In this light we may see the sea gull as a symbol of innocence or beauty. Nina, who is both innocent and beautiful at the opening of the play, is used by Treplev and Trigorin, the two artists; but if she were nothing more than a sea gull, she would be destroyed. "No that's not it," she cries. "I'm an actress."

As an actress she has strength, faith, devotion to her work, and that extraordinary power of endurance people have when they are possessed by a cause. Nina finds the purpose both Treplev and Trigorin lack. This is what Chekhov is talking about in his famous letter to Suvorin of November 25, 1892:

> Remember that the writers whom we call eternal or simply good and who intoxicate us have one very important characteristic in common: they move in a certain direction. . . . The best of them are realistic, and paint life as it is, but because every line is permeated, as with sap, by the consciousness of a purpose, you are aware not only of life as it is, but of life as it ought to be, and that captivates you. And we? We! We paint life as it is, and beyond that . . . we cannot go a step farther. We have neither immediate nor distant aims and our souls are a yawning void.[11]

Now we can put together a synthesis. It is almost a Blakean world that Chekhov has created. A is innocence, B is experience, and C is that third world that can convert the suffering of experience into a new and deeper vision. Ganz notes that the central symbol in each of the last plays—"the sea gull, Astrov's forests in *Uncle Vanya*, Moscow in *The Three Sisters*, and in Chekhov's final play the cherry orchard itself"[12]—is associated with the romantic longings, the innocent hopes of the characters with whom we most sympathize. These symbols are all associated with the world of innocence. Opposed to this world is that of experience, the hard world where one must be practical to succeed. In Chekhov the illusion-reality conflict takes, first of all, the form of the conflict between innocence and experience. In the *real* world, innocence is destroyed over and over again. It is an illusion to believe that it can be maintained. Perhaps that is the problem of the central figures in *The Three Sisters* and *The Cherry Orchard*. The members of the Prozorov family and the Gayev family keep living with the illusion that they can go to Moscow and that they can keep the cherry orchard. They want to remain children forever. But if the destruction of innocence is inevitable, the victory of realism is hardly enough. The real world is not the final reality for Chekhov any more than it is for Ibsen and Strindberg. Beneath the surface Chekhov is a lot more like Ibsen than he looks. There is a Chekhovian synthesis that combines hard work with the joy of life, paralleling Ibsen's hoped-for synthesis of Christian and pagan. In both playwrights this synthesis is postponed, unreachable until human beings and society will have changed. It is a synthesis suggested in Chekhov's last play by the two characters who stand for the future—Lopakhin, the hardworking merchant, and Trofimov, the idealistic student. The best qualities of each must be combined for a better society to come about.

Of all Chekhov's characters Nina comes closest to embodying the ideal. She does go from A to B to C, as Ellie Dunn will in Shaw's *Heartbreak House*. The problem is that we don't see B, because it takes place during the two-year passage between Acts III and IV. She does what Natasha and Lopakhin cannot do: she becomes immersed in reality without being destroyed by it. She goes from being a sea gull to being an actress, without losing the element of beauty embodied in the sea gull.

And as for death, the final reality, the good Dr. Chekhov seems not to have worried much about it. He knew it too well to romanticize it, and he loved life too much to welcome it. "I hear people are rejoicing over the death of Tolstoy," he wrote to Suvorin, "and this joy strikes me as gross beastliness. I have no faith in the future of those Christians who, although they hate gendarmes, at the same time hail the death of another and see death as an angel of deliverance."[13]

Like Ernest Simmons, I believe the extraordinary trip Chekhov took to Sakhalin Island in 1890 was one of the central events of his life, and I like particularly the mood of his letter to Suvorin at the moment of his return:

> God's world is good. Only one thing isn't good: ourselves. How little there is in us of justice and humility. . . . What is needed is work; everything else can go to the devil. The main thing is to be just—the rest will be added unto us.[14]

Chekhov was not, by reports, a particularly warm person. He knew how to hold himself aloof. But he gave something more important than that—his knowledge, his skills as a doctor, his art as a playwright for the betterment of human life. He worked tirelessly as a physician, particularly in the area around Melikhovo, and he was always willing to see people who came to him with manuscripts. He especially liked young writers, such as Maxim Gorky, who might have some effect on the future. He retained an extraordinary sense of humor in the face of his own mortal illness and toasted his wife and the attending physician shortly before his death.

In our own age, when so many illusions have established themselves as seeming truths, in an era when extremists on both sides pray to their gods to smite their enemies, when demagogues pass for statesmen and unadulterated greed is gilded with patriotism and religious piety, we would do well to listen to Chekhov's voice. It is a sane and sensible one that encourages us to work for our dreams rather than to blame God or fate for our own failures. It was Christopher Fry who called comedy "a narrow escape into faith."[15] That definition might well apply to the four last plays of Chekhov, whose faith in the future was built both on the belief that human beings can change and the knowledge that change is a slow and treacherous path along which many, like two and twenty misfortunes, will stumble before they reach the end.

5

George Bernard Shaw

When you are asked, "Where is God? Who is God?"
stand up and say, "I am God and here is God, not as
yet completed, but still advancing towards completion,
just in so much as I am working for the purpose of the
universe, working for the good of the whole world,
instead of merely looking after my personal ends."

—"The New Theology"

Of the playwrights in this study, Shaw is the most self-consciously and consistently concerned with the breakthrough to the higher life; and, as many recent studies, such as those by Alfred Turco and Warren Sylvester Smith, have made clear,[1] it is extremely important to understand Shaw's philosophy-religion, "Creative Evolution," before proceeding to a study of the plays, because it is really from the perspective of this philosophy that all the plays are written. While the dramatic means Shaw employs to express the philosophy evolve considerably, the position he asserts tends to be pretty consistent from *Mrs. Warren's Profession* to *Saint Joan*, a period of thirty years.

Paralleling the work of Henri Bergson (whom Shaw claims not to have read until after he had formulated his ideas), and strongly influenced by Nietzsche, Samuel Butler, and the scientific theories of Lamarck, Shaw's philosophy presents the fundamental point that we must evolve or perish.[2] The central tension in Shaw's work is between life and death, between those forces and individuals that contribute to the evolution of the race and those forces and individuals that contribute to stagnation. Just as Lamarck posited the inheritance of acquired characteristics— the giraffe's neck becomes longer because he *wills* it, and that longer neck is passed on to his descendants—so Shaw believed that society could improve only if men self-consciously willed the evolution of the race.

Like many Christians, Shaw could not reconcile the presence of evil and suffering in the world with a benevolent-omnipotent God, and so he solved the problem by making his "Life Force" benevolent but not omnipotent. The Life Force wills the elimination of evil but is helpless to accomplish its ends without human beings. Men and women are the tools, the "hands" of the Life Force, and to the degree that people seek to know and do the will of the Life Force, civilization has a chance to evolve. But humans prefer their own selfish little wills, their own pleasures; they will death rather than life, as the Devil makes abundantly clear in the "Don Juan in Hell" sequence in *Man and Superman*. And so the struggle ensues between those forces that would destroy life and those that battle for its enhancement.

Thus the central purpose of Shavian drama is to elicit change. Smith sums it up nicely: " . . . one of the characteristics of Shavian drama is that all the characters find themselves challenged in such a way that they have an opportunity to learn something if they will."[3] And Shaw outlines in *The Quintessence of Ibsenism*, first published in 1891, when he was on the verge of his playwrighting career, what it is he hopes people will learn and how he would like them to change. Most people—whom he calls "Philistines"—do not care very much about anything. They are indifferent to ideas and are usually opposed to change because it is uncomfortable; it represents something different from what they are used to. The vast majority of people who are not Philistines Shaw calls "idealists." By this term he means those who are committed to an institution or religious or philosophical position because it is an ideal. They may not be happy with the institution. That is not the point, say the idealists. The institution must be defended because it has been established for all time as "the right." Thus marriage, private property, nationalism may be idealized in Shaw by characters who will defend those institutions to the death. A final group Shaw calls in *The Quintessence* "realists." The realist is "the man strong enough to face the truth the idealists are shirking."[4] He is an iconoclast, an anti-idealist. He says that all institutions, all beliefs must be examined critically and that if they are no longer useful, applicable to the needs of society, then they should be discarded. The realist is the Shavian hero, the one who stands alone, like Ibsen's Dr. Stockmann, to try to bring about those changes that will allow both social and human evolution. The realist is by definition a heretic, a revolutionary, a gadfly to the priests and politicians of the world. Every genuinely religious person, Shaw reminds us in *The Revolutionist's Handbook*, is a revolutionary, because true religion has little to do with the defense of religious institutions.

Hence, Shaw's plays, beginning with *Widowers' Houses* in 1892, are essentially conflicts between realism and idealism, between those who are struggling to bring into being a new way of life and those who stubbornly (and often very humorously) defend outmoded ideas and institutions. In this light, we can understand Shaw's basic comic formula, which is the reverse of Molière's. Molière, whom Shaw greatly admired, usually constructed a relatively rational world and then placed at the center of it a foolish or irrational figure who threatens to upset that world—a Tartuffe, a Don Juan, an Alceste, a Harpagon, or an Arnolphe. At the end of a Molière play the intruder, the imposter, is ousted and order is restored. Shaw, in contrast, tends to place a superior character in a stupid and irrational world. The superior character tries to change the world. If the hero succeeds, then there is a happy ending, or at least a truce. If the protagonist fails, as in many of the later plays, then the play becomes a tragedy like *Saint Joan* or a semitragedy like *Heartbreak House*. Shaw's heroes, male and female alike, are those who hold before the world reality in its deepest sense. They invite the world to join them in the pursuit of that reality. The world usually prefers its own illusions. If we like our illusions very much, we are offended. If we think Shaw is writing about other people's illusions, we laugh and praise Shaw for his wit. That is basically how the plays work.

We see his essential stance as early as *Mrs. Warren's Profession*, written in 1893 but not publicly performed in England until 1925 because of the censorship that found the play, to use one of Shaw's later titles, too true to be good. The play has become, during the past ten years or so, one of the favorites in the Shavian repertoire because of its feminist elements, and recent productions have put the emphasis where it belongs—not on the sensational element of prostitution, but on the play's central character, Vivie Warren. The play might well have been called *The Education of Vivie Warren*, for though the surface theme lay in Shaw's attempt to shock the audience into a realization that they were the ones really responsible for prostitution, the play's deeper issue involves Vivie's choice of life-styles. She is offered essentially four choices: Frank (romantic love), Praed (escape from reality into art through aestheticism), Mrs. Warren (sentimental attachment to mother, no matter what mother does), and Sir George Crofts (co-opting with an evil system for the sake of money). Vivie's decision to join the law firm of Honoria Fraser is neither cynical nor misanthropic. She simply makes the wisest and most mature choice available to her, a choice clearly superior to the other four alternatives.

During the first act she expresses some attachment to Frank and, during the second, moves from Frank to her mother, because she is convinced, and rightly so, that the choice between the paint factory and prostitution was no choice at all and that her mother was justified in choosing prostitution. Her alliance with her mother is the first major step in her education; but when she finds out in the third act that Frank might well be her half brother and that her mother is now an international madam making money off girls similar to the one she once was, then she runs for London, disgusted by love's young dream, Crofts's capitalism, and the hypocrisy of the whole scene. Praed makes a last ditch appeal in Act IV to get her to go to Italy and look at paintings, but she turns that down by reminding him and the pursuing Frank that holidays are more tedious to her than work—which she finds quite exhilarating. Vivie, in the play's closing scene, concludes the pattern by rejecting her mother, not because she is a prude but because she has grown, has changed, has found a higher stage of morality where she wants neither her mother's money nor her life-style. She wants the joy of work.

In his next major play, *Arms and the Man* (1894), Shaw creates a more fully developed version of the hero, the chocolate cream soldier, Captain Bluntschli. In *Mrs. Warren's Profession* Vivie grows into the heroine by becoming disillusioned with what society has to offer. Bluntschli, having become disillusioned before the play opens, serves the central function of disillusioning others. If the world is going to change, people must change, and one of the primary roles of the Shavian hero is to change others by teaching them, one might even say converting them. We see that process of conversion as we look at the way Bluntschli handles the play's romantic figures, Sergius and Raina, both of whom have been playing at life because that was what they felt obliged to do. In *Arms and the Man*, as in most of Shaw's plays, there is an equation between romanticism, idealism, and illusion. Shaw believed that most people lived their lives governed by childish romantic illusions, fed by art, literature, and music. His art, he was determined, would explode these romantic myths. Raina and Sergius conduct their lives according to a romantic script, and the turning point in the play comes when Raina, caught in her high romantic style by Bluntschli, asks, "How did you find me out?" She is *glad* to have been found out, because keeping up the romantic pose is tiring; likewise, Sergius is glad to make love to Louka because his romantic wooing of Raina is exhausting. The happy ending of *Arms and the Man* is possible because the younger characters of the play— Bluntschli, Sergius, Raina, and Louka—are able to form, in Northrop Frye's terms, a new, more realistic, more pragmatic society, based on values that are less artificial than those of that older society represented by Raina's parents, the Petkoffs, and by their former selves.[5]

But happy endings like that of *Arms and the Man* are not particularly characteristic of Shaw. In *Candida* (1895), *Caesar and Cleopatra* (1898), and *Man and Superman* (1903), the next three centrally important plays, something always happens to mute the triumph of the hero. The conversion of the other characters is incomplete. The poet Marchbanks goes out into the night with the secret in his heart, Caesar returns to Rome to face an early death, Don Juan leaves hell to seek out a deeper reality in heaven. Those who are left in charge of society at the end of each of these plays—Candida, Cleopatra, the Devil (in the Hell sequence), and Ann Whitefield—do not promise to make any changes in their worlds based upon what they have learned from the exiled figures. In their respective worlds the women rule supreme. Candida tells her husband, the Reverend James Mavor Morell, that she has let him pretend to be master in her household, and he does not quarrel with her on that point. Cleopatra is glad to see Caesar go, because his presence has cramped her life-style, and Ann Whitefield listens to Jack Tanner's philosophical speeches with amusement. "Go on talking," she says to him in the play's next to last line.

Shaw's Life Force is tricky. Nothing in Shaw's universe exists without some purpose, and so Shaw conceives of sexual attraction between man and woman as an indication that the Life Force has selected them for purposes of breeding. Sterile men, such as Octavius Robinson, the Life Force passes by, but Ann and Jack it endows with powerful sexual attraction toward one another. That is precisely why Jack runs for his life. Of all the conflicts, none is so powerful, Tanner tells Octavius, as the conflict between the artist-man and the mother-woman, because *both* are in the grip of the Life Force, in the hands of something greater than themselves. The mother-woman wants to create life, to bear children, and to find a mate suitable to father and raise those children. She wants to *use* the male for her own purposes, purposes she may not be consciously aware of. Ann, Shaw insists, does not deliberately and self-consciously manipulate Jack. She cannot help being what she is any more than Jack can. He, in turn, has his own calling, that of the artist-philosopher, whose mission it is to reform society. Thus Jack has written *The Revolutionist's Handbook*. He wants to use Ann—for inspiration, for sexual gratification—but he hardly wants to set up domestic housekeeping. He wants the freedom to create. Artists make notoriously bad husbands and fathers, and that is the point of *Candida*. That play could well be a portrait of Jack and Ann fifteen years later if Ann were to have succeeded in taming Jack, for Candida is the ultimate mother-woman. She runs her household with love and with care, and Marchbanks's passion for her forces her to show her hand, something she would never have done otherwise. "Choose between us," they demand, and choose she does, "the weaker of the two." "Do you mean me?" her husband asks, and in doing so, he begins to understand their relationship. He has been the perfect mate for the mother-woman, and Marchbanks, the artist, realizes at the same moment that he must leave to follow his career in silence, in exile from the family, like one of Synge's wandering bards.

Disillusionment may be the prelude to despair; it may be the preface to growth. The marriage between Candida and her husband may never be the same because Morell's idea that he was the master of his home could well have been his vital lie, and vital lies may be necessary for most human beings. But for Marchbanks, the realization of the truth that Candida loves her husband and children is a painful but necessary step forward, a step from adolescent adoration to the recognition that his art will demand of him many hours of lonely toil, something Shaw, his creator, was deeply familiar with. Thus we have in *Candida* one of the central paradoxes of Shaw's work—that only through the transcendence of sexual love can the hero achieve the freedom necessary to create the higher reality toward which we must strive, a higher reality symbolized by the values of the two central male figures in this group of plays— Caesar and Don Juan.[6]

Of all the characters in Shaw's plays, Caesar comes closest to embodying the qualities that Shaw insists the human race must have if it is to survive. He is first of all a practical man capable of quick and efficient decisions in times of crisis. He knows that power is part of life and that the renunciation of power can lead only to useless martyrdom. But he also knows that power can be used in different ways, and his primary purpose for being in Egypt seems to be to teach Cleopatra how to rule. When Caesar finds her in Act I, she is a frightened little girl crouching like a kitten between the paws of the sphinx. As she gets her first taste of power at the end of the act and during Act II, she uses it viciously, striking out at Ftatateeta and her young brother with the claws of a cat. The animal imagery reinforces the play's theme. Caesar wants to turn Cleopatra into a queen. She may turn from a kitten into a cat, from a girl into a woman (note that one of her primary desires is that Caesar leave and send her Mark Antony), but does she ever become a queen? At the beginning of Act IV it would seem so. Charmian, Iras, and the rest of the court are bored because Cleopatra seems so serious. She walks around like Caesar, talks like Caesar, she *appears* to be like Caesar. But the play's climactic action—Ftatateeta's murder of Pothinus by Cleopatra's order— reveals that Cleopatra has not really learned anything except how to scratch more effectively.

At the heart of Caesar's character is his famous clemency, which is born not of weakness, but out of his realization that until human beings put aside vengeance and murder and pride, until they cease killing in order to save face, then murder will continue to beget murder until (in Caesar's words) "the gods become tired and create a race that can understand." Shaw's use of historical perspective here adds to the tragedy, for Caesar is prophesying both his own death and the crucifixion of Christ. He will return to Rome at the end of Act V to be killed by Brutus and Cassius, who will in turn be killed by Mark Antony, who will in turn be killed by Octavius Caesar, all in the name of right and justice until the end of time. Caesar understands that words such as *love* and *honor* and *justice* can be twisted and distorted to cover up the evil done in their name, and he also knows that anyone who tries to speak the truth about such things had better have the power to conquer the world or be prepared to be crucified for speaking the truth. The point of *Caesar and Cleopatra* is blunt: people don't want to change. The Christs, the Caesars, the Galileos, the Socrateses, the Joans of Arc—the archetypal Shavian heroes—come with the inspiration of the Life Force to change humanity, to push and cajole human beings to a deeper knowledge of themselves and the workings of the universe, but each of these figures is rejected and destroyed by a world that does not want to listen. Progress, it seems, is an illusion.

There is, however, another way—the way of the superman, and this becomes Shaw's theme in the most famous of his plays, *Man and Superman*. The most significant use of the term comes at the close of the "Don Juan in Hell" sequence when Dona Ana ends the dream by running off to heaven after Don Juan, crying "A father, a father for the superman." We must understand her cry in the context of what Don Juan has said to her during the act. Juan has been sent to Hell for slaying Dona Ana's father, the Commander; and the Commander has been sent to Heaven. The thrust of the play's action brings about an exchange: Juan is bored to death in Hell, which is not a place of fire and torment, as Milton and Dante described it, but a place where men and women amuse themselves with art, music, conversation, sex presumably, and other forms of irresponsible self-indulgence. Sartre's hell may be other people; Shaw's is polite society, where people have nothing better to do than to have fun. The Commander, bored in heaven, yearns for such a life, but Juan is disgusted:

I sing, not arms and the hero, but the philosophic man: he who seeks in contemplation to discover the inner will of the world, in invention to discover the means of fulfilling that will, and in action to do that will by the so-discovered means.

The threefold process of contemplation, invention, and action is the method by which progress may take place. "I tell you," says Juan to the Devil, "that as long as I can conceive something better than myself I cannot be easy unless I am striving to bring it into existence or clearing the way for it." That which Juan is trying to bring into existence we may term *superman*; and, to remain within the metaphor of the play, Heaven is a place where men are striving to become or to create supermen, and Hell is a place where people are content to drift. Dona Ana's cry is her affirmation of her role in the process of creating the superman.

The implications of Shaw's metaphor are radical. If supermen are to be created, it must be through the mating of superior men and women, symbolized in the Hell scene by Don Juan and Dona Ana. Their offspring would be of superior intelligence and would continue the work that their parents had begun. What Shaw has in mind seems quite similar to the vision of the future presented by the great French Jesuit theologian-scientist, Teilhard de Chardin, a world in which human intelligence has magnified to the point where the more animal elements in the human pysche, such as aggression, greed, and sexuality, have been refined away.[7] The superman can come about, Shaw argues, only if we approach the question of human breeding as scientifically as we have approached the breeding of plants and animals. Shaw disguises his most radical ideas by placing them in *The Revolutionist's Handbook* and imputing them to Jack Tanner, under whose pseudonym he can hide. Here Shaw-Tanner raises direct questions concerning eugenic breeding, changes in the marriage laws, and the possibility of raising children in kibbutzlike communes rather than in families. It is here that he says, "We must eliminate the Yahoo, or his vote will wreck the commonwealth."

How seriously is all this to be taken? Given the history of the twentieth century, we might attempt an answer. Our power of destruction, as the Devil so brilliantly points out early in the Hell scene, has increased at an alarming rate; our technological and scientific knowledge has continued to develop at a pace that even Shaw might not have predicted. But our moral capacity, our intelligence, our capacity to make fair and just decisions—as Albert Einstein so eloquently reminded us—has remained in the Dark Ages. Such outmoded policies as nationalism, racism, sexism, and economic opportunism remind us daily of the gap between our human growth and our technical development. It is useless, says Shaw, simply to call this Original Sin, throw up one's hands, and pray to God to help us. That is defeatism, pure and simple. It is the most blatant of illusions to believe that God will get us out of the mess we have created, because the only God that exists (Shaw's Life Force) cannot work without the help of human beings. We must take responsibility for controlling and improving our own world. God may inspire us, but God will not do *our* work. No real change will come about until human beings face the reality of their situation and set about to eliminate poverty, disease, brute animality, mental cretinism, and the like. We cannot afford to have sexual freedom, if, in the name of freedom, we simply keep breeding ourselves into a world full of millions of starving human animals who, having nothing to live for, are willing to die by the thousands for some illusion called honor. *Superman* means a world where every human being has the space to develop mind and body in a healthy environment, where common laborers work both with their hands and their brains, where religion is not the promise of a panacea called heaven, but the inducement for all human beings to develop the best that is in them. It is, says Peter Keegan, in *John Bull's Other Island*, the dream of a madman.

But Shaw believed in these kinds of dreams, and in *Major Barbara* (1905) he writes a parable that tells us how these dreams might come about. The play turns on Andrew Undershaft's version of Plato's idea of the philosopher-king. Undershaft says that the world cannot be saved until the munitions makers become professors of Greek or the professors of Greek become munitions makers—the professor of Greek in this case being his prospective son-in-law, Adolphus Cusins, whom he has selected as the next Andrew Undershaft. Throughout most of the play Cusins and Undershaft's daughter, Barbara, a major in the Salvation Army, have both despised Undershaft. He has proved to them dramatically that salvation can be bought when he presents the Army with a huge gift, one that Barbara on principle refuses to accept. If Undershaft can buy the Army, then he can undermine its principles. Barbara wants no part of it. But Cusins is curious. "What is your religion?" he asks Undershaft. "Money and gunpowder," answers the munitions maker, meaning "freedom and power."

By buying the Salvation Army, Undershaft is trying to teach Barbara and Cusins a moral lesson. The Army's system of demanding confessions in return for bread is only a kind of moral blackmail. A man who is starving will confess to anything in order to get a decent meal, as Rummy Mitchens and Snobby Price demonstrate. The Rummies and Snobbies, the Bill Walkers and Peter Shirleys of the world, Undershaft suggests, will *never* be changed until they have good jobs and the chance to develop fully as human beings. Food and shelter must precede moral instruction, but they do not preclude moral instruction. Undershaft symbolizes the practical material power that is the prerequisite for change. What Barbara and Cusins finally realize is that "turning our backs on Bodger and Undershaft is turning our backs on life."

When Cusins finally accepts the position as the future Andrew Undershaft, he does so with the knowledge that he and Barbara may be able to use their intellectual and spiritual power to give direction to the massive physical power that the Undershaft enterprise symbolizes. Andrew Undershaft himself is only a stage in evolution; he is not an answer, but a beginning. If the Barbaras and the Cusinses drop out, then Andrew Undershaft will continue to sell weapons to the highest bidder. For Undershaft, moral questions are subservient to economic questions. Barbara and Cusins will attempt to make economics serve humanity. In *Major Barbara* Shaw attacks neither religion nor economics, but the myth that they are two separate and conflicting disciplines. As Ganz notes cleverly, "The commitment to spiritual progress never precludes a commitment to material progress." Shaw is both Marxist and mystic.[8] Just as he had presented the triumvirate of Broadbent, Doyle, and Keegan in *John Bull's Other Island* the year before as a symbol of the union of body, mind, and spirit that might save Ireland, so he uses Undershaft, Cusins, and Barbara to dramatize the process of social salvation.

Throughout the decade he continued to warn his civilization that it would have to change its ways or perish. In 1914, the outbreak of World War I proved him tragically right; and he withheld his new play, *Heartbreak House*, from public performance until the war was over, because

> . . . you cannot make war on war and on your neighbor at the same time. War cannot bear the terrible castigations of comedy, the ruthless light of laughter that glares on the stage. When men are heroically dying for their country, it is not the time to shew their lovers and wives and fathers and mothers how they are being sacrificed to the blunders of boobies, the cupidity of capitalists, the ambition of conquerors.

Heartbreak House (1919) is Shaw's masterpiece, fuller and more complex in characterization than his other plays. He begins his preface, "Heartbreak House is not merely the name of the play which follows this preface. It is cultured, leisured Europe before the war." *Heartbreak House* is Shaw's portrait of a culture where "the best lack all conviction." The inhabitants of Heartbreak House—Captain Shotover, his daughter, Hesione, and her husband, Hector Hushabye—are the intelligentsia: still bright and imaginative, but withdrawn from the practical world, drifting aimlessly toward destruction. The house, designed by the captain in the form of a ship, is England herself: "The captain is in his bunk, drinking bottled ditch-water; and the crew is gambling in the forecastle. She will strike and sink and split." The world has been left to others—to Sir Hastings Utterword, Ariadne's husband, who is a "numbskull"; and to Boss Mangan, who can manipulate other men's money but who has only the power to destroy not to create. The split between practical power on the one hand and wisdom and creativity on the other hand has become complete. And England will surely be destroyed unless the Shotovers and the Hectors learn their business. "And what may my business as an Englishman be, pray?" asks Hector. "Navigation," answers Shotover. "Learn it and live; or leave it and be damned."

Into the drifting world of *Heartbreak House* steps the play's heroine, Ellie Dunn, a little like Alice into Wonderland. Her education, like that of Vivie Warren, supplies the play's central thread. The process of heartbreak is the process of disillusionment, the process of moving step-by-step, painfully, from one level of awareness to the next. That is what Ellie does during the course of the play. She begins as a naive romantic in love with Marcus Darnley, who it turns out is only Hector in disguise. In bitter reaction against her loss, she turns to practical Boss Mangan, whom she claims she will marry, because "if I can't have love, that's no reason why I should have poverty." But toward the end of the second act she is taught by the captain, her spiritual father and husband in heaven, that in the end it's not prudent to sell your soul for money. She moves during the course of the play from romance to materialism to a kind of spiritual insight. But *Heartbreak House* is not *Major Barbara*; there is no real breakthrough. The captain's seventh degree of concentration turns out to be rum, and Ellie is left wiser, but without clear direction.

If the play's primary metaphor is heartbreak, or the process of disillusionment, its other major metaphor is dynamite, suggesting the judgment of God. As the bombers come over the house at the play's end, Mangan and the burglar run for cover in the dynamite pit and are blown to bits, the two "practical men of business" destroyed because they are finally only scavengers, leeches on their worlds. On the remaining residents of Heartbreak House judgment is temporarily suspended, but Hector knows that it will come: "Either out of that darkness some new creation will come to supplant us as we have supplanted the animals, or the heavens will fall in thunder and destroy us."

Heartbreak House is Shaw's judgment on his own class and its failure to prevent the most tragic waste of life in human history. What is new in Shaw is the Chekhovian flavor, the combination of judgment and love with which he treats Hector and Hesione, Shotover and Ellie, and her father, Mazzini Dunn. For the inhabitants of Horseback Hall, Ariadne and Randall, there is more satire and less compassion, and still less for Mangan until he is stripped bare, shorn of his illusions in the final act. "Let's all strip stark naked," cries Mangan in despair. "We may as well do the thing thoroughly when we're about it. We've stripped ourselves morally naked: well, let us strip ourselves physically naked as well." Mangan dies, because once he has stripped there is nothing left. The hope of the play lies in Ellie Dunn, who, stripped of her illusions, has a new strength. "Are you one of those who are so sufficient to themselves that they are only happy when they are stripped of everything . . . ?" asks the captain. "It seems so," she answers. Ellie is the younger generation with a chance for a new beginning. Armed with her father's idealism, the captain's wisdom, and the strength born of her learning experience in Heartbreak House, she will survive the war to begin a new generation.

But people are stubborn, and old institutions and ideas give way with great resistance. Nowhere is this theme so clear as in Shaw's last great play, *Saint Joan* (1923). When the playwright's epilogue was criticized as being unnecessary, Shaw claimed he wrote it so that the play would not end with the catastrophe of Joan's burning; but he might have defended the epilogue on more relevant ground. The epilogue presents the true ending of Joan's story, as one by one, Dunois, Charles, the Archbishop, and de Stogumber inform Joan that they could not have her come back again. It is not the burning but the continued rejection of the saint by the world that Shaw wants to emphasize. The epilogue reminds us that *we*, not the inhabitants of the eleventh or fourteenth centuries, reject our saints. We don't want Joan around. For just as Caesar, with his higher morality, makes Cleopatra, Charmian, and Iras uncomfortable, so Joan places demands on her civilization that exhaust Charles and Dunois and Cauchon.

The clash between Joan and the church is the clash between realism and idealism in pure form. The church and state, personified by Cauchon and Warwick, are pledged to the defense of their systems by their very natures. Even the Inquisitor, the most thoughtful of Joan's opponents, is committed by the nature of his office to the defense of the Catholic Church. He cannot concern himself with the possibility that Joan might be right, that her vision is a step forward in the evolutionary process. Joan's answer is hardly the final one. It is important for us to understand that. She brings Protestantism and nationalism to a world that had been Catholic and feudal, and in turn her religion and politics will be replaced by a higher vision. None of Shaw's saints has final answers, but their morality, their vision, is always superior to that of their world. What destroys Joan is not her vision, but her innocence, her inability to understand the people against whom she is struggling. Their pride will not allow them to give way to her; and rather than trying to work with them, she only fights harder against them in her moments of crisis. What strikes us in *Saint Joan* is the immaturity of both Joan and her accusers. More and more in Shaw we sense the playwright's belief that the human animal is simply too immature to perform the tasks that civilization demands.

Immaturity is the title of Shaw's first novel; it is also the theme of the most complete statement of his philosophy, *Back to Methuselah*, written between 1918 and 1921 and first performed in 1922 by the Theatre Guild in New York. Like Ibsen's *Emperor and Galilean*, it is Shaw's most sustained attempt to explain his weltenshauung. He calls it a metabiological Pentateuch, by which he means that it is five plays (like the first five books of the Bible) that illustrate mythologically his religion, itself a combination of biology and metaphysics. The central metaphor of the Shavian religion is longevity. In Part II the brothers Franklyn and Conrad Barnabas put forth the central proposition of the play: just when humans reach the age of wisdom, they become senile and die. We are but children; if we could live longer, say for three hundred years, we might attain real maturity. As Conrad Barnabas puts it, "They will live three hundred years, not because they would like to, but because the soul deep down in them will know that they must, if the world is to be saved." Most of the ideas by which the world is governed, Shaw argues, are "boyish cinema-fed romanticism." If people are to be governed by more mature ideas, they must live longer, and the world must be governed by these long-livers.

What it comes down to in the long run is that Shaw has, in *Back to Methuselah*, created his own version of the Faust story. The play ends with the voice of Lilith, the mythic precursor of Adam and Eve, whom Shaw uses as a symbol of the Life Force itself. She speaks:

> I say let them dread, of all things, stagnation; for from the moment I, Lilith, lose hope and faith in them, they are doomed. In that hope and faith I have let them live for a moment; and in that moment I have spared them many times. But mightier creatures than they have killed hope and faith, and perished from the earth; and I may not spare them forever.

Just as Faust is spared by Goethe's God for never having been satisfied, so Shaw's human race is spared by Lilith as long as it continues to strive.

57

The crucial word is *stagnation*. Once hope and faith have been killed, once stagnation sets in, then the Life Force becomes tired. Within the framework of the Shavian philosophy, all truth is relative. The process of disillusionment is continual, and reality is always changing as we learn more both about our world and about our purpose in it. All that we know now is the merest illusion compared to that which we will know, that which we *can* know, *if* we use the minds that we have been given. The human animal is but a child in the universe. How old that statement sounds, and yet how recent. In the Phi Beta Kappa address at Harvard University in 1980, distinguished scientist and essayist Lewis Thomas made this precise point.[9] We are, he argues, a very young species, and should we evolve to our full potential, then we will have the power, the intelligence, and the maturity to solve our problems. In species years, we are but infants, at best adolescents. That was always Shaw's point, and the history of the twentieth century has made it abundantly clear that if we do not listen to him now, we may not have the opportunity to listen to him in the future.

6

John Millington Synge

*On the stage one must have reality and
one must have joy.*

—Preface to *The Playboy of the Western World*

That John Millington Synge should have a place in a study of reality and illusion in modern drama needs no defense, but we must be careful to define terms. Early French critic Maurice Bourgeois wrote that the "perpetual antagonism of Dream *versus* Reality is the theme of all his dramatic writing." Yeats held the same view, and Alan Price, in his *Synge and Anglo-Irish Drama*, sees "the tension between dream and actuality" as a unifying theme in Synge's work. Donna Gerstenberger, in her excellent study *John Millington Synge*, sees this view as something of a distortion but admits both to the importance of Price's work and the significance of the theme in some of Synge's plays. A more recent critic, Weldon Thornton, in *J. M. Synge and the Western Mind*, sees the contrast between illusion and reality as crucial in *The Well of the Saints* and *The Playboy of the Western World*.[1] I will take the position that the tension between dream and actuality as understood by Price is the central theme of three of Synge's plays—*In the Shadow of the Glen*, *The Well of the Saints*, and *The Playboy of the Western World*; and I will restrict my analysis to these three plays.

It is significant that both Bourgeois and Price use the word *dream* rather than *illusion*. They might also have used the word *imagination*, and I think Synge would have liked it had they used the word *joy*. To quote perhaps the most famous and most important line that Synge ever wrote: "On the stage one must have reality and one must have joy." The Irish audiences of his time never understood this, and that is precisely why *In the Shadow of the Glen*, *The Well of the Saints*, and *The Playboy* were so violently attacked by the Irish nationalist press. They thought Synge was being unpatriotic. They considered Nora Burke and Pegeen Mike slurs on Irish womanhood. Yeats realized that under such conditions it would be impossible to produce *The Tinker's Wedding* at all. Reactions to that play would have made the *Playboy* riots look like kid stuff. The audiences simply did not understand or did not want to understand what Synge was doing.

"On the stage one must have reality and one must have joy." Here "reality" may be defined as life as it is usually lived in Ireland—with all of its physical hardships, the threat of death, the shadow of poverty, the loneliness, the starkness, the terror of night, the tyranny of the British. Synge seems to be saying that it is the artist's obligation to depict life realistically, to present life as it really is. The Irish didn't like this. They wanted to see stage Irishmen; they wanted to see romantic images of glorious Ireland or comic images of humorous Ireland. But, God knows, they didn't want to see themselves; and so they reviled their two great-est playwrights, Synge first, and O'Casey afterward, because both were so uncompromising in their honesty. But Synge goes on, and this is where he differs from many modern dramatists. It is not enough to depict reality in the manner of Ibsen and Zola. One must also depict joy. Here is the paradox and heart of Synge's drama. What he means is "real-ity *nevertheless* joy." Reality by nature is not very joyful; yet life without joy is not worth living. So where does joy come from? The answer is—it comes from within. It is a quality imposed on reality by one's inner vision, by one's poetic imagination, by one's capacity to dream, by one's capacity to create illusion. And, says Synge, we needn't choose between reality and joy—though many of his characters do, as we shall see—but we can have both if we learn how to face reality armed with the joy of a poetic imagination. For the wonder of Synge's world is that it is a world where illusion or dream may *become* reality. George and Martha's imag-inary son can never be real; Christy Mahon's imaginary bravery *can*. Thus we might group Synge's characters as follows: (1) the fully heroic—those who actualize their dreams by living rich, imaginative lives while remaining fully aware of the harsh nature of reality; (2) the dreamers—those who retreat from reality into the world of illusion; and (3) the literalists—those who allow their lives to be circumscribed by the limits of reality and who thus have no joy.

In the Shadow of the Glen was the first of Synge's plays to be per-formed (1903), and it sets the pattern for all the others. There are four characters, each of whom will be developed in *The Playboy* on a larger scale: Dan Burke, the crusty old man, who will reappear as Christy's father; Nora Burke, the imaginative young woman, who will become Pegeen Mike; Michael Dara, the unimaginative young herdsman, who will be re-created as Shawn Keough; and the Tramp, who is a clear precursor of the exiled bard, Christy Mahon. Reality as symbolized by Dan Burke is (I can't resist the pun) a kind of living death. The whole point of the play is not that Nora is a bad wife, as Dan complains, but that Dan is a bad husband. He's a bad husband because he is a dead man. He thinks that life consists of nothing but work. As Nora puts it, "Maybe cold would be no sign of death with the like of him, but he was always cold, every day since I knew him—and every night, stranger . . . " The allusion to sexual coldness is explicit and deliberate, for sexual love is one of the great joys of life; and the Irish propensity to treat sex as dirty and sinful is one of Synge's targets in the play. What Synge's audiences seemed to miss was that Nora wanted much more than sex. They considered her a dirty woman because they assumed (1) that sex was dirty, and (2) that sex was all that Nora was missing. But what Nora wants is not very different from what that other more famous Nora who walks out on her husband wants—freedom to be a complete person, freedom to find herself. She realizes that Michael cannot give her that freedom any more than Dan could. Perhaps he could give her a sex life; but he is too timid, too conventional, too much afraid of life to supply her needs. Throughout the play the symbol of what Nora needs is Patch Darcy, and the Tramp shares her admiration for him:

> That was a great man, young fellow, a great man I'm telling you. There was never a lamb from his own eyes he wouldn't know before it was marked, and he'd run from this to the city of Dublin and never catch for his breath.

Apparently Patch had stopped by the house in days gone by for more than conversation, and so Dan in pharisaical fashion casts the adulterous woman out into the harsh world to die; but the ending of the play makes clear that Dan and his symbolical heir, Michael, are the ones who will die, for they have cast out life from their house. The Tramp tells Nora of the power of the imagination to transform reality, if we will only pause to respond to the rich beauty of the world around us:

> Come along with me, now lady of the house, and it's not my blather you'll be hearing only, but you'll be hearing the grouse and the owls with them, and the larks and the big thrushes when the days are warm . . . it's fine songs you'll be hearing when the sun goes up, and there'll be no old fellow wheezing, the like of a sick sheep, close to your ear.

Nora is no sentimental idealist. She knows that life on her own in the country will be rough, but she can also sense its possibilities: "I'm thinking it's myself will be wheezing that tune with lying down under the Heavens when the night is cold; but you've a fine bit of talk, stranger, and it's with yourself I'll go." "Talk" is the central theme of *The Playboy*, and since I will discuss Synge's use of language at length in relation to that

61

play, I will not comment on it here except to say that "fine talk" is insep-arable from the fully lived life, but it is not a replacement for it. I think Nora knows that.

In *The Well of the Saints* (1905) Synge makes his first attempt to treat the dream-reality theme in a full-length play. It's a good play, but like *The Tinker's Wedding*, it shows evidence of Synge's trying to stretch material that would have been more effectively handled in shorter form. The theme may be clearly stated through a summation of the central action. Martin and Mary Doul, a blind couple, have developed a happy marriage based on illusions of their own comeliness, cultivated by the townspeo-ple. Mary, in reality a weather-beaten old hag, believes herself to be "the beautiful dark woman of Ballinatone." Her illusions are fed by the men, and Martin's by the women. They dream of having their sight so that they might appreciate one another fully; and, ironically, their wish is granted. When the traveling saint pours holy water on them to restore their sight, there ensues the most touching and pathetic scene in the play. Martin, the first to be cured, rushes up to the beautiful Molly Byrne, certain that she is Mary; but when he hears her voice, he turns away saddened. Then, taking heart, he turns to Bride, another fair girl, but she too repulses him. Then Mary, having returned from the church also cured, asks, "Which of you is Martin Doul?" He hears her voice and turns: the two confront each other in utter disbelief and horror. They curse one another, and as Act I ends it seems that sight brings only misery. In Act II the same theme is continued. Both Martin and Mary continue to be miserable in their new state. Martin, unable to bear the ugliness of real-ity, proposes to Molly Byrne; if Mary is not the beauty he dreamed she was, then he will have beauty rather than Mary. But Molly, who is going to marry Timmy, the smith, refuses him, and Timmy casts him off his land. As Act III opens, Martin and Mary are blind again, back where they were at the start of the play. Each has seen the real world, and each has come to the conclusion that it's better to be blind. But having had their former illusions—vital lies, if you like—about one another shattered, on what basis can they build a new relationship? The answer is—by creat-ing new illusions. Mary tells Martin:

> For when I seen myself in them pools, I seen my hair would be gray or white, maybe, in a short while, and I seen with it that I'd a face would be a great wonder when it'll have soft white hair falling around it, the way when I'm an old woman there won't be the like of me surely in the seven counties of the east.

Martin responds:

> **MARTIN:** I've this to say, Mary Doul. I'll be letting my beard grow in a short while, a beautiful, long, white, silken, streamy beard, you wouldn't see the like of in the eastern world . . . Ah, a white beard's a grand thing on an old man.
>
> **MARY DOUL:** (*laughing cheerfully*) Well, we're a great pair surely, and it's great times we'll have yet, maybe, and great talking before we die.

At this point we must remember Synge's injunction: "On the stage one must have reality and one must have joy." The movement in *The Well of the Saints* has been from joy to reality to joy; but at no point in the play have the two been combined. The saint, representing reality, returns with his holy water at the end of Act III to restore their vision once more (apparently the second dousing is permanent), but Martin manages to knock away the saint's can of holy water before he can sprinkle them. As a penalty for their sin, the two are exiled, a fate common to all Synge's major protagonists, as Arthur Ganz reminds us.[2] Exile is a price they are willing to pay to preserve the joy that they have found in their new illusions. They will not have reality back again at any cost.

In her analysis of the play Donna Gerstenberger makes a most perceptive comment about the implications of the ending:

> . . . it would seem that in this play Synge makes one of the few partial compromises to be found anywhere in his work, for the play ends with *a preference for the lie, an insistence upon illusion in the place of reality* [italics mine]. Synge accepted the dramatic implications of his material and the dramatic irony it provided, and these implications suggest a position which Synge had not taken elsewhere. Moreover, it is a position which the evidence of the notebooks and his other work would indicate that he could not seriously have accepted beyond his commitment to this particular dramatic situation.[3]

What makes her comment so valuable is her understanding that the ending *is* appropriate to this play, while at the same time *not* representing Synge's attitude toward the desirable relationship between illusion and reality. To understand Synge's position we must turn to *The Playboy of the Western World* (1907), because, in Weldon Thornton's words, "In any event *Playboy* offers a more subtle and in this sense a truer presentation of this theme than does *The Well of the Saints*."[4]

As Synge's masterpiece opens, we find a picture of reality without joy.

The Hegelians

Pegeen Mike sits, tending to the business of running her father's pub, and talks with her fiancé, Shawn, about their coming wedding:

> **PEGEEN:** It's a wonder, Shaneen, the Holy Father'd be taking notice of the likes of you; for if I was him I wouldn't bother with this place where you'll meet none but Red Linahan, has a squint in his eye, and Patcheen is lame in his heel, or the mad Mulrannies were driven from California and they lost in their wits. We're a queer lot these times to go troubling the Holy Father on his sacred seat.
>
> **SHAWN:** If we are, we're as good this place as another, maybe, and as good these times as we were for ever.
>
> **PEGEEN:** As good, is it? Where now will you meet the like of Daneen Sullivan knocked the eye from a peeler, or Marcus Quin, God rest him, got six months for maiming ewes, and he a great warrant to tell stories of holy Ireland till he'd have the old women shedding down tears about their feet.

Upon this opening dialogue the entire action of the play is built. Pegeen is a woman obviously bored with the likes of Shawn Keough, reality is drab and tedious, and Father Reilly controls all. Though he never appears in the play, he dictates every move that Shawn makes. Pegeen yearns for a time when exciting things happened: she emphasizes two things, violent acts and storytelling. Enter Christy Mahon. We must remember, if we are surprised by the villagers' reactions to Christy, that he is the first interesting thing that has happened to them in a long time. As they question him, they do so out of curiosity. When he reveals his crime, they respond with amazement and respect, because a violent crime committed far away in another part of the country is a piece of romance, and romance can bring some joy, some excitement into the drab life of this miserable village. They accept Christy as an exotic figure from a storybook. They also accept Christy because he is a storyteller, and a good one. When Christy tells the story of how he killed his father to the girls at the beginning of Act II, he has embellished it quite a bit since the first-act version. He has dramatized it. He plays his father, then himself. He leaps back and forth, acting out each moment. He builds toward his climax:

> He gave a drive with the scythe, and I gave a lep to the east. Then I turned around with my back to the north, and I hit a blow on the ridge of his skull, laid him stretched out, and he split to the knob of his gullet.

The words are carefully chosen for rhyme and rhythm, for assonance and alliteration. Every word contributes to the evocation of the scene.

64

But notice that the girls do not necessarily believe it. "That's a grand story," says Susan. "He tells it lovely," answers Honor. The artist—the man who tells the story, not the man who committed the crime—is the man who excites Pegeen and the girls.

Synge has established an extremely complex tension between dream and reality by this point in the play. For even as Christy is telling his story to the girls, his father—very much alive—is nearing the village. Thus we have the paradox of a man building his whole character on a lie; and yet, because the lie is accepted, and because he is such a good liar, and because the people aren't really interested in the truth, Christy begins to become less and less of a liar as the play progresses. In other words, he begins to become the man he has pretended to be. At first nothing more than a shy, frightened runaway, he gains confidence because the people respond to him. The more they love him, the more self-esteem he gains. In the famous shaving scene at the opening of Act II he says:

> Didn't I know rightly I was handsome, though it was the devil's own mirror we had beyond, would twist a squint across an angel's brow; and I'll be growing fine from this day, the way I'll have a soft lovely skin on me and won't be the like of the clumsy young fellows do be ploughing all times in the earth and dung.

Because of his imagination, because of his imaginative ability as a poet, his reality is changing. He goes off to the games, and he does *in actuality* become the playboy of the Western world. The Christy of Act I would not have. And after the games he makes love to Pegeen in rich and confident imagery:

> It's little you'll think if my love's a poacher's, or an earl's itself, when you'll feel my two hands stretched around you, and I squeezing kisses on your puckered lips, till I'd feel a kind of pity for the Lord God is all ages sitting lonesome in his golden chair.

And so, admiring the confidence and strength of the young stranger, Michael James gives him the hand of his daughter, for "a daring fellow is the jewel of the world, and a man did split his father's middle with a single clout should have the bravery of ten, so may God and Mary and St. Patrick bless you, and increase you from this mortal day." Christy and Pegeen shout, "Amen, O Lord!" and thus the curtain would fall on a romantic comedy much as the curtain would have fallen on *A Doll House* after Torvald's "I'm saved" had it been a conventional well-made play.

Synge, like Ibsen, is interested in that fusion of reality and joy; if the play had ended here we would have only what Synge calls in the preface "the false joy of the musical comedy."

Christy has not yet confronted reality. He has grown, it is true; but the ultimate reality he must confront if he is to become a man is his father. And that is the primary difference between *The Well of the Saints* and *The Playboy*. Martin and Mary run off at the end, content to live out an illusion. Christy and Pegeen are not allowed that luxury. In the closing moments of *The Playboy* Christy confronts the very grim reality both of his father and of Ireland. Old Mahon appears, and the fickle crowd, hungry for excitement, turns on Christy, waiting for the confrontation between the two. And poor Christy, who really has changed, though the crowd doesn't understand (nor the original Irish audience), has to knock the old man on the head again to prove his manhood. Now the crowd is really incensed; and tying him up, they prepare to turn him over to the law. Pegeen herself condemns him:

> I'll say, a strange man is a marvel, with his mighty talk; but what's a squabble in your back-yard, and the blow of a loy, have taught me that there's a great gap between a gallous story and a dirty deed. Take him on from this, or the lot of us will be likely put on trial for his deed today.

This is the moment of Pegeen's tragic loss, though she will not recognize it until the end of the play. For the people of the village, Christy's presence as a murderer is a joy as long as the murder was committed far away. He remains a figure of romance until he commits the "dirty deed" in their own backyard. Now it is a hanging matter, and the law is likely to be put on them. Reality, in the form of the law, has overcome joy, and it has overcome love. Christy realizes this. He turns on the treacherous villagers, berating them for their folly:

> Shut your yelling, for if you're after making a mighty man of me this day by the power of a lie, you're setting me now to think if it's a poor thing to be lonesome, it's worse maybe to go mixing with the fools of earth.

And Old Mahon, who comes staggering back after his second "murder," echoes his son's sentiments: "We'll have great times from this out telling stories of the villainy of Mayo, and the fools is here." Nearly all of Synge's plays end with the protagonists leaving society: Nora and the Tramp, Martin and Mary, Christy and his father, Deirdre and Naisi. The full life cannot be lived within the social context. It is too limiting. There is always Father Reilly or the law or some other representation of the stifling power of authority such as Dan Burke or the priest in *The Tinker's Wedding* or Conchubor in *Deirdre of the Sorrows*. Within this kind of world there is no room to dream, to develop the self fully. Christy realizes this, and he also realizes that there can be no joy or freedom if he remains under the thumb of a tyrannical father. And so since he can't kill him, he decides to declare himself master of the house. "Come on now," says Old Mahon:

> CHRISTY: Go with you, is it? I will then, like a gallant captain with his heathen slave. Go on now and I'll see you from this day stewing my oatmeal and washing my spuds, for I'm master of all fights from now. Go on, I'm saying.
>
> MAHON: Is it me?
>
> CHRISTY: Not a word out of you. Go on from this.
>
> MAHON: Glory be to God! (*With a broad smile.*) I am crazy again!

Mahon, of course, can hardly believe his ears. At first he is shocked, but really he is delighted. His son has become the man he has always wanted him to be, and the two go off together sharing the joy of their newfound relationship:

> CHRISTY: Ten thousand blessings upon all that's here, for you've turned me a likely gaffer in the end of all, the way I'll go romancing through a romping lifetime from this hour to the dawning of the judgment day.

And if the play were not a masterpiece, it would end here, for this is a magnificent curtain line; but Synge is true to his credo. On the stage one must have reality and one must have joy. If the play ended here we would feel the joy of the now mature Christy ready to face reality with his newfound power of imagination, but Synge wants us to feel the sense of loss generated by Christy's departure.

The play ends as it began, with Pegeen Mike and Shawn. They are back to the drab, dull reality of the joyless life. And Shawn, for the life of him, cannot understand why Pegeen is upset. "O my grief, I've lost him surely. I've lost the only Playboy of the Western World." Pegeen's lament is more than personal. One thinks again of the preface, this time of Synge's closing lines:

> In Ireland, for a few years more, we have a popular imagination that is fiery and magnificent, and tender; so that those of us who wish to write start with a chance that is not given to writers in places where the springtime of the local life has been forgotten, and the harvest is a memory only, and the straw has been turned into bricks.

67

It is with Christy that I associate the popular imagination of which Synge speaks; Pegeen's loss is Ireland's loss, and all of Synge's drama is an appeal to the Irish people to cultivate the imagination which is such a rich part of their heritage and not let it be destroyed either by the encroachment of priest or the coming of modern urban life.

Part Two
Lost and Found

7

Luigi Pirandello

> SOME ACTORS: He's dead! dead!
> OTHER ACTORS: No, no, it's only make believe, it's only pretense!
> THE FATHER: Pretense? Reality, sir, reality!
> THE DIRECTOR: Pretense? Reality? To hell with it all! Never in my life has such a thing happened to me. I've lost a whole day over these people, a whole day!
>
> —Six Characters in Search of an Author

If there is one playwright who cries out to be included in this study it is Luigi Pirandello. Pirandello and the reality-illusion theme are almost synonymous, so much so that the unwary reader is apt to be trapped into thinking that it is his foremost concern, almost his only concern. But as Eric Bentley and, more recently, Roger Oliver have reminded us, the reality-illusion theme serves more as a means than an end. Pirandello's central concern, Oliver tells us in his important 1979 study *Dreams of Passion: The Theater of Luigi Pirandello*, is "suffering and a compassionate response to that suffering." He goes on to elaborate: Pirandello "is less concerned with hope or despair than with the need for people, both as individuals and in groups, to try to understand the suffering of others so that no actions will be undertaken that will increase the victim's pain."[1]

In this chapter I will be concerned with the relationship between the reality-illusion conflict and the presence of human suffering in five of Pirandello's plays: *It Is So (If You Think So)* (1917), *Henry IV* (1922), and the "trilogy of the theater in the theater"—*Six Characters in Search of an Author* (1921), *Each in His Own Way* (1924), and *Tonight We Improvise* (1929).[2] The plays in the theater trilogy will require different treatment from the first two because they force us to use the terms *reality* and *illusion* in a completely new way. In the trilogy we, as audience, are constantly reminded that we are in a theater seeing characters portrayed by actors on a stage, and we are pushed by this process to reexamine our own view of what reality is. We cannot escape into the "story" of the play or the lives of the characters. In fact, in the theater plays the story becomes a kind of illusion, which we are continually forced to examine freshly from the perspective of the "new" reality of the theater itself, where we remain—not transported into the world of "art" but accosted by an action that demands of us a reevaluation of the relationship between art and life, pretense and reality. But the "theater trilogy"—as radical as it is in the history of European drama—is not a complete innovation when viewed as part of Pirandello's dramatic development. It is a natural outgrowth of techniques he had developed in earlier plays; it is another means of presenting the theme of human suffering that so obsessed him throughout his career. Thus the theater plays can be understood best after we have examined the treatment of reality and illusion in the two plays that do not depend directly on the theater itself as a technique of development.

It Is So (If You Think So), the first of Pirandello's major plays, dramatizes the playwright's concern with the individual's need for both privacy and compassion. Signor Ponza, his wife, and his mother-in-law, Signora Frola, arrive in a small provincial town where he has taken the position of secretary to Commendatore Agazzi, a local official. Within days of their arrival the local citizens—the women in particular—are gossiping fiercely about his peculiar living habits. It seems that rather than having his mother-in-law, Signora Frola, live with himself and his wife, he has rented for her an apartment in the fashionable part of town and has chosen to live with his wife on the fifth floor of a tenement on the town's outskirts. The mother-in-law is not permitted to visit her daughter but is forced to communicate with her by messages placed in a basket and hauled up to the fifth floor by a pulley. The strangeness of these arrangements both fascinates and distresses the townspeople, and the Ponza family becomes the primary topic of conversation in the town. What is to be done? Well, they decide, the only thing to do is to find out the *truth*, so they call in the old lady—who explains to them that Signora Ponza is her daughter, whom Ponza believes to be dead. He imagines that his wife is a different person, and he cannot bear to see the old lady together with his new wife. Mother and daughter consent to the arrangement to protect Ponza's vital lie, to keep him from becoming overly agitated. In short, Ponza is *mad*. No sooner is this explanation received than Ponza comes in and tells a very different story: it is Signora Frola who is mad, and it is he, Ponza, who is protecting *her* vital lie. His second wife is *not* her daughter; the first wife, her daughter, really is dead, and he has created this elaborate arrangement to protect the old woman from the suffering she would face if she had to confront the truth.

The townspeople are not happy. They want to know the truth, and either Signor Ponza or Signora Frola must be lying. Who is really mad? Who is telling the truth? The only way to find out is to call in the daughter, which they do at the end of the play. And she tells them, "I am the daughter of Signora Frola . . . and the second wife of Signor Ponza. . . . I am she whom you believe me to be." Hence the title, *It Is So (If You Think So)*. Reality is subjective, and the truth—objective truth—cannot be known.

But this is not the main point of the play: the point is that ignoring this fact causes human suffering. Signora Ponza, when she is summoned at the end to clear up the mystery, says, "There is a misfortune here which must stay hidden: otherwise the remedy which our compassion has found cannot avail." These may well be the most important words in the play—"the remedy which our compassion has found." For compassion is exactly what the townspeople have forgotten in their search for truth. "You are trying to do me a favor," says Signora Frola, "but really, what you're doing is working me a great wrong. I've got to leave town this very day because he must not be aroused." Ponza himself puts the point most strongly: "I refuse to submit to this ferocious prying into my private affairs which will end by undoing a work of love that has cost me untold sacrifice these past two years."

What makes the play work so well theatrically is the unwitting identification of the theater audience with the townspeople until they are shamed into a more compassionate attitude at the end. We—as theatergoers—want to know the truth, but Pirandello says we can't. We can't because the arrangement Ponza, his wife, and his mother-in-law have made is personal, private, and subjective. It is meaningful only to them and cannot be explained to anyone else. Furthermore, it is no one else's business, which is what one of the play's most important figures, Lamberto Laudisi, has been telling us all along. Laudisi appears to be Pirandello's spokesman, articulating familiar Pirandellian truisms and acting as a kind of intermediary between the Ponzas and the townspeople and between the characters of the play and the audience. Early in the play he tells us: "What can we really know about other people—who they are—what they are—what they are doing, and why they are doing it?" He goes on to explain to Sirelli that we are a different person to each person we meet, and that, therefore, one can never know the truth about another person. And when the play ends with Signora Ponza's insistence that she is *both* Signora Frola's daughter *and* Ponza's second wife, Laudisi alone understands what she means, and his ironic laughter ends the play.

But we should not equate Laudisi's cynical laughter at the folly of the play's characters with the laughter of Pirandello. Pirandello is far more understanding than his character. Laudisi has one very important job, and he does that well. As the ironic man he unmasks the pretensions of the townspeople. He reveals the stupidity and arrogance of provincial people whose own lives are so boring that they have nothing better to do than to play with the private lives of others. But Laudisi is not the "compassionate ironist" described by Susan Bassnett-McGuire in her recent study.[3] Like the Director in *Six Characters* and Diego Cinci in *Each in His Own Way*, whom we will examine later, Laudisi fails to see the hurt he is doing to the characters. When Sirelli suggests bringing Ponza and his mother-in-law together, Laudisi responds, "Well, bring them together if you want to! All I ask is permission to laugh when you're through!" In Act III Laudisi himself conceives the idea of inviting Ponza's wife to speak. One of the points of the play is that he ought to know better, but he doesn't, because he has not integrated the intellectual and emotional parts of his life. Viewing the Ponza family only as a fascinating intellectual puzzle that will prove his theory of subjective truth, he cannot see them as real human beings. Pirandello hopes to jolt us as audience into a deeper awareness than that of any of the characters in the play. In short, he challenges the audience to break through to a deeper level of reality, one that is more real than traditional theater can depict. In *Henry IV* he pushes us even further.

In *It Is So* Pirandello presents the world of the Ponza family from the point of view of the townspeople. We see them as Agazzi, Sirelli, Laudisi, and the others see them. In *Henry IV* we experience Henry's world from his point of view—we *live* the play as Henry lives it, and as a result, our experience of the mystery and complexity of human personality, of the subjectivity of reality, is much more direct, more profound and immediate.

To understand the play, we must first understand the facts of Henry's history. Eighteen years before the action of the play takes place, a group of Italian noblemen and noblewomen decided to hold a pageant in which each participant would play a historical character. Henry selected the role of Henry IV of Germany because Donna Matilda, with whom Henry was in love, had chosen the part of the Marchioness Matilda of Tuscany, the ally of Pope Gregory VII, Henry's implacable enemy. During the pageant, Henry's horse reared, making him fall and injure his head. Late in Act III Henry says that the fall was caused by those "who, behind my back, pricked my saddled horse till it bled." Accident or not, the fall injured Henry so that he regained consciousness believing that he actually *was* the Emperor Henry IV. To allow him to live his illusion, his sister, the mother of Charles di Nolli, had a villa arranged to look like Henry's palace, and she hired a group of young men to act the roles of Henry's private counselors. For twelve years Henry played his role, unconscious of his delusion, until gradually his sanity returned. Then came the crucial decision of his life. He elected to remain "mad" (a choice he will have to make again at the end of the play), to continue playing the role of Henry IV. Why? Because he realized that only as Henry IV could he have any life:

> **HENRY IV:** Look at my hair!
> **BELCREDI:** But mine is grey too!
> **HENRY IV:** Yes, with this difference: that mine went grey here, as Henry IV, do you understand? And I never knew it! I perceived it all of a sudden, one day, when I opened my eye; and I was terrified because I understood at once that not only had my hair gone grey, but that I was all grey, inside; that everything had fallen to pieces, that everything was finished; and that I was going to arrive, hungry as a wolf, at a banquet which had already been cleared away.

Thus, as the play opens, Henry has been consciously "playing" the role of Henry IV for approximately six years, because only as Henry IV can he live with any intensity, only as Henry IV can he defeat time, which may destroy him as a human being but not as a character in history. The others—Tito Belcredi; the Marchioness Matilda; her daughter, Frida; Henry's nephew, Charles di Nolli; and the Doctor whom they have brought to examine Henry—do not know this, nor do they really care. The Doctor comes to see Henry out of scientific interest in the case, Belcredi and Matilda out of curiosity, di Nolli out of sense of obligation to his mother, and Frida because di Nolli and her mother have dragged her there. They are like the chorus of townspeople in *It Is So*: they would like to know the "truth" about Henry so that they can do whatever science or propriety demands that one does in such a case. Then they can get the problem of Henry off their backs, out of their lives. None of them cares, and it is only by caring that anyone can know who Henry is.

Pirandello develops the motif of caring in two ways: through the counselors and through the visitors. In the case of the counselors, the lack of caring comes in part from their having no real artistic sense. They are bad actors, hired to play roles they have no aptitude for, and one of them, Berthold, who has just been hired, goes to pieces under the stress of the situation. None of the hired help at the villa cares, except for the old waiter, John, who at the end of the second act comes in to play the monk. Henry and the others talk about him:

ORDULPH: Yes, yes! Let's make him do it!
HENRY IV: Fool, why? Just to play a joke on a poor man who does it for love of me?
LANDOLPH: It has to be as if it were true.
HENRY IV: Exactly, as if true! Because, only so, truth is not a jest.

Earlier in the same scene Henry lashes out at them:

I say that—you are fools! You ought to have known how to create a fantasy for yourselves, not to act it for me, or anyone coming to see me; but naturally, simply, day by day, before nobody, feeling yourselves alive in the history of the eleventh century, here at the court of your Emperor, Henry IV.

Two statements, one from each passage, compel our attention. The first, "It has to be as if it were true . . . because, only so, truth is not a jest." And the second, "You ought to have known how to create a fantasy for yourselves." In Pirandello's world there is a close relationship between what the individual does in creating a fantasy and what the actor does in creating a role. In each case the traditional line between reality and illusion is broken down. The fantasy, the role, may be more real than what we call reality, if it is fully created and lovingly performed. At the same time the role may be morally justified if it is done for love, if it is done as if it were true. The counselors, except for old John, fail on both counts; and the visitors, in their masquerade, fail even more dismally on the moral level because their roles are performed without compassion, and their final piece of role playing drives Henry to kill Belcredi and forces him to retreat into his "madness" as a protection from prosecution for murder.

In the first act the Doctor pretends to be Monsignor Hugh of Cluny, Donna Matilda takes the role of the Duchess Adelaide, and Belcredi pretends to be a monk; but all of them act their parts badly because they are there on false pretenses, playing roles they do not understand in order to spy on Henry. Henry not only sees through them but turns their masquerade against them by accusing Belcredi, his enemy, of being Peter Damiani and letting them know that he recognizes their disguises as clumsy attempts to conceal themselves.

Unaware of Henry's perception, they plan during the second act the trick that will bring about the denouement—the substitution of Frida and Charles di Nolli into the frames of the portraits that stand on either side of the throne. The trick, performed at the opening of Act III, very nearly drives Henry mad again, and when he explains to them that for him the only *real* Marchioness of Tuscany is Frida, not Donna Matilda, who has aged nearly twenty years, the horror of what they have done becomes fully apparent to the audience for the first time. Theoretically, the Doctor's plan should have worked, just as, theoretically, the plan of bringing Ponza, Signora Frola, and Signora Ponza together should have worked. Both plans fail, (1) because reality and illusion can no longer be separated, since there is no such thing as *the* truth which can be rationally or scientifically discovered and demonstrated, and (2) because the characters who are concocting the plans lack the insight into and compassion for the characters with whom they are dealing.

Thus, in *It Is So* and *Henry IV* we find the archetypal Pirandello situation. At the center of each play is a character or a group of characters who suffers. Surrounding the inner group is an outer circle, made up of characters who are after the truth with a capital T. The characters in the outer circles try to understand the action that goes on within the group at the center, but they always fail, and the harder they try to prove the truth, the more they cause the characters at the center to suffer.

When we turn to the theater trilogy, we find the same pattern present, but complicated and enriched by the fact that we must reevaluate our understanding of reality and illusion by keeping in mind that the reality of theater itself undergirds all other depictions of reality. Roger Oliver, in his remarks on *Six Characters*, puts the matter very well. Pirandello, he tells us, is

> insisting on absolute realism, a realism the original audience was unwilling to accept. This audience, as seen by their violent reaction at the play's premiere, apparently did not want to be reminded that they were seated in a theater. Instead they desired to be transported out of that reality into the illusion of a new reality, with a new environment and new characters whose problems they could become involved with. They paradoxically wanted "realism" in order to escape. Pirandello, on the other hand, gave them "reality" in order to confront them with insights about themselves and their lives.[4]

Pirandello, like Brecht shortly after him and like so many of the playwrights of our own time, refuses the audience the luxury of escaping from themselves into the story. Each of the plays in the theater trilogy has an inner action, a story—in all three cases, one that is violent, melodramatic, "theatrical" in a sense, but one that, if told by itself, would not work. Try to tell the story of the six characters and see what happens. Bentley does so very well in his fine essay on the play in *The Theater of War*,[5] and the result is a piece of cheap Sicilian melodrama. The stories of the LaCroce family in *Tonight We Improvise* and of Delia Morello and Michele Rocca in *Each in His Own Way* are similar: by themselves they would make second-rate plays. But when the inner action is enriched by the outer action of the play in the theater, then Pirandello is not only able to create more interesting and complex characters, because we experience them from multiple viewpoints, but he can also make the conflict between the inner action (the story) and the outer action (the play in the theater) the central conflict of the play, commenting on and forcing us to reinterpret the inner action.

Thus the conflict between the Father and the Director in *Six Characters* makes us view the conflicts among the characters in a different light. The conflict in *Each in His Own Way* between the "characters of the comedy on the stage" and the "real" characters appearing in the theater lobby makes us understand the action of the comedy differently, and the conflict between Hinkfuss and his actors places the story of the LaCroce family in a new setting. Because the ultimate reality in all three plays is the theater itself, we must ask whether it is possible for art to depict life truthfully at all. Are all attempts at art doomed to be illusionary, in some sense, because life, which is formless and chaotic, refuses to be restrained by form? All the plays in the theater trilogy collapse into chaos at the end, and rightly so, because the life that chaos represents cannot be constrained by art as symbolized by the Director in *Six Characters*, the stage comedy in *Each in His Own Way*, and the controlling hand of Hinkfuss in *Tonight We Improvise*.

Paradoxically, Pirandello's theater plays, on the surface a rebellion against stage realism, are in a genuine sense more "real" than the plays he is reacting against. Granted, Pirandello is still employing the "fiction" of a stage play to present his reality, but he has not, as Robert Brustein says, "merely multiplied illusions";[6] rather, in Oliver's words, he has substituted "an illusion that is one step closer to the truth than the old illusions."[7] To see how he does this, we must look at the three plays more closely.

In *Six Characters* it is best to begin at the center and work toward the outside. At the center is the Father, who is to *Six Characters* what Henry is to *Henry IV* and Ponza is to *It Is So*. He is, as Bentley points out, a kind of ancient mariner whose primary raison d'être is to buttonhole people and tell his story.[8] Within the framework of the inner play his main antagonist is the Stepdaughter who refuses to allow him his drama, because she wants the drama played from her point of view. She wants *her* story told, and the central scene of the play within a play, the sequence at Madame Pace's dress shop, becomes the means by which she will have her revenge against him. But the Father struggles against her interpretation of his character:

> We believe this conscience to be a single thing, but it is many sided. There is one for this person, and another for that. Diverse consciences. So we have this illusion of being one person for all, of having a personality that is unique in all our acts. But it isn't true. We perceive this when, tragically perhaps, in something we do, we are as it were suspended, caught up in the air on a kind of hook. Then we perceive that all of us was not in that act, and that it would be an atrocious injustice to judge us by that action alone, as if all our existence were summed up in that one deed.

The Stepdaughter, he goes on, wants to judge him on the basis of a single action, his surprising her at Madame Pace's; he demands to be understood as a complex human being, something neither the Stepdaughter nor the Son is willing to do. They are defining his reality on the basis of a small portion of him, the Stepdaughter on the basis of his sexual needs and the Son on the basis of his initial decision to abandon his family. As Arthur Ganz summarizes the issue, "Since each observer has his own idea of the person he sees, there are in effect as many persons to be seen as there are observers."[9]

The inner conflict of the play, then, is the conflict among the six characters themselves as to how the play is to be presented. Each has his own play within him. The Son attacks the Father: "He thinks he has got at the meaning of it all. Just as if each one of us in every circumstance of life couldn't find his own explanation of it." The Stepdaughter adds her feelings: "He wants to get at his complicated 'cerebral drama,' to have his famous remorses and torments acted; but I want to act my part, *my part*." We must remember that if the play were presented as realism, none of this argument could take place; Pirandello would simply have to select a point of view from which to dramatize the story. But because the figures on the stage are characters rather than figures in a story, they are allowed to argue among themselves as actors might discuss their roles in the process of rehearsal or improvisation. Therefore, even within the inner play Pirandello has overcome some of the limits of traditional realism.

But the central and overriding conflict in the play is that between the characters, primarily the Father, and the actors, especially the Director (I am using the American term *director* rather than the English term *manager*, which appears in the Edward Storer translation). In this conflict Pirandello found his most successful stage metaphor for the reality-illusion conflict, one that functions on two different levels, both important and neither subordinate to the other.

The first is the level so fascinatingly described by Eric Bentley in the essay to which I referred earlier.[10] Here Bentley jokingly suggests that what the Father wants is a father, not a playwright, and for him the Director would be a perfect father, because in the two figures we see the split between the internal and external, intellectual and practical parts of the self—we see the essentially schizophrenic nature of modern man. The Father cannot function without adopting some special strategy (like Ponza, like Henry) which he uses to protect himself from what R. D. Laing calls the implosion of the world. He has no capacity for survival in the world. The Director has the practical capacity for survival, but no real sense of what is happening to the Father, nor any inkling that the same kind of thing might happen to him. He never recognizes that the Father is a part of himself. And so we have the practical part of the self totally separated from the introspective, analytical, philosophical part of the self. The Father needs the approval and protection of the Director in order to survive. That is his search. In terms of reality and illusion, we might argue that both are parts of reality that have become separated from one another and that Pirandello is showing us, as in *It Is So* and *Henry IV*, the tragic consequences of that separation.

In terms of the theater, the conflict between these two different manifestations of reality takes the form of the limitations of the theater of Pirandello's day, as symbolized primarily by the Director, when confronted with a different kind of reality. There is no place for the kind of reality suggested by the characters in the theatrical world represented by the Director and his troupe. When the Stepdaughter insists that their story is "the truth," the Director responds: "What does that matter? Acting is our business here. Truth up to a certain point but no further." *Truth up to a certain point* is the motto of the theater, and as a result, the Director will finally reject the characters because he cannot fit them into his scheme of reality, which involves type characters, three acts, two intermissions, and no changes of set except between the acts. His exasperated confession, which forms the epigraph for this chapter, ends the original version of the play (the one reproduced in *Naked Masks*). But in the revised version, the characters return to the stage after the actors have left and quite frighteningly implant *their* reality upon the audience in a way that the actors have not. The Director and his troupe may not have been changed by the intrusion of the characters into their world, but we have been changed by our viewing of the play, and it is significantly into *our* world, the world of the street, that the characters make

80

their final exit, looking perhaps for another theater, another audience to hear and understand their story and their suffering.

Each in His Own Way, the second play in the trilogy, shifts the focus from the relationship between the characters and the actors to the relationship between the play and the audience. Once again there is an inner play that is commented on by an outer action taking place during the intermissions or "choral interludes," as Pirandello calls them. One problem with *Each in His Own Way* is that, while the action of *Six Characters* seems to be a *real* rehearsal of *real* actors on a *real* stage interrupted by *real* characters, the choral interludes in the second act are clearly *not* real—they do not take place in the *real* theater lobby, and the characters being portrayed in the interludes are clearly actors pretending to be members of the audience. Pirandello will solve this problem brilliantly in *Tonight We Improvise* by actually moving the play into the lobby during the "real" intermissions. Thus the interplay between various levels of reality is not as convincing in *Each in His Own Way* as it is in the other two plays in the trilogy. Nonetheless, it is important to understand what the playwright is attempting here.

The inner action involves the triangle of Delia Morello, Michele Rocca, and Giorgio Salvi. At first it looks as if we are going to have *It Is So* all over again, as Doro Palegari and Francesco Savio get into an argument over why Delia Morello went off with Rocca on the night she and Salvi were supposed to be married, thereby causing the suicide of the sculptor. What business of theirs, we might ask, is it to interfere in the private life of two very happy people? But Pirandello is working with a very different question in *Each in His Own Way*, because both Delia Morello and Michele Rocca, rather than resenting the interference of Palegari and Savio, find their interest welcome. Why? Delia and Rocca have each been having an identity crisis of sorts. Since the suicide of Salvi, both have felt guilty, and so each has fabricated a vital lie to salvage some kind of personal dignity. Delia has convinced herself that she ran off with Rocca in order to save Salvi, since she knew the marriage would ruin him; Rocca attempts to persuade himself that he ran off with Delia to save his friend's artistic career, which would have been destroyed had the marriage taken place.

Diego Cinci, who plays the role of *raisonneur* in this play, as Laudisi had in *It Is So*, reviews the positions of all the characters, concluding that our reality is determined by the views other people hold of us and that, as the views of others change, so our own self-image changes. And that is exactly what happens. Delia welcomes Doro Palegari's defense of her, because she cannot sustain her vital lie unless the position is held by someone else. But when Doro confronts Delia with Francesco Savio's position, she begins to believe that Savio is right. The issue is further complicated by the fact that Palegari and Savio then reverse positions, having been persuaded by one another's arguments.

Pirandello leaves the issue of who is "right" hanging until the end of the second act when he brings on Delia Morello and Michele Rocca in a *coup de théâtre* that resolves the conflict of the inner play and sets up the conflict in the second choral interlude, which will become the play's final and most significant action. Pirandello's stage directions indicate the nature of their encounter:

> The moment SHE sees MICHELE ROCCA, so changed from what he had been, another person in fact, she suddenly finds the mask, the fiction, which both she and he have hitherto been using to defend themselves against the secret passion by which from the very beginning they have been madly attracted toward one another, a passion which they have been translating before their own minds into terms of pity and interest for GIORGIO SALVI, each pretending to be trying to save him from one or the other.

Their suffering has revealed their true passion for each other to each other, a passion that Palegari, Savio, and Diego Cinci—who have been engaged in the issue only on an intellectual level—cannot comprehend. Thus the second act ends with Delia and Rocca's exit and Cinci and Savio alone onstage gasping in disgust and disbelief.

At this point Pirandello unleashes his most original device, one carefully prepared for, but, as Roger Oliver explains, one that readers of the Livingston translation may not fully understand. Pirandello's subject in *Each in His Own Way* is the relationship between theater and life. To explore that relationship he makes the inner action a *commedia a chiave*, a play in which the characters are based on real-life models. Pirandello's primary trick is to have the models on whom Delia Morello and Michele Rocca are based in the audience, and his original instructions, not included in the Livingston translation, place actress Amelia Moreno (the model for Delia Morello) and the actor playing Baron Nuti (the model for Michele Rocca) in the lobby area before the curtain opens so that members of the audience coming in may overhear their conversation. The audience is also to be given a flyer indicating that because the subject of the play is so scandalous, "some unpleasant incident may occur tonight in the theater."[11]

Thus prepared, the audience is not surprised to find Amelia Moreno and Baron Nuti, who have been seated in the audience, rushing onto the stage during the second interlude, disrupting the action of the play and sending the actors home before the supposed third act can be performed. The play, like *Six Characters*, ends in total chaos, but in the midst of the chaos Signora Moreno and Baron Nuti, who have been horrified by the stage action they have just seen, have also been moved by that action to acknowledge their love for one another. In this way art, as theatrical representation, has directly influenced life by changing two "real" people. Here is where Pirandello wants the audience to become involved, for it is clear that the whole first choral interlude, devoted largely to the reactions of the imaginary theater audience and the critics, represents the playwright's view of how an audience is *not* to take the play. Just as Palegari and Savio are more interested in their own quarrel than in Morello and Rocca, so the defenders and attackers of Pirandello are more interested in their own critical positions than in what is really happening on the stage. The chaos at the end and the juxtaposition of Morello-Rocca with Moreno-Nuti is there for us, just as the ending of *Six Characters* is there for us, to shock us into an awareness and a compassion deeper than that of the fictitious audience in the play.

As I indicated earlier, one of the difficulties with *Each in His Own Way* is that the choral interludes, which supposedly take place in the theater lobby, are too clearly staged pieces. Pirandello overcomes this disadvantage in part by having Amelia Moreno and Baron Nuti in the audience, but the play as a whole is so dominated by the inner action that the "theater in the theater portions" are not strong enough to balance them. Such is not the case with *Tonight We Improvise*, the most daring and the most technically complex play in the trilogy. Not only is the theater dimension present from beginning to end, but the leading actors are asked to play both themselves *and* their characters, thus creating a dimension of reality that Pirandello has not attempted before. In *Tonight We Improvise* the conflict is between the director, Hinkfuss, and the actors, both as characters and as themselves. Pirandello is searching, in this play, for some way within the medium of theater to allow art to reflect more fully the confusion and fragmentation of "life." By using the device of a theatrical improvisation created by the director, Hinkfuss, against whose control the actors rebel, Pirandello succeeds magnificently. In Oliver's words:

> Theater is still reflecting life but is now doing it more accurately, since improvisation is one step closer to "reality." The director's loss of control

reflects the belief that life becomes fragmented and disrupted by the constant struggle between the freedom of impulse and the constraint of form.[12]

The inner action of the play is based on a Pirandello short story that concerns the LaCroce family—the mother, Signora Ignazia; the father, called Sampognetta ("the toy whistle"); their four daughters, Mommina, Totina, Dorina, and Nene; and a group of Air Force officers. Among the daughters the primary figure is Mommina, who marries one of the officers, Rico Verri, and then finds herself, in the play's most important scene, trapped within the walls of her apartment by her jealous husband, where she dies singing from *Il Trovatore*, the opera in which her sister Totina is scheduled to perform that very evening in their town. Mommina's death scene and the other major sequence which precedes it in Act III, the death of Sampognetta caused by knife wounds in a nightclub brawl, raise major questions about the relationship between life and art—because in both scenes it is the freedom of the actor to improvise and to make us, as audience, identify with the suffering of the actor that causes the sequences to be so powerful.

After Mommina's "death" there is a reaction onstage similar to that at the end of *Six Characters*:

THE CHARACTER ACTRESS: (*pointing again to* MOMMINA, THE LEADING ACTRESS, *lying on the floor*) But why don't you get up, Miss _____? She's still lying there—

THE CHARACTER ACTOR: She couldn't really be dead, could she? (*All gently bend down over* THE LEADING ACTRESS.)

THE LEADING ACTOR: (*calling to her and lifting her up*) Miss _____.

THE CHARACTER ACTRESS: Are you really sick?

NENE: Good God, she's fainted. Let's lift her up.

THE LEADING ACTRESS: (*getting herself up*) No—thank you. It really *is* my heart, though. Let me get my breath. Let me get my breath—

The same kind of confusion occurs after the "death" of Sampognetta. The actor has entered, complaining that he cannot play the scene the way it has been improvised, because all of the elements that he as an actor needs to "play" his death have been either removed or omitted. Then he goes on to *describe* how he would have played it and in doing so creates a death scene which paradoxically elicits more emotion than the original scene would have:

He drops his head on the breast of THE NIGHT CLUB SINGER. *His arms go limp after a moment, and he falls on the floor dead.*

NIGHT CLUB SINGER: Oh God! (*She tries to hold him up and then lets go of him.*) He's dead! He's dead!

MOMMINA: (*throwing herself on him*) Papa, my Papa, my Papa— (*and she begins to cry. This outburst of actual emotion in* THE LEADING ACTRESS *provokes emotion in the other actors, who give themselves up to tears, too.*)

In each case our emotion is directed as much, if not more, to the actors than to the characters, and we are, as audience, both more distanced from the action because of this device and yet more moved by it because of the distancing. The distancing from the inner action (the story of the LaCroce family) allows us to be more moved by the "lifelike" problems created for the actors as human beings. And I think that is precisely what Pirandello was after in all the plays of the theater trilogy. The failure of the Director and the actors in *Six Characters* may be their failure to accept the characters in this way; and on one level, Dr. Hinkfuss, the director in *Tonight We Improvise*, is guilty of the same failure.

Hinkfuss is the most important character in the play, but one toward whom we feel a profound ambivalence. He is guilty, like the Director in *Six Characters* and like Laudisi and Diego Cinci, of seeing life too much on the intellectual level, of reducing everything to an intellectual problem that can be solved. He wants, as director, to control everything. He wants to reduce the control of the playwright by eliminating the script, except for the scenario; and he wants all the actors and actresses to do exactly as he says. Thus, ironically, the so-called improvisation is not an improvisation at all, but an exercise in which the director replaces the playwright as the author of the play. Audiences of the 1980s used to the work of directors such as Peter Brook, Richard Foreman, and Arianne Mnouchkine would have no difficulty understanding what Hinkfuss is doing. But Pirandello is suspicious of this attempt by theater as art to overwhelm theater as life. The actors, craving the freedom that Hinkfuss says he is giving them, take the final step by banishing him from the stage so that they can *truly* improvise, truly play out their feelings without the controlling hand of the director. This will really be life, they argue. And so they play the final scene by themselves, and it ends with the terrifyingly moving "death" of Mommina and the near-death of the leading actress. But even here Hinkfuss has not really been absent. He has been up in the light booth adding to the beauty of the scene with particular lighting effects. Some direction, after all, is needed not only for theater as an art form to work but also to protect the actors from the chaos that would result if they carried the process of living their roles too far.

Tonight We Improvise, like Pirandello's other major plays, does not answer questions; it presents them. *It Is So*, *Six Characters*, and *Tonight We Improvise* all leave us with a sense of open-endedness; we leave the theater asking questions about ourselves, about reality, about the relationship between art and life, much in the way that we leave a Brecht production, *forced* to think about the issues, the questions, because the playwrights have taken away from us the pure emotional catharsis of traditional theater. Pirandello, Brecht, and O'Neill—the three playwrights who began their theatrical careers during or shortly after the First World War—were all restless experimenters, trying to make the theater do things it had not done before. They wanted their audiences to experience reality in a more profound way. Sometimes their experiments made their plays seem artificial, even crude. But when they succeeded, they did so magnificently.

Pirandello's great contribution to the reality-illusion question is that he makes us see the whole issue freshly. If reality truly is subjective, then vital lies may not be vital lies at all. Who is to say that the Ponzas are living a vital lie? Is not the term itself based on the notion that there is a *truth* being averted by a life-giving lie? And on the level of theater itself, who is to say which is more real—the action being depicted onstage or the action in the theater being conducted by actors, directors, and technicians? Pirandello's theater plays both influence and anticipate much of the interplay between reality and illusion that will take place in the plays of Peter Weiss, Jean Genet, Tom Stoppard, and Peter Handke in the sixties and seventies. Here the whole theme of playing with reality, introduced by Pirandello, is picked up and further developed. The ending of *Marat/Sade*, for example, when the chaos of "reality" breaks violently out of the confines of art, seems strikingly similar to the endings of Pirandello's theater plays, where art cannot control reality. After Pirandello it is only in America that the tradition of psychological and social realism continues with any real power. Pirandello's gift to modern theater, especially European theater, seems more alive than ever in our postmodern world of artistic and theatrical self-consciousness. In Stoppard's plays, *Jumpers* and *The Real Thing* especially, we see the spirit of Pirandello at his best—his playfulness, his wit, his intellectual curiosity, and his uninhibited love of the theatrical.

8

Bertolt Brecht

> ANDREA: "Unhappy is the land that breeds no hero."
> GALILEO: No, Andrea: "Unhappy is the land that needs
> a hero."
>
> —Galileo

Drama proceeds by dualities. Drama is conflict. The conflict between reality and illusion as we have examined it thus far tends to take the form of a kind of Hegelian triad: thesis, antithesis, synthesis, with an attempt to break through to a deeper reality in the synthesis thwarted by the inexplicable and final reality of death itself. Failing to find a new breakthrough, the hero may retreat to a world of dreams, drugs, or drunkenness, an escape from the unbearable nature of reality without purpose. But there is usually that sense of the glimpsed vision, the moment of release or insight that precedes either death or the failure to sustain the vision.

In Brecht we have all kinds of dualities: instinct versus reason, the individual versus society, the dramatic theater versus epic theater, capitalism versus Marxism. Nearly all Brecht's major protagonists are forced to struggle with dualities in their own natures, so much so that the concept of the split character may be the key to understanding Brecht. But Brecht, like Pirandello, is different from the playwrights considered in Part One of this study, because he does not treat the dualities in Hegelian fashion. There is not in either Pirandello or Brecht the sense of conflict (thesis versus antithesis) leading to synthesis. Pirandello is too much of a relativist, too subjective in his view of the human situation, to be a Hegelian. Brecht rejects the Hegelian idea of progress for different reasons, reasons that are ably described by Austin Quigley in his new study *The Modern Stage and Other Worlds*. Quigley notes, "For Korsch and Brecht, the dialectical progress of human society is no longer a Hegelian dialectic leading inevitably toward a pre-conceived social and spiritual synthesis, but a mode of social interaction that leads us to examine the need for, and possibility of, intervention in domains neither fully understood nor in their final form."[1] Brecht rejects both the concept of transcendence and the idea that change is a movement toward a necessarily better or more permanent mode of social interaction. Synthesis implies an end to contradiction. At the end of a Brecht play contradictions are seldom resolved, but the audience is invited to choose a course of action that would be appropriate for that particular situation at that particular time in history. I find it interesting that Martin Esslin uses the title *Brecht: A Choice of Evils* for the English edition of his influential book on the playwright to underline the theme of choice in Brecht. His central characters must always make difficult, almost excruciating choices, and those choices are, by necessity, a choice of evils. We as audience must learn, through our participation in the action of the plays, how to choose the lesser of two evils. Both Pirandello and Brecht hope to humanize us with their plays. They both remind us frequently that we are in the theater so that we cannot escape from the reality of the *human* issues into the make-believe of the story. We may best understand reality and illusion in Brecht through the motif of choice. To explain what I mean I would like to begin with a fairly late play, *The Good Woman of Setzuan* (1943), and then go back and examine the playwright's overall development in light of my thesis.

Three gods arrive in the city of Setzuan. Atheists are saying, "The world must be changed because no one can *be* good and *stay* good." The gods hope to refute the atheists by finding at least one good person, but thus far not only have they failed to turn up a good person, they have not even found a place to spend the night. Finally, Wang, the water seller, persuades Shen Te, the play's title character, to take them in. Pleased that they have found a good person, even though she is a prostitute, the gods reward her with enough money to set up a tobacco shop. The results are disastrous. An almost indescribable family of eight takes advantage of her, she falls in love with an unemployed pilot who needs money, and the gift of the gods turns into a curse. How can Shen Te be good and stay good? Her role as "the Angel of the Slums" is driving her out of business, and her love affair runs directly counter to the dictates of reason and good sense. Her lover, Yang Sun, is really a scoundrel.

So Shen Te "invents" a cousin, the shrewd and practical Shui Ta, who drives off the spongers, finds out the truth about Yang Sun, the pilot, and parlays Shen Te's small nest egg into a thriving business, even employing the erstwhile lover as a foreman, thus bringing out his true character. But there is one problem even the astute Shui Ta cannot solve: Shen Te is pregnant. He can hide it for a time under the cover of his own increasing weight as a successful entrepreneur, but sooner or later the truth will come out, and it does—in the form of a concluding trial in which the three gods act as judges. Accused of murdering Shen Te, Shui Ta asks that the court be cleared, takes off his mask, and makes this confession:

Your injunction
To be good and yet to live
Was a thunderbolt:
It has torn me in two . . .
When we extend our hand to a beggar, he tears it off for us
And so
Since not to eat is to die
Who can long refuse to be bad . . .
I truly wished to be the Angel of the Slums
But washed by a foster-mother in the water of the gutter
I developed a sharp eye
The time came when pity was a thorn in my side
And later, when kind words turned to ashes in my mouth.[2]

It is the archetypal Brechtian situation. The gods are useless. "We never meddle in economics," they say at the beginning and go off on a pink cloud at the end, a classic deus in machina that reverses the traditional happy ending, leaving poor Shen Te-Shui Ta as split as ever and with no advice except to try and be as good as she can. "Help!" screams Shen Te. "Help," asks the audience. If ever there was a Brecht play that works the way he wanted it to, it is this one. The audience is given no help. They must take their brains home after the play and figure it out. As Brecht wrote, "Epic theatre turns the spectator into an observer, but arouses his capacity for action, forces him to make decisions. . . . "[3]

What kind of questions does the audience ask itself? This is important. We do not ask ourselves the kinds of questions about reality and illusion that we might after viewing a Pirandello play. We do not ask whether or not Shen Te is more "real" than Shui Ta, though we might. We do not ask whether Shen Te represents illusion and Shui Ta reality, though we could. We do not ask these questions, because the performance of the play has convinced us of the innate reality of the split character. Both Shen Te and Shui Ta are real. If she invents him, it is only that she is calling forth an aspect of herself that she needs in order to survive. We accept the device as a symbol and the play as a parable. What Brecht makes us ask is quite a different question: Does reality have to be that way? And, is there something we can do about it? The answer to the first question is "no" and to the second "yes."

Human beings, according to Brecht's Marxist view, develop the traits, values, and institutions necessary to be successful in the economic system within which they live. Competitiveness, resourcefulness, avarice, shrewdness, practicality are all qualities that enable one to survive in a capitalistic system. Man is an adaptable animal. In Brecht's famous table of contrasts between dramatic and epic theater, man is described under epic theater as "alterable and able to alter."[4] Brecht believes both in fate and in freedom. Within the framework of a capitalistic system, Shui Ta will inevitably succeed and Shen Te will inevitably fail. But the system itself is not inevitable, and if the system can be altered, so can human beings. In Brecht's universe extreme heroism, goodness, and unselfishness of the sort exhibited by Shen Te or Grusha are, in part, marks of an aberration in the social and economic system. In a good society these traits would not be necessary. "Unhappy is the land that has no heroes," says Andrea to Galileo after his leader's capitulation to the Inquisition. "No, Andrea," answers Galileo. "Unhappy is the land that needs a hero." It is a point Brecht makes frequently.

From this look at *The Good Woman of Setzuan* we may derive some working generalizations that seem, at least on the surface, consistent with the views Brecht put forward during the early thirties when he did most of his writing on epic theater. There is no such thing as the innate nature of man. Man is not by nature good or evil, heroic or nonheroic. Man is a "process," and the nature of that process is determined by social conditions. "Social being determines thought" is one of Brecht's favorite terms. There are two sides to man—the feeling or instinctual side (Shen Te) and the rational, practical side (Shui Ta). Feelings, instincts are dangerous because they lead people to commit irrational acts or acts inconsistent with their welfare. The difference between Brecht's theory and his practice as a playwright is most emphatic at this point. In Brecht's theory the instinctual or feeling side is viewed negatively. Brecht's reactions to productions of his plays are like Chekhov's responses to Stanislavsky. Audiences were moved to tears by *Mother Courage*, so Brecht rewrote the play to make her less sympathetic. Chekhov insisted that his plays were comedies. Both playwrights insisted that they wrote plays with the intention of making their audiences see their lives in order to change them. It takes rationality, objectivity to make changes. The real purpose of the celebrated *Verfremdungseffekte* (principle of alienation) is to keep the audience rationally involved, thinking, throughout the production. Brecht did not want a cathartic, emotional release that would send the audience out of the theater saying, "Wasn't that a powerful experience?" Rather, the audience should leave asking, "What can be done?"

The premise of Brechtian theater then is that reality can be changed, and that people who go to the theater can do something in the process of change. While the characters in the plays seem to be victims of their circumstances, we do not have to be victims of ours. Brecht leaves us with the same paradox that Marx does: he is both an environmental determinist (social and economic conditions determine behavior) and a revolutionist (workers, cast off your chains). The two seem contradictory. How are we expected to change the world if our ideas are simply the outgrowth of conditions we have no control over. Paradox upon paradox. Brecht's plays are more humanly moving than he meant them to be. Why? Because from the very beginning of his career his rationalism is a kind of protection against his own natural instincts, which he saw both as decadent and practically debilitating.

The process really begins during the First World War when Brecht, as an eighteen-year-old medical orderly, was called up to the front:

> I was mobilized in the war and placed in a hospital, I dressed wounds, applied iodine, gave enemas, performed blood transfusions. If the doctor ordered me: "Amputate a leg, Brecht!" I would answer: "Yes, Your Excellency!" and cut off the leg. If I was told: "Make a trepanning!" I opened the man's skull and tinkered with his brains. I saw how they patched people up in order to ship them back to the front as soon as possible.

Martin Esslin's analysis of this passage is illuminating:

> . . . even Brecht's ostentatious display of defiant toughness in later life, the disgusted rejection of anything even remotely smacking of high-minded sentiment, whether religious or patriotic, can be seen as the reaction of a basically tender mind, shaken to its core by the sheer horror of existence in a world where such suffering was allowed to happen. The blatant cynicism of his public *persona* in later life is all too obviously the mask of one whose faith has been shattered and who has decided to meet the world on its own inhuman terms.[5]

I could not improve on Esslin's statement. Brecht goes in two directions. Distrusting the gentler emotions, he sees that pity, compassion, feelings about what happens to soldiers in war or workers in peacetime are useless. They accomplish nothing and only open the self to further victimizing by the state. One alternative is personal rebellion, the pose of the decadent artist—the Baal, Kruger, Garga figures in the early plays—a self-indulgent sensationalism, an exploration of the world of the senses for its own sake, a total giving in to instincts.

Brecht at first rejects all social solidarity. The title character of *Baal* (1918) destroys his women and turns mindlessly on the composer, Ekart, his best friend, because Ekart leaves him for a waitress. At the end of *In the Swamp* (1923), Shlink announces to his opponent, Garga, "the union of organs is the only union, and it can never bridge the gap of speech. . . . If you stuff a ship with human bodies till it bursts, there will still be such loneliness in it that one and all will freeze." The world of the early plays as well as Brecht's personal pose during the time he wrote them—that of the bohemian artist—is obviously a defense against his horror at the world he lived in. But it was a dead end, quite literally. All the early heroes—Baal, Kragler in *Drums in the Night* (1922), Shlink, and Garga—are essentially self-destructive.

By 1926, he has made the turn in the other direction. He has read Marx's *Das Kapital*, he has developed around him a group of friends and collaborators—Kurt Weill, Elisabeth Hauptmann, and Erwin Piscator being the best known—and he has begun to shape, under Piscator's influence, the fundamental ideas of the epic theater. As early as 1927, he writes, "It is understood that the radical transformation of the theatre can't be the result of some artistic whim. It has simply to correspond to the whole radical transformation of the mentality of our time."[6]

Plays like *A Man's a Man* (1926) and *The Threepenny Opera* (1928) illustrate the change. Here Brecht is able to experiment more fully with the development of social themes, the use of music for educative purposes, and the juxtaposition of bawdy comedy with political and sociological commentary in order to shock audiences into new perceptions. If in *A Man's a Man* the gentle porter, Galy Gay, can be transformed before our very eyes into the fiery soldier, Jeremiah Jip, what then can society as a whole do to any man? "One man is just like all the others," says Polly Baker. "A man's a man." With Peachum and Macheath in *The Threepenny Opera*, Brecht presents subtle yet acerbic criticism of the modern bourgeois. Frederic Ewen points out perceptively that there are two, overlapping Brechts in this play:

> There is the sky-storming nihilist, laureate of the asphalt jungle; and there is the initiate into Marxism, who was attempting to parallel the lesser duplicities and betrayals, the thievery of the netherworld with the more seemingly respectable but crasser and more thoroughgoing iniquities and corruption of the upper world.[7]

By 1930, the Marxist had won the day; in this year Brecht finished his most overtly economic and political play, *Saint Joan of the Stockyards*. Inspired in part both by Shaw's *Saint Joan* and *Major Barbara*, which Brecht admired, the play shows how capitalist power in the mammoth figure of Pierpont Mauler can utilize religious figures like Joan for its own ends. Mauler works on a basic premise: if you can't beat them canonize them; a dead saint is better than a live protester. Joan, who has been converted to Marxism in the course of her struggles to help the workers, cries out:

> Therefore, anyone down here who says there is a God
> When none can be seen
> A God who can be invisible and yet help them,
> Should have his head knocked on the pavement
> until he croaks. . . .
> And the ones that tell them they may be raised in spirit
> And still be stuck in the mud, they should have their heads
> Knocked on the pavement.

No one wants to hear this, and so the black strawhats, the packers, and the stockbrokers all combine to sing a magnificent closing chorale in order to drown her out. It may well be that Joan dies as much of discouragement as of pneumonia. The play closes with a kind of anthem which is both a brilliant parody of the ending of Goethe's *Faust* and an illuminating comment on the future of the Brechtian hero:

> Humanity! Two souls abide
> Within thy breast!
> Do not set either one aside:
> Be torn apart with constant care!
> Be two in one! Be here, be there!
> Hold the low one, hold the high one—
> Hold the straight one, hold the sly one—
> Hold the pair!

Here is Brechtian irony at its finest, and it is but a step from this speech to the position we find ourselves in the three great plays Brecht wrote first between 1938 and 1940—*Mother Courage and Her Children, Galileo,* and *The Good Woman of Setzuan.* In these plays we see the Brechtian dualities in their clearest and most mature form. Having rejected instinct, whether in its early anarchistic-nihilistic form or in its later self-sacrificial form embodied in the heroic Joan Dark (Jeanne d'Arc), Brecht explores in the later plays the development of the rational, pragmatic side as a survival mechanism. Before we look closely at these plays, however, we must look somewhat more generally at one of the central problems with which they deal—human nature.

In *Saint Joan of the Stockyards* the cynical Mauler explains to Joan that he would like to help the poor but that human nature is evil and help would not really do any good. "Mankind's not ripe for what you have in mind," he says. "Before the world can change, humanity must change its nature" (a blunt version of the conservative argument paraded so much in the eighties). We know that Brecht as a Marxist would not agree with this position. We know in fact that Mauler uses the argument to defend the status quo. "Don't give the poor money, they'll just abuse it." Brecht's position is that before human nature can change, the world must change. Man is, we remember, "alterable and able to alter." If the soldiers can make Galy Gay into Jeremiah Jip, cannot a good environment perform the reverse process? Yes, we argue theoretically. The trouble is that plays don't change the world. Do we ever in Brecht or in any other major playwright see the world actually changed by someone? "The world is out of joint," says Hamlet. "O cursed spite / that ever I was born to set it right." The heroes we have looked at in this study are not much different from Hamlet in this regard. They all want to change the world and almost always at the moment of climax find that the world cannot be changed—so they leave it, transcend, adopt their own philosophy, and die, or they go into exile, literally or symbolically. It is the movement we have been watching: that from illusion to reality to ideal or dream. Even Pirandello, who has, as we have seen, rejected the Hegelian pattern, dramatizes this sort of action.

But Brecht won't have that. Except in *The Caucasian Chalk Circle*, which we will examine at the end of this chapter, the world is not changed. Nor do the heroes make the leap we have been discussing. Instead, they *adapt*! They want to live. "Better a live dog than a dead lion," is Galileo's motto. Thus, we *appear* to have almost a reverse of the paradigm that has guided us thus far. Brecht's heroes go from dreams and ideals to reality to illusion, if we define illusion as a kind of necessary game or role that allows one to survive, a kind of putting on of the mask instead of taking it off. We must, therefore, examine the pattern and ask how Brecht wanted his audiences to respond to such adaptations.

We begin with Anna Fierling, known as Mother Courage. As a young woman she was full of dreams; she believed she was special. "With my looks and my talent and my love of the Higher Things," she sings in the "Song of the Great Capitulation,"

Our plans are big, our hopes colossal.
We hitch our wagon to a star. . . .
"We can lift mountains," says the apostle.
And yet how heavy one cigar!

She has three children—Eilif, brave and foolhardy; Swiss Cheese, the honest one; Kattrin, good and loving. How can she support them except to adapt and conform? There's a war on: the only way to make a living is to adapt to the values of wartime—cunning, avarice, business acumen. How else is she to save her children? This is the central irony of the play—that Mother Courage is involved in a business deal each time one of her children is killed. The pattern is devastatingly obvious. Eilif is drafted by the recruiting officer while she is selling the sergeant a belt; Swiss Cheese is executed while she is debating whether to pay the ransom; Kattrin is shot while her mother is in the town of Halle buying up stocks "because the shopkeepers are running away and selling cheap." But is she wrong? What would happen to the children if she didn't do this? "The Song of the Great Souls of This Earth" makes it clear that none of the children could survive alone. Solomon (Mother Courage), Julius Caesar (Eilif), Socrates (Swiss Cheese), and Saint Martin (Kattrin) represent the virtues of wisdom, bravery, honesty, and unselfishness. Mother Courage argues, "for the virtues are dangerous in this world, you're better off without." In Brecht's play there is no reward for virtue; on the other hand, vice doesn't help much either.

Brecht's notes on the play, written largely for his classic 1949 production in Berlin, suggest an answer to Mother Courage's problem:

> What is a performance of *Mother Courage and Her Children* primarily meant to show?
> That in wartime big business is not conducted by small people. That war is a continuation of business by other means, making the human virtues fatal even to those who exercise them. That no sacrifice is too great for the struggle against war.[8]

The last sentence is telling. Mother Courage's sacrifices do *nothing* to stop war. She lives and acts as if the condition of war is both natural and inevitable. Brecht wants the play to illustrate the fact that "Courage has learned nothing from the disasters that befall her." He goes on, "But even if Courage learns nothing else at least the audience can, in my view, learn something from observing her."[9] Paradoxically, what audiences seem to have learned from seeing the play was not what the playwright wanted them to learn. Audiences, again and again, have seen Courage as the symbol of the common person, battered by the forces of war and big business, who gets up from near-death to keep going. But to Brecht she was an antihero, and it is worthwhile to note that the revisions the playwright made both in this play and in his other masterpiece, *Galileo*, attest to his desire to make his heroes less sympathetic rather than more.

Galileo is one of Brecht's great creations. Like Mother Courage, he has so much energy, so much pure vitality, that he tends to appeal to audiences for what Brecht would argue are the wrong reasons. "He has more enjoyment in him than any man I ever saw," says the Pope. "He loves eating and drinking and thinking. To excess." Perhaps this is the key to his character. Instinct versus reason again. For Galileo, even the thinking process has become instinctual. He gorges himself on it. For this we love him more than we would a cool, rational type. But Galileo himself knows better. The two scenes critical for an understanding of his character are the seventh and the thirteenth—the dialogue with the Little Monk and the revelation scene when Andrea comes to visit at the end.

"I take it the intent of science is to ease human existence," says Galileo to Andrea. In other words, Galileo's role in a rational universe is not to indulge in thinking bouts but to use reason to improve the lot of humanity (Marx again). Galileo explains this point to the Little Monk in the earlier scene: "virtues are not exclusive to misery. If your parents were prosperous and happy, they might develop the virtues of happiness and prosperity. Today the virtues of exhaustion are caused by the exhausted land." The Little Monk's parents need God (illusion) because they have nothing else. God gives their lives meaning. "How could they take it," cries the Little Monk, "were I to tell them that they are on a lump of stone ceaselessly spinning in empty space, circling around a second-rate star?"

Galileo understands that the purpose personified in God must be internalized. People must learn to think for themselves, to use the instruments of reason and scientific technology to help themselves. The central issue of the play becomes the moral responsibility of the scientific community. This is the point that Galileo stresses to Andrea:

> As a scientist I had an almost unique opportunity. In my day astronomy emerged into the market place. At that particular time, had one man put up a fight, it could have had repercussions. I have come to believe that I was never in real danger; for some years I was as strong as the authorities, and I surrendered my knowledge to the powers that be to use it, no *abuse* it, as it suits their ends. I have betrayed my profession.

It is important to understand that this emphasis was not in the original (1938) German version but was added by the playwright in collaboration with Charles Laughton for the 1947 English version Brecht and Laughton prepared together in California. The new emphasis, Brecht pointed out, was made necessary by Hiroshima. Brecht's explanation of the change is instructive:

96

The "atomic age" made its debut in Hiroshima in the middle of our work. Overnight the biography of the founder of modern physics had to be read differently. . . . In the first version of the piece, the last scene was different. Galileo had written his *Discorsi* in the greatest secrecy. When his favorite pupil Andrea visits him, he arranges to have the book smuggled abroad across the frontier. His recantation offered him the possibility of creating a crucial work. He was wise. In the California version Galileo interrupts the pupil's encomium and proves to him that the recantation was a crime, and not to be balanced by the work, no matter how important. *Should it interest anyone, this too is the opinion of the playwright* [Brecht's emphasis].[10]

Galileo was Brecht's favorite play. He never tired of tinkering with it, and at the time of his death he was preparing another version of it for production by the Berliner Ensemble. In this version Galileo's self-criticism, while in substance the same as the Laughton version, is even more severe. The playwright's fascination with the play surely stems in part from the parallels between the creature and his creator. Galileo is Brecht's portrait of the artist as an old chameleon. It certainly raises questions about Brecht's personal life-style and his relations to both East and West. Did Brecht, like Galileo, tell the authorities what they wanted to hear so he could get on with his work? Did Brecht, also like Galileo, feel he had betrayed humanity by not speaking out more forcefully? "Better stained than empty," cries Galileo, but the playwright himself seems to undercut that position.

We are now back to *The Good Woman of Setzuan*, and the question here is: Does Shen Te, in creating the cousin, Shui Ta, commit the same crimes as Mother Courage and Galileo? Is she one more antihero who chooses adaptation first and humanity second? The issue reminds me of the perennial argument about ethics. If you use an evil means to a good end, does the means itself destroy the end for which you are working? If a person says, for example, "I wish to do good in this world and help my fellow man, but I cannot do any good without real power," does his use of evil means to gain power thereby destroy his potential for doing good? This is the question Shaw raises with the character of Undershaft in *Major Barbara*. To consider Brecht's position, we must examine both the Shen Te/Shui Ta character and the Grusha/Azdak figures in *The Caucasian Chalk Circle*, completed in 1945 and the last of Brecht's major plays.

Shen Te and Grusha are variants of the same character (Kattrin in *Mother Courage* and Joan Dark are others). Both are young women, gentle and motherly. Both love easily and naturally; both take risks to help others, Shen Te in putting up the gods, Grusha in caring for the child.

Both are moral in an "immoral" kind of way. Both pause and consider for a long time before committing the acts that start their plays. "Terrible is the seductive power of goodness," exclaims Grusha when she finally takes the child. Shen Te might have said the same. The way the world is, Brecht implies, being good will inevitably get you into trouble. It may kill you, as it does Joan Dark and Kattrin. But Shen Te and Grusha have protectors: Shen Te has Shui Ta, and Grusha has Azdak. And there is a difference between the two. The Shen Te/Shui Ta relationship will not change the world. The Grusha/Azdak relationship might. It is not so much that Shen Te's ends are defeated by Shui Ta's means, because Shui Ta exists to help Shen Te; the issue is that nothing happens during the course of the play to make the world any different. It is exactly the same at the end of the play as it was in the beginning. So is the world of *Mother Courage* and, to some extent, the world of *Galileo*. But at the end of *The Caucasian Chalk Circle* the world is, at least momentarily, different:

> And after that evening Azdak disappeared and was not seen again.
> The people of Grusinia did not forget him but long remembered
> The period of his judging as a brief golden age
> Almost an age of justice.
> But you who have listened to the story of the Chalk Circle
> Take note what men of old concluded:
> That what there is shall go to those who are good for it
> Thus, the children to the motherly, that they prosper
> The carts to good drivers, that they are driven well
> And the valley to the waterers, that it bring forth fruit.

There is at the end of this play an unusual environment of festivity. The traditional images of comedy—marriage, the feast, the dance—are observed. The usurpers are cast out, the blocking characters defeated, Grusha and Simon married. *All the couples dance off.* Of course, we know that Brecht, the practical theater man, gave *The Caucasian Chalk Circle* a happy ending because he thought he could more readily get it produced in the United States; but it would be pure cynicism to think of the ending as crafted for that purpose alone.

Finally it's a matter of *being* versus *doing*. There seem to be two fundamentally different ways of viewing the world. Some view it primarily in terms of being (with its concomitant sides of experience and perception—"being" as experiencing, "being" as seeing). Others view it primarily in terms of action. Brecht is one of the latter. It is not so much a question of who Azdak is, but of what he does. Azdak is a good judge. He awards the child to Grusha, as Eric Bentley reminds us, because of what she has done. She deserves the child *because* she has been a good mother, just as the valley of the prologue will be awarded to the fruit growers because they have proved themselves better for the valley.[11]

Thus, the term "epic theater" *is* appropriate for Brecht's work. As audiences we are placed in front of actions and asked, as a result of the choices characters make, to evaluate their decisions and to try to discover how the world might be changed so that those decisions might have been different. Quigley asserts, correctly I think, in *The Modern Stage and Other Worlds* that Brecht is asking his audience to "participate in an inquiry" rather than "assent to pre-existing values."[12] Epic theater invites us to participate in an inquiry, and that is, finally, why it is so difficult to discuss Brecht in terms of the reality-illusion conflict. The pattern in the action of Brecht's plays really redefines the conflict by eliminating the Hegelian synthesis, by subordinating the idea of being to that of action, and by asserting that reality—the tough, tangible stuff of life—is what there is. It is an illusion to believe in some inner being, some "real" self that transcends this life. For Brecht those high ideals of the Ibsenian and Chekhovian heroes are the real illusions. We must face reality squarely, but facing it does not mean *adapting* to it. For reality is "alterable and able to alter." The function of the hero in Brecht is not to separate himself from the impurities of the world, to keep inviolate some illusionary sanctuary of the self. The function of the hero is to immerse himself in reality, as Azdak does, as Galileo does, and to use his creative powers to remake the world so that the sacrifices of the gentler figures will not be necessary. Ronald Hayman, one of Brecht's recent biographers, reminds us that his first play, *The Bible*, written when the playwright was fifteen, deals with the question of whether an innocent girl should be sacrificed to save her native city. Brecht's interest in the necessary sacrifice of the good person to save the community was literally lifelong.[13] And that life's work is a reminder to us as human beings that the sacrifice will continue as long as we permit it. In a good society such sacrifices would not be called for.

9

T. S. Eliot

Humankind cannot bear very much reality.

—Thomas in *Murder in the Cathedral*

In a study of reality and illusion in modern drama, the place of T. S. Eliot is both central and unique, central because reality and illusion are the major concern of all his plays and unique because he is the only major modern dramatist to treat the theme from a Christian perspective. His work seems particularly interesting when placed in direct contrast to the materialism of Bertolt Brecht, an artist whose career parallels Eliot's both chronologically and in their attempts to establish a theater radically different from that to which their audiences were accustomed. Both had visions of reality that required fundamental changes in theatrical method, and both wrote vigorous critical prose in defense of their methods.

Eliot's plays from *Murder in the Cathedral* (1935) to *The Elder Statesman* (1958) form both a unity and a continuum. All five plays deal with the difference between the saint and the common man and the degree to which each is able to confront reality as Eliot perceives it. All five plays contrast reality as normally understood by human beings with reality as understood by the Christian. As Michael Goldman perceives, all of Eliot's major figures suffer from "an isolation in unreality. They are trapped in a world of make-believe."[1] The action of each play is the story of the characters' attempts to deal with that unreality. However, each play is quite different from the others, because each represents a different stage in Eliot's campaign as an artist to restore verse drama to an important place in English theater. He wanted, as he stated in "Poetry and Drama" in 1950, to get his audiences to accept verse not only from characters in historical plays but from figures in contemporary plays:

> What we have to do is to bring poetry into the world in which the audience lives and to which it returns when it leaves the theatre; not to transport the audience into some imaginary world totally unlike its own, an unreal world in which poetry is tolerated. What I should hope might be achieved by a generation of dramatists having the benefit of our experience is that the audience should find, at the moment of awareness, that it is hearing poetry, that it is saying to itself: "I could talk in poetry, too!" Then we

should not be transported into an artificial world; on the contrary, our own sordid, dreary daily world would be suddenly illuminated and transfigured.[2]

The story of Eliot's development as a playwright is the story of his attempt to put this theory into practice by moving in each of his plays more and more fully into the world of his audience. In *Murder in the Cathedral* the poetry works effectively and the choral device seems natural because of the twelfth-century setting and because of the almost superhuman status of Becket. In *The Family Reunion* (1939) Eliot writes his first play in a contemporary setting, but it is a kind of compromise, a cross between drawing room comedy, melodrama, and expressionism. The choral speeches, the appearances of the Eumenides, and the long, difficult exchanges between Agatha and Harry all suggest Eliot's discomfort: he is halfway between *Murder in the Cathedral* and his later plays, and the result is far from satisfactory. *The Cocktail Party* (1949) is, in my opinion, Eliot's masterpiece. In it he has solved successfully the problem of meeting the audience on its own ground and yet utilizing the play as a means of transfiguring the audience's daily life. *The Confidential Clerk* (1953) and *The Elder Statesman* (1958) move further in the same direction, too far I think. Both plays rely heavily on popular West End theatrical devices, much in the manner of Noël Coward or even Gilbert and Sullivan. *The Confidential Clerk* is built around the question of the parentage of both Colby and Lucasta, and Eliot even resorts to the melodramatic device of bringing in the mysterious Mrs. Guzzard to reveal all in Act III. *The Elder Statesman* is somewhat less contrived, but the accumulation of Lord Claverton's past sins in the shape of Federico Gomez (alias Frederick Culverwell) and Mrs. Carghill (once Maisie Montjoy) is overly stagy. The last two plays are certainly more readily understandable by an average theater audience than the first three, but I agree with Carol Smith that Eliot has lost more than he has gained:

In giving up the intellectual appeal of the early plays, and by substituting none of the compelling effects of naturalism, Eliot has lost the best of both theatres. His goal of developing a new theatre, and training an audience to respond to it, had thus been frustrated by the inability of his current dramatic methods to reach the emotions of his audience, on the one hand, or to fascinate and stimulate their intellect, on the other.[3]

Though the question of form may not seem directly related to the study of reality and illusion in Eliot's plays, it is a crucial one, because all his plays are, in Smith's words, "theatrical fables meant to disclose religious meanings."[4] If this is so, then the *form* that the fable takes will have tremendous bearing on how effectively the playwright communicates his religious meanings. One of Eliot's problems is that in some cases the audience perceives only the surface of the play (illusion) and misses its depths (reality). Thus, as we move through the plays in an examination of their themes, we will keep in mind the relation between form and substance as it affects the transmission of the religious content.

Murder in the Cathedral, despite Eliot's claim that it was artistically a dead end, is still his most exciting play, because the verse is of such a high order and because Eliot is so successful in varying the verse forms to the needs of the dramatic situation and the character who is speaking. There are many different kinds of verse and even two different kinds of prose in the play, and this is what prevents the boredom that overtakes the audience in the later plays, where all the characters seem to sound alike. A character's perception of reality is closely connected to the kind of language he speaks. Thus the knights, who represent the lowest level of humanity in the play, speak colloquial modern prose. Their defense of themselves in Act II makes use of all the common clichés of modern life. Their language is entirely secular and without imagery. Thomas, who understands the mentality of secular society, anticipates the audience's identification with the knights when he says in Act I:

> I know
> What yet remains to show you of my history
> Will seem to most of you at best futility,
> Senseless self-slaughter of a lunatic,
> Arrogant passion of a fanatic.

The world represented by the knights, the world that judges Thomas dead "of Suicide while of Unsound Mind," is one kind of reality; it is the lost world of "Prufrock" and *The Waste Land* and "The Hollow Men." Eliot's purpose is to make us aware that this reality is the merest illusion. This world, which we call reality, is unreal:

> Man's life is a cheat and a disappointment;
> All things are unreal,
> Unreal or disappointing:
> The Catherine wheel, the pantomime cat,
> The prizes given at the children's party,
> The prize awarded for the English essay,

The scholar's degree, the statesman's decoration.
All things become less real, man passes
From unreality to unreality.

Like the knights, the first three tempters represent aspects of our daily reality, each of which Thomas is able to reject as unreal. The First Tempter with his sensuous, lyric sweetness suggests the life of the senses, the pleasures of youth. The second—more blunt and short-spoken—stands for political power. The third, with his snakelike rhetoric, is a symbol of intrigue and revolution. Only the fourth is a true temptation for Thomas, because at this point in his life, he has already rejected the other three as unreal. For Thomas, spiritual dedication to God is the only reality, but the Fourth Tempter hits him from an unexpected angle: "But think, Thomas, think of glory after death." Thomas realizes that the Fourth Tempter presents a critical problem: "Is there no way, in my soul's sickness, / Does not lead to damnation in pride?" He sees that what he thinks is ultimate reality may be his ultimate illusion if he is going to be martyred for the sake of his own pride. And that is precisely why Eliot includes Thomas's Christmas sermon, because the audience must understand fully the distinction between the true martyr, made by God's will, and the false martyr, made by his own will. In the light of the sermon the lines spoken first to the Chorus by Thomas and then to Thomas by the Fourth Tempter take on added meaning:

You know and do not know, what it is to act or suffer.
You know and do not know, that acting is suffering.
And suffering action. Neither does the actor suffer
Nor the patient act. But both are fixed
In an eternal action, an eternal patience
To which all must consent that it may be willed
And which all must suffer that they may will it,
That the pattern may subsist, that the wheel may turn and still
Be forever still.

The Chorus will never know what these words mean, but the Fourth Tempter is wrong. Thomas will come to understand the meaning of his own action, which is not his own action. He comes to realize that his action is taken by God out of time, and that his job is to consent that God's pattern may be worked out. At the still point of the turning wheel is God, and once he has seen God, had his "wink of heaven," Thomas sees that the true madman is the man of this world:

You think me reckless, desperate, and mad.
You argue by results, as this world does,
To settle if an act be good or bad.
You defer to the fact.

But this does not mean that Thomas's martyrdom has no earthly purpose. That it does is brought home by the play's second most important character, the Chorus. The play is called *Murder in the Cathedral*, not *Becket*. If the play were merely about Becket, we could do without the Chorus, but Eliot wants us to ask ourselves why this murder occurred and how it has significance for us. We are forced to explore the meaning of the murder for ourselves by becoming the women of Canterbury and sharing in their experience of Thomas's death. If we do not accept our role, then the play fails.

Like the women, we are drawn to the center of action by curiosity, by a compulsion to be present at that which is about to take place. But we are afraid. We want to be left alone. "We do not wish anything to happen." Content with "living and partly living," we are accustomed to the injustices of life, the regular cycle of birth and death, of marriage and scandal, of taxes and high prices. We understand the calamities of this world, the so-called real things—but we do not want to be drawn into something we do not understand. We do not want God to enter our lives. This is precisely why Thomas must be martyred. As he says in his sermon, "A martyr, a saint, is always made by the design of God, for His love to men, to warn them and to lead them, to bring them back to his ways." The Chorus does not want to be brought back, and it takes the shock of Thomas's death to jolt them into a realization that they are creatures dependent on God for their very being. If Act I is the story of Becket's struggle for salvation, Act II is the story of the Chorus's growing realization of their part in Becket's death and their need for regeneration. The play is dominated by seasonal imagery. The time is winter, and unless a spiritual rebirth takes place, there will be no spring: "And the world must be cleaned in the winter, or we shall have only / A sour spring, a parched summer, an empty harvest. / Between Christmas and Easter what work shall be done?" The Chorus begins that work by confessing to Thomas that they have participated in the martyrdom. They are as guilty as the knights, because they have been afraid to intervene, afraid to give themselves to God. Thomas understands and is compassionate toward them, for "humankind cannot bear very much reality." As the play ends, the Chorus confesses its sins and prays for God's mercy:

Forgive us, O Lord, we acknowledge ourselves as a type of the common
   man,
Of the men and women who shut the door and sit by the fire;
Who fear the blessing of God, the loneliness of the night of
   God, the surrender required, the deprivation inflicted;
Who fear the injustice of men less than the justice of God;
Who fear the hand at the window, the fire in the thatch, the
   fist in the tavern, the push into the canal
Less than we fear the love of God.

The choral confession bears out the truth of Thomas's assertion:
"Humankind cannot bear very much reality." We the Chorus will avoid
God wherever possible, fearing both God's love and justice, fearing the
surrender, the demand, the commitment that loving God may place
upon us. And so saints come from God—Joan of Arc, Thomas, Jesus
Christ—and we crucify them, stab them, burn them to death. We do not
like to be reminded of reality, for if *they* are right, our life is the merest
sham, an illusion of illusions. We cannot bear to be told that; so we kill
anyone who dares demand too much of us. But their deaths jolt us, and
for a moment our lives are changed. We become part of God's world:
"This is one moment," Thomas tells the Chorus, "But know that another /
Shall pierce you with a sudden painful joy / When the figure of God's
purpose is made complete." The revelation will be brief. We will glimpse
God's presence momentarily, and then the clouds will close, and we will
return to our daily round, living and partly living. So there will have to be
another saint, another martyr to remind us of where the more abundant
life really is. Thus the cycle goes.

How fascinatingly similar *Murder in the Cathedral* is to Shaw's *Saint
Joan*. Despite the fact that the two figures had little use for one another,
their positions in these two plays are remarkably alike. Both define reality in spiritual terms, both create as central figures saints whose vision
is deeper and more penetrating than the average person's, and both
handle the reality-illusion conflict in terms of the growth that the average person may make through the aid or intervention of the saint. Both
see the function of the saint or genius to teach man about reality; and
both, for all that they have written about their religious views, are best
described as mystics. While they may be far apart in style and tempera-
ment, they are closer in basic attitude than critics have usually acknowl-
edged.

Eliot's second play, *The Family Reunion*, is his least successful theatrically. It is his first play in a contemporary setting and the first of four

plays to be based deliberately on classical models. One of the main problems with the play is that the classical models, Aeschylus's *Libation Bearers* and *Eumenides*, are too obtrusive, thrusting the characters into roles too big for them. Harry, in particular, has not the depth of his classical counterpart, and as a result, his final departure seems rather anticlimactic. Agatha, who has no real counterpart in the Greek story, is the most interesting character in the play, but we are left pretty much up in the air as to what becomes of her. The play is too long, and many of its scenes tedious; but it is important because it shows the playwright trying to learn how to treat the theme of salvation in a contemporary setting.

The Chorus of *Murder in the Cathedral* is replaced by the choral quartet of Ivy, Violet, Gerald, and Charles. Like the women of Canterbury, they are a type of common person who doesn't know what is really going on. As Harry says, "You are all people / To whom nothing has happened, at most a continual impact / of external events." They themselves state the nature of their reality in the choral speech that closes the first scene:

> Why do we all behave as if the door might suddenly open, the
>   curtains be drawn,
> The cellar make some dreadful disclosure, the roof disappear,
> And we should cease to be sure of what is real or unreal?
> Hold tight, hold tight, we must insist that the world is what we
>   have always taken it to be.

Like the women of Canterbury and the inhabitants of *The Waste Land*, they fear the coming of spring, the disclosure that might reveal the unreality of that which they call real. Unlike the women of Canterbury, they are not redeemed by Harry's presence. Except for Charles, who says at the play's end, "I think that I might understand," they continue to deal on a very superficial level with what they think of as reality:

> But the circle of our understanding
> Is a very restricted area,
> Except for a limited number
> Of strictly practical purposes
> We do not know what we are doing.

Harry and his mother, Amy, the Dowager Lady Monchesney, also have their parallels to characters in *Murder in the Cathedral*. Harry, like Becket, must undergo a series of temptations before he can find the right way. He must come to an understanding of how God works, and his major antagonist is his mother, who wants him to accept a purely material definition of reality. Wishwood, the appropriately named family estate, represents what the world would be like if Amy's wishes were fulfilled—a world of snobbery and material comfort protected from the reality of suffering. Her death symbolizes Harry's victory over this world, the same world that paralyzes J. Alfred Prufrock.

But there has been a major change in Eliot's thinking since the days of "Prufrock" and *The Waste Land*, and nowhere in the play is that change better illustrated than in a new type of character he introduces, the "watchers and waiters," Mary and Agatha. There is no one to help Prufrock or the characters of *The Waste Land*, no one to help the "hollow men." But in the world of Eliot's plays, all written after his conversion to Christianity, a dominant figure is that of the helper, the guardian, the watcher—a Beatrice or Virgil figure who guides the fallen human through the inferno and purgatory on the way to paradise. Eliot projects in *The Family Reunion* a division of humanity into four groups: (1) the saint or future saint in Harry; (2) the watcher or guardian in Agatha; (3) the self-seeking materialist in Amy; and (4) the unaware common person in the aunts and uncles. Eliot's view of the possibility of salvation for the ordinary human is most pessimistic in *The Family Reunion*. Agatha makes it clear that ultimate reality is spiritual and that Harry has crossed from this world into the spiritual world:

> Here the danger, here the death, here, not elsewhere;
> Elsewhere no doubt is agony, renunciation,
> But birth and life. Harry has crossed the frontier
> Beyond which safety and danger have a different meaning.
> And he cannot return. That is his privilege.
> For those who live in this world, this world only,
> Do you think that I would take the responsibility
> Of tempting them over the border?

If the real world, as Eliot views it, is the world into which Harry has crossed, then what hope is there for those who live in "this world only"? Agatha, the guide, will not take the responsibility of "tempting them over the border." Are they, then, condemned to a life of illusion? It would seem so, but in his last three plays Eliot will develop a more affirmative theology of the salvation of the ordinary person.

In *The Cocktail Party*, the strongest of the last four plays, Eliot shifts the focus for the first time from the saint to the ordinary human. The saint is there in Celia, but her salvation may well be considered the secondary action of the play, while the redemption of the rest of us, symbolized by Edward and Lavinia, is the primary action. The play is very carefully patterned, and the awkward and obtrusive elements of *The Family Reunion* expunged. Though the play is based on Euripides' *Alcestis*, it is not necessary to know that; the allusions to *Alcestis* serve mainly to enrich the play for those who are aware of them, without disturbing or distracting those who are not. Eliot here is attempting to make use of what he has learned from the study of Shakespeare: that a work of art may appeal to a widely heterogeneous group of people on several different levels at the same time. On the simplest level *The Cocktail Party* is a play about how a psychiatrist, Sir Henry Harcourt-Reilly, and his aides restore a dead marriage to life. Eliot gives the ordinary West End theatergoers enough plot to keep them interested (Edward's affair with Celia, Lavinia's with Peter, Peter's with Celia), but he constantly works on the more perceptive viewer beneath the surface. The verse is natural enough to pass as the witty urbane chatter of polite society, but at moments of great tension it rises to poetry, particularly in the second act.

Eliot's view of reality and illusion has changed in this play. At the center of *The Cocktail Party* is Reilly's exposition of the two ways. In *Murder in the Cathedral* and *The Family Reunion* there had been but one way—the way of the saint. But the way that Reilly outlines to Edward and Lavinia, pessimistic as it may seem on the surface, indicates a new apprehension of reality. One's first reaction is to be insulted. Edward says to Lavinia, " . . . we must make the best of a bad job. That is what he means." Reilly agrees. And this does seem like a rather dismal fate, but making the best of a bad job is not that bad. Reilly describes it to Celia:

> They . . . learn to avoid excessive expectation,
> Become tolerant of themselves and others,
> Giving and taking, in the usual actions
> What there is to give and take. They do not repine;
> Are contented with the morning that separates
> And with the evening that brings together
> For casual talk before the fire
> Two people who know they do not understand each other,
> Breeding children whom they do not understand . . .
>   In a world of lunacy,
> Violence, stupidity, greed . . . it is a good life.

Edward is incapable of loving, Lavinia is unlovable. Both must accept these limitations and go on, each trying to be considerate of the other, trying to be thoughtful, trying not to use the other merely to gratify personal needs. And so they do. In Act III they have changed: Edward compliments Lavinia on her dress, and they speak to one another with a new sensitivity. One must choose one's own way and then face the consequences; the consequences of Edward and Lavinia's way is the cocktail party that is about to begin as the play ends. Edward understands finally what that means:

> Oh it isn't much
> That I understand yet! But Sir Henry has been saying
> I think that every moment is a fresh beginning;
> And Julia, that life is only keeping on;
> And somehow, the two ideas seem to fit together.

The life Edward and Lavinia are to lead contrasts dramatically with the saint's life that Celia chooses. The way of the saint, Reilly maintains, is no better than the way of this world—it is simply the inevitable result of the saint's inability to reconcile the self to this life. Yet—and I think this is the main difficulty with *The Cocktail Party* as a play—despite Reilly's insistence that Celia's way is no better than Edward and Lavinia's, we feel that it is. We can feel the change that has taken place in the Chamberlaynes, and we can see how the process of disillusionment has brought both Edward and Lavinia to greater self-knowledge. We can even sense the beginnings of a real Christian marriage at the end of the play. Still, Eliot loads the deck. Celia's way *is* better. Her crucifixion, however ludicrous, makes us feel guilty, and we cannot help but agree with Edward that there is something wrong with giving a cocktail party immediately after having received the news of Celia's death. It is almost as if Eliot is trying to convince himself that the way elected by the Chamberlaynes is really as good as Celia's, when what he really believes is that different people have different levels of capability. Eliot is essentially an elitist, and *The Cocktail Party* confirms it. Not all of us can be saints, and the Chamberlaynes, being one-talent people rather than five-talent people, simply do the best they can with the talents they have. If reality is defined as union with God, then God seems to have designed the pattern so that only the saints are capable of that union. The rest of us must settle for cocktail parties.

In his last two plays Eliot turns even more fully than in *The Cocktail Party* to the plight of the ordinary human. Eliot seems to have realized between 1949 and 1953 that he had left out of his dramatic canon a type of character superior to the women of Canterbury, the aunts and uncles of *The Family Reunion*, and even to Lavinia and Edward—yet not in the same category with Becket or Harry or Celia. This new type becomes a central figure in the last plays: Colby Simkins and Sir Claude Mulhammer in *The Confidential Clerk* and Lord Claverton and his daughter Monica in *The Elder Statesman.*

Eliot's tone is more compassionate and more humane in these plays. In *The Confidential Clerk* we see that each person must have, behind the facade of the workaday world, which Eliot still treats as illusion, a private world into which he can retreat. The paradox is that this retreat can be a withdrawal into either illusion or reality. Lady Elizabeth has been sustained by a series of illusions, one of which is that Colby is her son. But Sir Claude, like Colby, hungers for the real world:

> I want a world where the form is the reality,
> Of which the substantial is only a shadow. . . .
>
> There are occasions
> When I am transported—a different person,
> Transfigured in the vision of some marvellous creation,
> And I feel what the man must have felt when he made it.

Sir Claude divides men into two groups: truly religious people and geniuses who can find some unity in their lives, and the rest like himself: "others . . . who have at best to live / in two worlds—each a kind of make believe. / That's you and me." In this sequence Eliot is establishing both a religion and an aesthetic. The saint or genius (the creative artist) can communicate directly with reality, but Sir Claude is a second-rate potter and Colby a second-rate organist and pianist. Thus each is denied the direct experience of the ecstasy that the saint or the artist feels. Yet, Eliot implies, they can share something of the artist's ecstasy by their participation in the work of art as audience. They do not fool themselves about their own abilities. Colby has no illusions at the end about how far he will get as a church organist or a parish priest; Sir Claude has no illusions about his pottery making. What they have had is illusions about their personal relationship:

> COLBY: You've become a man without illusions
> About himself and without ambitions.
> Now that I've abandoned *my* illusions and ambitions
> All that's left is love. But not on false pretences.
> That's why I must leave you.

The obvious fault in *The Confidential Clerk* is that Eliot has started to talk down to his audiences. He gives them too much farce, too much mistaken identity, too much last-minute discovery of parentage; but the fact that Colby is not Sir Claude or Elizabeth's son is important, because it teaches us that we must live within the limits that life imposes on us. We can choose neither our parents nor our children. Nor can we make people into something they are not. Sir Claude is guilty of trying to make Colby in his own image. Colby's final discovery frees him to be himself. It also frees B. Kaghan and Lucasta to be what Sir Claude and Lady Elizabeth really need, a son and daughter.

The *Elder Statesman* completes the cycle that *Murder in the Cathedral* had begun, both thematically and formalistically. Eliot continues, in this his last play, the movement away from an elitist view of life. Though *The Confidential Clerk* treats human love with more compassion and understanding than the earlier plays, there is still in both Eggerson and Colby at least the suggestion of the saint. Colby, Lucasta observes, "has his own world, / and he might vanish into it at any moment." Eggerson has his garden. They both have retired from the workaday world, symbolized by Sir Claude's office. Sir Claude, though treated sympathetically, must be content to live in two worlds, and Colby's final departure is an indirect comment on the inadequacy, from Eliot's point of view, of Sir Claude's compromise. His is a good life, but Colby's is better.

The Elder Statesman is a world without saints. There are no Beckets, Harrys or Celias, not even any Colbys or Eggersons. There is only everyman, Dick Ferry, alias Lord Claverton. There is a saintlike guardian, but Eliot is always careful to differentiate the saints from the watchers. Monica belongs with Agatha and Mary, Sir Henry and Alex and Julia. She and Charles will aid Lord Claverton in his last months, as Lucasta and B. Kaghan will aid Sir Claude and Lady Elizabeth in their last years. But this is emphatically a world of human love, and a play that emphasizes human sin, repentance, and forgiveness. The play is very carefully patterned. Lord Claverton, near death, is visited by three ghosts from his past.[5] The first, Federico Gomez, actually Fred Culverwell, reminds him both of the old man he ran over without stopping and of his responsibility for Culverwell's disgrace and metamorphosis into Federico Gomez. A second ghost, Mrs. Carghill, alias Maisie Montjoy, reminds him of his callousness in their love affair and his concern only with his reputation. A third ghost, his son Michael, reminds him of his failure as a father and his inability to accept his son as a separate person. Finally Lord Claverton is reminded by the ghost of his former self, Dick Ferry, that he has lived his whole life as a pretense and that he has used everyone around him to create a false image of himself. The play concludes with a moving scene of recognition, in which he asks his daughter for forgiveness and passes his newfound wisdom to the younger generation, freeing Monica and Charles from the bondage of service to him:

I feel at peace now.
It is the peace that ensues upon contrition
When contrition ensues upon knowledge of the truth.
Why did I always want to dominate my children?
Why did I mark out a narrow path for Michael? . . .
Why did I want to keep you to myself, Monica? . . .
I've only just now had the illumination
Of knowing what love is. We all think we know,
But how few of us do! And now I feel happy—
In spite of everything, in defiance of reason,
I have been brushed by the wings of happiness.

As all of Eliot's critics have noticed, *The Elder Statesman* is Eliot's *Oedipus at Colonus*, his *nunc dimittis*. Did the playwright have a premonition that it was to be his last play? It has the peace and serenity, the sense of completeness that is represented by Sophocles' play and Milton's *Samson Agonistes*, "and calm of mind, all passion spent." Like Oedipus, Lord Claverton comes to a new awareness of himself. He sheds his illusions, and his disillusionment leads not to bitterness but to peace. He has learned both how to love and what love is. Eliot's moving dedication of the play to his second wife, Valerie, suggests that, finally freed from the agony of his lifelong struggle with his first wife, Vivienne, he is able at last to love fully and to *see* in his closing years that there are other paths than the choice between sainthood and "the best of a bad job."

10

Eugene O'Neill

Stammering is the native eloquence of us fog people.

—Edmund in *Long Day's Journey into Night*

Perhaps the place to begin is with Edmund's library in *Long Day's Journey into Night*. Much of the great scene in the fourth act between father and son is a kind of literary conflict, with Edmund throwing his authors against his father's—Balzac and Whitman, Strindberg and Shaw and Ibsen, Baudelaire and Dowson, against Shakespeare, Dickens, and the Bible. James and Edmund are like debaters, quoting their favorite passages as evidence to support their positions. Edmund's books, of course, are pretty much the ones Eugene O'Neill himself read at that time or would read and reread during his period of confinement at the Gaylord Farm Sanatorium in 1912 and 1913. O'Neill was twenty-four in 1912, and his ideas had been strongly shaped both by his reading and by the turbulent experiences of his adolescence and early manhood. By the time he began to write one-act plays in 1913, he had been married and divorced, he had fathered a son, he had spent two years at sea, and he had almost committed suicide while living at Jimmy the Priest's, a waterfront dive in lower Manhattan that would become the setting for two of his most famous plays, *Anna Christie* and *The Iceman Cometh*.[1]

This tension between literature and life, between those books that embody the playwright's vision and ideals and those life experiences that continually thwart the fulfillment of those ideals, forms the central subject matter of O'Neill's plays; and though both the dramatic form in which the playwright expresses the tension evolves and the attitude toward the subject changes with the evolution of form, the subject is there from the beginning, and it never ceases to obsess the playwright. In some ways O'Neill belongs more with Ibsen and Shaw and Strindberg, his heroes, than with Pirandello and Brecht, his contemporaries. He is, like the earlier playwrights, a frustrated idealist, a dreamer, almost one of the Hegelians. But finally, his dream of a breakthrough fails him; and in the late plays he joins Pirandello in asking for human compassion rather than some encompassing vision of truth.

In his perceptive essay "O'Neill's Search for a 'Language of the Theatre,'" Robert F. Whitman describes the central tension of O'Neill's plays

113

in this way: "Characteristically, the impulse toward the ideal, frustrated by life, brings cynicism and despair; the impulse toward faith, frustrated by life, leads to skepticism; the impulse to love, frustrated by life, leads to hate or smothering possessiveness; the impulse to create, frustrated by life, becomes destructive."[2]

The quest theme is obvious. The natural impulses of human beings are toward the ideal; toward faith, love, creation; toward a higher order of being. But life frustrates our dreams and aspirations. Thus O'Neill's theme, as Whitman sees it, is "the eternal conflict between Man's aspirations and some intransigent, ineluctable quality in life which circumscribes and limits him, and frustrates the realization of those dreams which seem to make life worth living."[3]

The quest motif is evident from the time of O'Neill's first full-length play, *Beyond the Horizon*, which opened at the Morosco Theatre in February of 1920 and won O'Neill his first Pulitzer Prize. Robert Mayo is O'Neill's archetypal hero in embryo. He is a dreamer who longs for the sea, trapped on the farm. He reads books. Throughout O'Neill's work, books and the sea will stand as symbols of the search for a higher, deeper, fuller life. Robert sees that fuller life "beyond the horizon," and he has made up his mind to go in search of it, when "reality" intervenes in the form of Ruth. Ruth loves him, not his brother, Andy, whom he has supposed she loves, but she will not encourage him in his search, nor will she go with him. She is rooted in the farm. The joining of the two farms, so critical in the value system of the father, becomes possible with the marriage of Robert and Ruth, but it will also bring about Robert's destruction. Andy replaces Robert as the voyager, but the sea is not a natural life for him. He is not an explorer, a thinker, and he writes back prosaic postcards from ports of call, describing only the dirt in places Robert would have gloried in seeing.

The second and third acts work out the tragic consequences of the choices made in the first act. Both Robert and Andy destroy themselves because each has made the wrong choice; Robert cannot farm, because it is in his nature to dream; Andy is rooted in the earth, and separated from the earth, he allows his desire for the material to lead him to disastrous speculation. The final irony of *Beyond the Horizon* is that the last movement of the play, which brings about Robert's death, is for Andy and Ruth a kind of happy ending. They will marry and have children and restore the farm. They are like Chekhov's stronger and more practical characters—Lopakhin, if you like—who will survive and even flourish within the limits of their vision and ability. It is always the dreamers who perish, who are somehow not fit for life on this earth, who are punished for their lack of practical ability with failure, and then with disease, and finally with death—a death that they do not fear but even look forward to as a kind of reunion with God, a return to the mother from whom they have been separated by birth. The classic statement of it is Edmund's in *Long Day's Journey*:

> I belonged, without past or future, within peace and unity and a wild joy, within something greater than my own life, or the life of Man, to Life itself! To God, if you want to put it that way. . . . It was a great mistake, my being born a man. I would have been much more successful as a sea gull or a fish. As it is, I will always be a stranger who never feels at home, who does not really want and is not really wanted, who can never belong, who must always be a little in love with death!

As Tom Driver adds, "more than a little."[4] In the moments before his death Robert Mayo feels the peace that has eluded him throughout the play, for if death is the ultimate reality, it is also the last hope for the fulfillment of those dreams and visions that life has not permitted us to achieve. If Edmund's presentation of that hope is more articulate and more dramatically appropriate than Robert Mayo's, it is both because of O'Neill's artistic development during the twenty years between the two plays and because Edmund has experienced the sea and has had at least his one moment of illumination.

The theme of "belonging" is picked up in the following year (1921) as the central issue of *The Hairy Ape*. Yank is another O'Neill dreamer, but a primitive and inarticulate one, a stoker on a transatlantic liner who has been shocked into awareness of himself by Mildred Douglas's terrified reaction to him when she visits the stokehole in the third scene. During the remainder of the play his characteristic pose is that of Rodin's *The Thinker*. He is trying to figure out something, but he can't. *The Hairy Ape*, whether consciously or not, bears the stamp of D. H. Lawrence. Yank is the passionate, elemental force in man. It is at peace with itself, comfortable in its primitive, animal joy. Mildred, her aunt, her father, and the characters who parade by on Fifth Avenue have lost that part of themselves. They have destroyed it, refined it to the point of nonexistence. They do not recognize Yank. Our human dilemma, as symbolized by Yank's, is how to move upward on the evolutionary scale, how to grow, without destroying the joyous or animal part of the self. This is a theme to which O'Neill will return again and again, especially in *Strange Interlude* and *Mourning Becomes Electra*.

It is a mistake to accept Yank as simply the "hairy ape" of the title. When asked about the play's theme by George Jean Nathan, O'Neill responded, "I must dig at the roots of the sickness of today as I feel it—the death of the old God and the failure of science and materialism to give any satisfactory new one for the surviving primitive religious instinct to find a meaning for life in, and to comfort its fears of death with."[5] Yank's desire to belong is a part of that "primitive religious instinct." Having lost his place in the world of the stokehole, he is groping hopelessly for meaning, for dignity, as Arthur Miller would call it, in a world that has nothing to offer him. As he stands before the gorilla cage, he reflects, "I ain't got no past to tink in, nor nothin' dats comin', on'y what's now—and dat don't belong." In O'Neill's world belonging means finding a place where a genuine self can be nourished and prosper. And that is all but impossible.

The third of O'Neill's important early plays, *The Emperor Jones* (1920), treats the theme somewhat differently. Less sympathetic than either Robert Mayo or Yank, Jones is farther back on the evolutionary scale. Robert and Yank have rejected the values of society and stand, however tentatively, at least on the edge of a breakthrough. Jones still believes in the material values of money and power, and the play is the story of his gradual movement toward self-understanding through what Doris Falk calls "the striking off of the masks of the self, layer by layer, just as bit by bit his emperor's uniform is ripped from his back."[6] Jones's basic illusion is that he has no illusions; and even at the end of his ordeal he continues to believe in the superstition of the silver bullet. Perhaps he dies more at the beginning of his quest than as a result of it.

In *Desire Under the Elms* (1924), the culminating play of the first period of O'Neill's career, we see the emergence of the reality-illusion theme in the form that will dominate for the next seven or eight years. The central figures, Abbie Putnam and Eben Cabot, are stronger figures than their predecessors in *Beyond the Horizon*. They are driven by darker and more complex passions, and their tragedy runs deeper than that of Robert Mayo, who is more a victim than a tragic hero. O'Neill's view of tragedy is closely related to the quest theme. In a frequently reprinted statement, O'Neill said to Arthur Hobson Quinn, "I'm always acutely conscious of the Force behind (Fate, God, our biological past creating our present, whatever one calls it—Mystery certainly) and of *the one eternal tragedy of Man in his glorious, self-destructive struggle to make the Force express him* instead of being, as an animal is, an infinitesimal incident in its expression" [italics mine].[7]

For O'Neill the center of *Desire Under the Elms* is Abbie and Eben's "glorious, self-destructive struggle" to overcome both the materialism of ownership and the repressive Puritanism symbolized by Ephraim. At the beginning of the play Abbie is motivated primarily by greed, the desire to own something. Her first line is "It's purty—purty! I can't b'lieve it's really mine." "Yewr'n?" asks Cabot. "Mine!" The desire to own the farm underlies the tragedy of the play. The sheriff, blind to the tragic implications of ownership, ends the play with the ironic line, "It's a jim-dandy farm, no denyin'. Wished I owned it." The painful process of moving from desire for things and sexual desire to love for one another ennobles Abbie and Eben. They attempt to make the force express them through that love, but the only way Abbie knows how to prove her love to Eben is to kill the child, and so the ending becomes both glorious and self-destructive.

We see the same kind of victory in defeat in O'Neill's most ambitious play, *Mourning Becomes Electra* (1931). Here again, as so often in O'Neill, reality finally defeats human attempts to gain freedom and happiness, but the victory of reality is less oppressive than in many of the other plays, because Lavinia, the Electra figure, freely chooses to close herself in the house in order to expiate the Mannon curse. Mourning does become Electra. The play is built around the familiar contrast between life and death. In Part I, *Homecoming*, death is represented primarily by Ezra Mannon and the Mannon house. We also sense death in the Puritan austerity of Lavinia, who is in every respect her father's daughter. Christine Mannon and Adam Brant try to break out of the repressive world of the Mannons through the life-giving freedom of sexuality. Sex in the Mannon household is associated with sin, and the only way that Christine and Adam can find to overcome this repressive attitude is to kill Ezra. But murder only begets murder, and all of the characters' attempts to gain freedom and peace, to find "the blessed isles," end in disaster.

In Part II, *The Hunted*, the life figures, Christine and Adam, are destroyed by Orin and Lavinia, the death figures, the life deniers; but the murder of Adam and Christine's suicide serve only to unhinge Orin and force Lavinia to realize that she can never live in the ordinary world. For a moment in the final play, *The Haunted*, it seems as if life will be victorious. Vinnie, changed by her trip to the South Seas, has cast off the death-in-life of the Mannon house, and we see her for the first time as a woman. Away from the sexually inhibiting world of New England, she has found sexual fulfillment. She has become her mother rather than her father. But O'Neill's tragic view is uncompromising. Orin's suicide shows her that marriage to Peter will only extend the Mannon curse, and she makes the life-denying decision to end the curse by locking herself in the house in order to save others from suffering. Her defeat is a defeat for life, but she has succeeded, to go back to O'Neill's words, in making the Force express her, "instead of being, as an animal is, an infinitesimal incident in its expression." There is dignity and nobility in her final renunciation; if the play depicts the final triumph of reality over dream, it also depicts in Vinnie a human being who is strong enough to live without illusions.

Abbie and Eben in *Desire* and Lavinia in *Mourning Becomes Electra* are the strongest O'Neill heroes in the plays of this period, but the most important figures for a consideration of the reality-illusion theme are Dion Anthony in *The Great God Brown* (1926) and Nina Leeds in *Strange Interlude* (1928). The period between *Desire Under the Elms* and *Mourning Becomes Electra* was one dominated by O'Neill's attempt to do for the theater what Joyce had done for the novel. He wanted to find some device whereby he could get the depth and complexity of characterization that stream of consciousness allowed the novelist. He began to believe, to use his own words, "that the use of masks will be discovered eventually to be the freest solution of the modern dramatist's problem as to how, with the greatest possible dramatic clarity and economy of means, he can express those profound hidden conflicts of the conscious and unconscious mind which the probing of psychology continues to disclose to us."[8] Dion Anthony and Nina Leeds are the most memorable results of that experimentation, the first existing as a character by means of the multiple masks O'Neill constructs to represent the different facets of his character's tortured and divided personality, and the second created through the experimental device of "unspoken" asides or soliloquies delivered to the audience while the other characters temporarily freeze.

There is a direct relationship between the stage devices and O'Neill's handling of the quest theme. In Dion's case it is clearest. His name, Dion Anthony, suggests the combination of Dionysus or Pan and the spirit of Saint Anthony—in O'Neill's words, "the creative pagan acceptance of life, fighting eternal war with the masochistic, life-denying spirit of Christianity."[9] It sounds like Ibsen's *Emperor and Galilean*, and it is, with a terrible difference. O'Neill never gives us the feeling that a new synthesis is possible. Dion seems doomed from the beginning to hide the creative, sensitive artistic part of the self behind the cynical mask of the mocker. Even Margaret, whom he loves, cannot bear to look upon his naked face. So from the time of his childhood, when Billy Brown destroys his sand pictures, Dion has repressed and distorted his real self, wearing the cynical mask until it becomes, late in the play, twisted with pain and anguish, never allowing him the breakthrough to the reality *beneath* the mask, as we are so close to doing in Ibsen and Shaw. For most of the play Dion's talents are used by the materialistic "Great God Brown," and when the physical Dion is dead, Brown can continue his work only by assuming for himself the Dion mask—that is, by stealing from Dion the creative imagination that he himself lacks. O'Neill is close to Pirandello's *Six Characters* here, dramatizing in Brown versus Anthony the same sort of split that Pirandello gives us in the Father versus the Director. The tragedy of the self in modern society is the tragedy of incompleteness. Grotowski says, "Civilization is sick with schizophrenia, which is a rupture between intelligence and feeling, body and soul."[10] *The Great God Brown*, while it does not work successfully as theater because its mask devices are too self-conscious and its dialogue too stilted and melodramatic, succeeds more clearly than any of O'Neill's plays in dramatizing the tragic split in the modern psyche and the failure of Western society, particularly in the period following World War I, to offer a framework within which the pagan and Christian elements can converge into a new synthesis.

Nina Leeds comes closer than Dion to healing the wounds, and at one point in the nine-act *Strange Interlude* she almost succeeds. Denied fulfillment with Gordon by her Puritan father, Professor Henry Leeds, Nina goes through a period of licentiousness, for which she compensates by marrying Sam Evans. Her life is a battle between the power of God the Father, the familiar Puritan God of Ephraim Cabot and the Mannon family, and the need for natural sexual and emotional fulfillment. Unable to find wholeness, she does the next best thing: she puts her needs into categories and finds a man to fulfill the needs of each one: Sam, the husband; Ned, the lover; Charlie Marsden, the substitute father. "My three men!" she exclaims to herself at the end of Act VI. "I feel their desires converge in me! . . . to form one complete beautiful male desire which I absorb . . . and am whole." But her happiness is only temporary, and her wholeness is an illusion. The very strategy that allows her to meet her needs destroys the men and drives them to actions that force her at the end of the play to renounce her happiness to keep from causing unnecessary pain to Sam.

"Man is born broken. He lives by mending. The grace of God is glue!" says Billy in the fourth act of *The Great God Brown*. "The mistake began when God was created in a male image," says Nina. The statements are closely related. There is a strong religious element in the plays written between 1925 and 1934, an element that shows O'Neill struggling with a symbolism adequate to express the spiritual statement the playwright is trying to make. Whether in the plays we have looked at or in the less successful experiments like *Dynamo* and *Days Without End*, there is always that thematic thrust toward reunion with the feminine figure, the mother God.

O'Neill combines his own obsessive Freudianism with a kind of latent feminist theology by attacking the identification of religion with the hard, masculine tradition of American Puritanism. His heroes struggle desperately to break through the "strange interlude" of this life, break through the meaningless electrical displays of the male God, "whose chest thunders with egotism," into a reunion with the natural, life-affirming force of the feminine. In a Jungian sense, O'Neill's male heroes are searching for a completion of the self, which the hard father God, whether it calls itself Mayo, Cabot, or Leeds, consistently denies. During this period O'Neill demonstrates most forcefully his affinity with Strindberg, especially the Strindberg of *A Dream Play*, the tortured and disillusioned idealist trying to fight through the masks of the material world to union with the spiritual or feminine element, symbolized in *A Dream Play* by the Daughter of Indra.

If O'Neill's dramatic career had ended in the early thirties, as the world of New York theater assumed it did, then we could conclude that O'Neill belongs in this study more with the playwrights of the first generation. His Hegelianism, as I mentioned at the outset of this chapter, has parallels to Ibsen's and Shaw's, and his dramatic struggle to depict some kind of spiritual breakthrough has striking similarity to the post-Inferno Strindberg. But, of course, O'Neill's career did not end with his reception of the Nobel Prize in 1936. The plays he worked on between 1936 and 1946, during that decade of absence from Broadway, became the plays by which we remember him today. These plays have a different thematic texture and a different voice.

In the last plays—*The Iceman Cometh, A Touch of the Poet, Long Day's Journey into Night, A Moon for the Misbegotten,* and *Hughie*—O'Neill returns, as Whitman notes, to the realism of the early plays but armed with alcohol:

> One of the most striking qualities possessed by all of these plays is the really impressive quantity of alcohol consumed in each of them. . . . This phenomenon might be passed off as irrelevant . . . were it not for the fact that it represents the *technique* which was to serve much the same dramatic function as the more mechanical devices of the earlier plays.[11]

Alcohol serves a dual function, not only in the late plays of O'Neill but in the plays of Tennessee Williams and Edward Albee. It brings about a release of inhibitions, a freeing of the self to speak more openly and honestly—*in vino veritas*. It also frees the playwright to create behavior that an audience would not believe if the characters were sober, and to create speech patterns at once natural and lyric. As the characters, especially those of Irish-Catholic background, become drunker, their speech becomes more lyrical, but it is not the strained and artificial lyricism of *Strange Interlude* or *The Great God Brown*; it is the natural, almost comic, lyricism of the drunk returning to his Irish roots.

Within the framework of the reality-illusion conflict, alcohol works in two ways at the same time. It allows the characters to see themselves more honestly, at least for a moment. It *frees* them from the restrictions their own value systems have placed on their ability to see the truth. At the same time alcohol allows them to escape from the real world into a world of dreams, particularly the world of the past, which now replaces the future as the keynote in the plays. Most of the central characters are older, and their lives have moved them further and further away from the fulfillment of their ideals. In their dreams they see the past as a time when they were in touch with something that has gone, something that they cannot live without. And so they re-create reality, both past and present, in C. W. E. Bigsby's words "by constructing pipe dreams, illusions and fantasies which can sustain the self in its battle with the world."[12]

The Iceman Cometh (1946) is the archetype for all the plays. It takes place in Harry Hope's saloon (in reality Jimmy the Priest's, where O'Neill stayed frequently between 1909 and 1912), in the year 1912, a critical year in the playwright's life and the same year in which *Long Day's Journey* is set. The characters may be divided into two groups: (1) Harry Hope and the workers and roomers, and (2) Larry Slade, Don Parrit, and Hickey. The members of the first group are all sustained by illusions about both their past and their future. The characters in the first group parallel, in ways, the members of the Ekdal family in Ibsen's *The Wild Duck*, and Hickey is clearly derived in certain of his traits from Gregers Werle. In O'Neill's play the term *vital lie* has been replaced by *pipe dream*. Whether they are the same and whether O'Neill's attitude toward illusion is different from Ibsen's we can only surmise after some analysis.

Harry, an old ward politician, has not left the rooming house since his wife died, and he dreams of the day when he will take a walk around the block and renew his political career. His brother-in-law, Ed Mosher, plans to get a job with the circus. Pat McGloin hopes to clear his name and have himself restored to duty with the police force, and Willie Oban, remembering his potential in law school, thinks of getting a job in the district attorney's office after his brilliant defense of Pat gets the policeman reinstated. Joe Mott, the Negro, dreams of running a black gambling house, while Piet Wetjoen, the Boer "General," and Cecil Lewis, the English "Captain," relive the Boer War and dream each of returning to his native land. James Cameron, "Jimmy Tomorrow," thinks of the day when he will return triumphantly to the newspaper, and the last of the group, Hugo Kalmar, periodically awakens from his drunken stupor to dream of the future triumph of the "Movement" (IWW). The help at the rooming house and bar parallels the clientele. Rocky Pioggi, the night bartender, thinks of himself as a "business manager," when he is really a pimp for Pearl and Margie, two prostitutes who comfort each other by thinking of themselves as tarts. Chuck, the day bartender, plans to marry another prostitute, Cora, and they dream of a farm in the country far from the corruption of Harry's bar.

Into this world of pipe dreams steps Theodore Hickman (Hickey), who, like Gregers Werle, is determined to make each of them start life anew on the foundation of truth. No longer will they need the escape of alcohol or foolish pipe dreams. Each of them must make his dream a reality, each must do the thing he has been talking about. The result is near-disaster. One by one, the characters are stripped naked, and deprived of drink and dreams, they become nervous, ugly, depressed. Conflicts that had been playful become real. Tempers flare, and racial prejudice erupts. One by one, the roomers leave the bar to go into the "real" world, and by night they have all returned—sullen, remorseful, defeated by life. It is only just before the very end of the play, when Hickey admits that he was crazy and, in a sense, gives them their vital lies back, that they regain their peace, their sense of humor, their fellowship. Like the members of the Ekdal family, they are best left with their pipe dreams. Dr. Relling has been vindicated.

But, as both Eric Bentley and C. W. E. Bigsby have demonstrated, the reality-illusion conflict is not the play's central theme.[13] *The Iceman Cometh* may be more O'Neill's version of *It Is So* than his version of *The Wild Duck*. The play's three central figures—Hickey, Parrit, and Slade—are best understood when approached from a different perspective, that of the love-hate conflict. Hickey, while he pretends that he no longer needs illusions, has really preserved the greatest illusion of all—the illusion that he loved his wife. Parrit, who parallels Hickey throughout, continually confesses that he is responsible for his mother's capture by the police, but like Hickey, he never confesses his true motive until he accidentally blurts it out near the end. Both Parrit and Hickey illustrate what can happen when love is replaced by hate. Torn by guilt themselves, neither can leave the others alone. Neither can develop what Bigsby calls "a level of imaginative sympathy,"[14] which would allow them to develop real compassion for others. Hickey destroys the peace of Harry's roomers because he hasn't the courage to face himself, just as Gregers Werle turns his own self-hatred on the Ekdal household. Parrit cannot face himself either until the very end, when he commits, with Larry Slade's support, the act he really came to Harry Hope's for—his own suicide.

O'Neill, much more pessimistic than Ibsen, finally, does not leave us truth as an option. *The Wild Duck* implies that truth is better under the right conditions. *The Iceman Cometh* gives us only, in Edwin Engel's words, "dreams, drunkenness, and death."[15] And neither dreams nor death are treated so romantically as in the earlier plays. Death is not a return to the earth mother or to the unity of things; death is the final reality—the end. This is the view embodied by Larry Slade. "I'm the only real convert to death Hickey made here," he says at the play's end, and he means it. His experience with Parrit and Hickey has destroyed the last of his illusions, and he will not return to his role as the grandstand "foolosopher" and friend of the outcast. At the play's end he stares grimly ahead, waiting for death to take him.

But while the stoic pose may be admirable, O'Neill does not present it in the last plays as preferable to dreams. Bigsby perceptively reminds us that in the final group of plays "no moral distinction is made between truth and illusion."[16] Dreams may well be the stitches holding together the fabric of life. In *Hughie* (1964), for example, "Erie" Smith, a down-and-out gambler, tells a listless night clerk at a cheap hotel stories of his escapades with Follies girls and big-time racketeers, all of which are fabrications. Hughie knows that they are lies, but the telling of the tales keeps both Erie and Hughie alive. The new night clerk, obviously another Hughie, will play the same role that Hughie had played and will thereby save both himself and Erie from despair. Lying becomes a form of creativity, a way of inventing through stories a self that doesn't otherwise exist.

In *A Touch of the Poet* (1958), the clearest example from the late plays of what can happen when there are no illusions left, Con Melody, a name that suggests a combination of con man and melody maker, has brought his wife to America where he can invent and play the role that life has denied him, that of the Byronic hero. He stands before the mirror, reciting lines from "Childe Harold's Pilgrimage":

I have not loved the World, nor the World me;
I have not flattered its rank breath, nor bowed

To its idolatries a patient knee. . . .
                              I stood
Among them, but not of them.

This is a role, says O'Neill in a stage direction, "which has become more real than his real self to him." He has played the part for so long that neither he nor the viewer knows where the real man ends and the part begins. He keeps a Thoroughbred mare as a status symbol, and each year on the anniversary of the battle of Talavera, he puts on his full-dress uniform and relives his imaginary past. Sara, his daughter, resents his role playing, because she sees that it has destroyed her mother and threatens to ruin her chances for happiness with Simon Harford. "Oh Father," she begs him, "why can't you ever be the thing you can seem to be? The man you were? I'm sorry I never knew that soldier. I think he was the only man who wasn't just a dream." The play reaches its climax when Melody challenges Mr. Henry Harford to a duel for insulting his daughter's honor and finds himself ignominiously beaten up by Harford's hired policemen. His illusions crushed, the hero of Talavera comes home and shoots his mare. Sara's wish has ironically come true. Her father will never more play the Byronic hero. But then in a masterstroke of irony O'Neill shows us what happens when a man like Melody becomes disillusioned. He cannot live with reality. To face his own failure would mean death, and so he adopts another role. He begins to affect an Irish brogue, the very same brogue that he has criticized his wife and daughter for using, and he plays the part of the poor Irish-American, loyal supporter of Andy Jackson, backslapper, and big drinker. One illusion is replaced by another, and as the play ends, Sara sadly understands that the former role was preferable to the latter:

> May the hero of Talavera rest in peace! (*She breaks down and sobs, hiding her face on her mother's shoulder—bewilderedly.*) But why should I cry, Mother? Why do I mourn for him?

As I have suggested, a primary difference between the late plays of O'Neill and the earlier ones is the role that time plays. In the earlier plays the heroes look forward to a fulfillment that never comes; and their energies are devoted, however fruitlessly, to the quest for love, faith, or creative productivity. Throughout the last plays there is a sense of "too-lateness," a sense that whatever possibilities for joy or faith or action existed did so long before the play itself opens. Nowhere is this so clear as in *Long Day's Journey into Night* (1956). In this play, deceptive in its symbolism, because it seems so realistic, the long day's journey into

124

night becomes a symbolic recapitulation of life, with the morning suggesting youth and innocence and clarity of vision, and the gradually oncoming night, with its increasingly heavy fog, standing for the process of life itself moving inexorably toward death. The play might well be called *A Long Life's Journey into Death*. Each of the three older characters struggles to overcome that darkness by adopting strategies of escape.

Mary is the most important of these three figures. For her the house in New London has become a living tomb. Having married an actor, she is excluded from the social circles of the community. More importantly, because of the blundering of an ignorant doctor at the time of Edmund's birth, she has become addicted to morphine; and despite periodic efforts to cure herself, she is unable to live without the drug. Her hands, which were once so beautiful and delicate, have become arthritic, and she can no longer play the piano. Her hair, of which she was once so proud, is no longer manageable. Like O'Neill himself, who was raised a Catholic and then lost his faith, she remembers a time, before she met James Tyrone, when she was a devout believer. In the final moments of the play, she muses, "I went to the shrine and prayed to the Blessed Virgin and found peace again because I knew she heard my prayer and would always love me and see no harm ever came to me so long as I never lost my faith in her." In her mind that faith is identified with her "true self," a self that she spends the play searching for, taking stronger doses of morphine until she can get beyond the pain, beyond the present, back to something she has lost, "something I need terribly. I remember when I had it I was never lonely nor afraid. I can't have lost it forever. I would die if I thought that. Because then there would be no hope."

It is Mary who articulates most clearly the central theme of this play, which O'Neill wrote in "pity and understanding and forgiveness for *all* the four haunted Tyrones," when she says in the second act:

> But I suppose life has made him like that, and he can't help it. None of us can help the things life has done to us. They're done before you realize it, and once they're done they make you do other things until at last everything comes between you and what you'd like to be, and you've lost your true self forever.

A part of Mary must know that she can never get back to that "true self," that her struggle to keep from losing it is Gatsby's "boats against the current," a fight to regain something that never existed except in the imagination. And yet without it life is not worth living. Call it "vital lie" or "pipe dream" or "illusion," it is the driving force of some characters' lives, to keep inviolate that idea of the self with which one can live. We all want to believe we are special, and some cannot live at all without that faith.

James, in his way, understands it too. His niggardliness with money, with which Edmund chides him in the brilliant fourth act, has been caused by the poverty of his childhood, and the niggardliness in turn causes him to hire a cheap doctor for Mary during her pregnancy with Edmund, and it finally drives him to buy the rights to *The Count of Monte Cristo*, which in turn made him rich. Liquor loosens his tongue, and he tells Edmund:

> I've never admitted this to anyone before, lad, but tonight I'm so heartsick I feel at the end of everything, and what's the use of fake pride and pretense. The God-damned play I bought for a song and made such a great success in—a great money success—it ruined me with its promise of easy fortune. I didn't want to do anything else, and by the time I woke up to the fact I'd become a slave to the damned thing and did try other plays, it was too late.

As Mary goes back to her convent days for solace, James returns to the night in 1874 when Edwin Booth, playing Iago to his Othello, said to the theater manager, "That young man is playing Othello better than I ever did."

Jamie has neither the convent nor the stage to turn to. He drinks to keep out reality and plays the role of the man-about-town. But beneath the facade of the playboy he is both miserable and potentially dangerous. He warns Edmund about himself:

> Made my mistakes look good. Made getting drunk romantic. Made whores fascinating vampires instead of poor, stupid, diseased slobs they really are. Made fun of work as sucker's game. Never wanted you to succeed and make me look even worse by comparison. Wanted you to fail. Always jealous of you. Mama's baby, Papa's pet!

Like his father, Jamie knows what he really is, but it is only at this critical moment under the influence of liquor, with Edmund about to leave for the sanatorium, that he can utter the truth, and he does so not with vindictiveness, but in love, a love that all four family members share. And in a play remarkable for the intensity of its quarrels, we find that almost every quarrel is followed by an apology or an expression of love. While the characters have momentary glimpses of their own faults and

126

those of the others, knowing the truth does not give them the power to change, and their love is a kind of admission of that powerlessness.

There are two characters in the late plays who stand as an exception to this pattern: Sara Melody and Edmund Tyrone. In the projected cycle that O'Neill never finished, Sara was to be the central figure. Her marriage to Simon Harford, which we suppose to have taken place after the end of *Touch of the Poet*, was to launch her into a series of plays in which her children would eventually be central figures. Sara is a woman of beauty, strength, and insight. In the tradition of Synge's female characters, she combines youth, lyricism, a tough-minded realism, and a capacity to dream. Early in the play she says to her mother, "Oh if I was a man with the chance he had, there wouldn't be a dream I'd not make come true." Like Christy Mahon, she does convert dream into reality by overcoming her shyness to marry the man she loves.

Edmund, we would like to believe, will do the same thing. The title, *Long Day's Journey into Night*, does not apply to him the way it does to the others. The most important technique in the play is that of confession, and it is to Edmund that the other characters confess, as if to pass on to him some knowledge he can use before he leaves them. His departure for the sanatorium is the beginning of his life, not its end. He is stronger than people realize. As Jamie remarks perceptively to his father, "His quietness fools people into thinking they can do what they like with him. But he's stubborn as hell inside and what he does is what he wants to do, and to hell with anyone else." He also has no illusions about himself. In his confession to his father, he summarizes both his strengths and his limitations:

> The *makings* of a poet. No. I'm afraid I'm like the guy who is always pan-handling for a smoke. He hasn't got the makings. He's got only the habit. I couldn't touch what I tried to tell you just now. I just stammered. That's the best I'll ever do, I mean, if I live. Well, it will be faithful realism at least. Stammering is the native eloquence of us fog people.

As Bigsby reminds us, "Edmund's comment on his own talent is essentially O'Neill's description of his own position as a playwright."[17] Edmund is O'Neill's Paul Morel, his Stephen Dedalus. He is both more and less than his creator. His own clear vision of his creative potential on the eve of his departure for the sanatorium shows far more vision and maturity than the young O'Neill had at the time. It took O'Neill a lifetime to comprehend enough to write, "Stammering is the native eloquence of us fog people," and the O'Neill who wrote that is an Edmund fulfilled, an Edmund who stammered away for twenty years trying to pierce the veil. Fog is the central image of O'Neill's masterpiece, and it may effectively stand as the best image with which to summarize his life and work. The truth is not available to "us fog people," only an occasional glimpse in moments of sunshine. In the simplicity of his final plays O'Neill creates a vision in which only compassion and a "touch of the poet" can combat the absurdity of a universe which leaves us "lost in the fog."

11

Arthur Miller and Tennessee Williams

> *We meet unblessed, not in some garden of wax fruit and painted trees, that lie of Eden, but after, after the Fall, after many, many deaths. Is the knowing all? And the wish to kill is never killed, but with some gift of courage one may look into its face when it appears, and with a stroke of love—as to an idiot in the house—forgive it; again and again . . . forever?*
>
> —Arthur Miller, *After the Fall*

In the world of Arthur Miller and Tennessee Williams, illusions are most frequently referred to as lies. The world of the Kellers, the Lomans, and the Carbones in Miller and the Wingfields, the Dubois, and the Pollits in Williams is a world where, as Big Daddy puts it, "mendacity" rules. "I've lived with mendacity! Why can't *you* live with it? Hell, you *got* to live with it, there's nothing *else* to *live* with except mendacity, is there?" These are Big Daddy's words to his son, Brick, and at the heart of the plays of these two men is the question he raises. Can men live with it? Some can and some can't. Biff Loman can and Big Daddy can and Quentin in *After the Fall* can. But Willy Loman, Joe Keller, Eddie Carbone, Blanche Dubois, and Brick Pollit—the most famous of these playwrights' protagonists—cannot and will not. They claim as their rightful due a certain innocence. They would return to life before the fall, to a simpler more virtuous past where they are not to blame, where they themselves and those they love are virtuous participants in an unglamorous and often evil world.

It's in the American character. In his influential study *The American Adam*, R. W. B. Lewis traces the theme of innocence from the time of the Puritans through the late nineteenth century, seeing it reach its fullest development in Thoreau, Emerson, and Whitman in the years just before the Civil War. And the notion of American innocence hangs on. During the Great Depression writers like Steinbeck see the people as good and the system as bad, while World War II only reinforced the idea of the Old World, symbolized by Hitler, as evil, and the New World as good. The

129

American illusion of innocence might be called our national vital lie. Even after Vietnam and Watergate, Ronald Reagan has used the rhetoric of American goodness and Soviet evil to reinforce both his foreign and domestic policies. Of all our playwrights, Arthur Miller and Tennessee Williams speak to us most fully and most honestly of ourselves as Americans. They understand and depict, with extraordinary compassion, characters who desperately *need* the illusion of innocence to stay alive, to retain their dignity as human beings. At the same time they depict the tragic results of that need, and the terrible things that those necessary lies do to the characters and the members of their families.

1. Arthur Miller

Much of what Miller is trying to say may be illustrated by a story. There once was a man who gave a party, and while the man was pleasantly drinking with his guests, there came a knock at the door, and when the man answered the knock, he saw that there stood on the threshold an uninvited guest. When the man saw who the guest was, he held the door shut against him, but the uninvited guest, instead of leaving, continued to push on the door, trying to force his way in. The man held his ground grimly, and for the better part of the evening the battle was a stalemate. Meanwhile, the guests were wondering about the peculiar behavior of their host. The story may end in a variety of ways, depending on how it is applied. In *Death of a Salesman* (1949) and *A View from the Bridge* (1955), it ends with the death of the central character. But to unravel the mystery, let me apply the story to the two plays.

As Miller tells us in the introduction to his *Collected Plays*, he first conceived of *Death of a Salesman* as a play that existed totally within the consciousness of Willy Loman. "In fact," he says, "*The Inside of His Head* was the first title."[1] The so-called flashbacks or past sequences are not past sequences at all; they are really dream sequences representing what Willy is thinking in the present, and they may represent distortions of what actually happened in the past. Once this is understood, we may see that Willy Loman (as the man in the story) has the obligations of the present with which to deal (the guests at the party)—his job, his family, his friends. But he cannot. He drives his car off the road, he imagines that he is still driving his old red 1928 Chevy in which the windshield opens, he talks to his brother, Ben, in the middle of his card game with Charley and then accuses Charley of cheating. The question is: Why can't Willy deal with the present (reality) anymore? The full answer doesn't come until the end of the play when the incident in Boston comes flooding into Willy's consciousness in the men's room of the restaurant. We realize that this is the single most important event, not only in Willy's life but in the life of his son Biff. Biff, the high school football hero who had won a scholarship to the University of Virginia, needed only to go to summer school to make up the math course he had flunked, but instead, after his trip to Boston, he "lay down and died." "Why?" asks Willy. "Why? Bernard, that question has been trailing me like a ghost for the last fifteen years." Biff knows:

> **BIFF:** Because I know he's a fake and he doesn't like anybody around
> who knows!
> **LINDA:** Why a fake? In what way? What do you mean?
> **BIFF:** Just don't lay it all at my feet. It's between me and him—that's all I
> have to say.

Biff's discovery of Willy in the hotel room with the woman marks the beginning of Biff's disillusionment with his father and with himself. To this point he had been motivated primarily by the desire to please his father, whom he had idolized. Now the idol has fallen, and Biff drags himself through fifteen long years of aimless wandering, finally bringing himself to the understanding he reaches at the end of the play:

> I am not a leader of men, Willy, and neither are you. You were never
> anything but a hard-working drummer who landed in the ash can like all
> the rest of them! I'm one dollar an hour, Willy! I tried seven states and
> couldn't raise it. A buck an hour! Do you gather my meaning? I'm not
> bringing home any prizes anymore, and you're going to stop waiting for
> me to bring them home!

For Biff the process of disillusionment is painful but positive. His growth is slow and uncertain, but he will be able to face life without the crutch of "mendacity" and without the need to maintain his own innocence. Biff's failure, as Bigsby points out, is that "it never occurs to him to transform the public world."[2] He will go west and try to live out that dream until it, like his father, disillusions him. But that is a story for another play in another generation (a Sam Shepard play perhaps). In *this* play Biff has a firmer grip on both reality and morality than any of the other major characters.

Willy cannot live with the knowledge that he is "a dime a dozen." He must not only have a sense that he is successful ("I'm vital in New England"), but more importantly, he must have the love and respect of his son Biff. Without these things he cannot live at all, but there is no way that he can have either of them, except in his dreams; and so he takes himself back in time, back to the days before the Boston incident when the boys were young and idolized him. He barricades the door against the uninvited guest of unpleasant memories and creates a golden, idealized world, symbolized not only by the dialogue of the dream sequences but by the music and the lighting. In these scenes we see Willy, in Bigsby's words, "engaged in recreating the world,"[3] a heroic but dangerous, and eventually destructive, activity.

The world will not be re-created. In Willy's psyche the memory of the Boston incident is intolerable—intolerable because it violates Willy's image of himself as a good husband and responsible father. It violates what Miller calls "his image of his rightful status."[4] Willy has almost succeeded in obliterating the incident, but the cost of keeping out the uninvited guest is the loss of his ability to deal with daily obligations. He is going crazy, spending most of his time muttering to himself. What that muttering really is—and I think we feel this more intently in Dustin Hoffman's recent portrayal of Willy than in any other version—is Willy's last desperate effort to create an imaginary world in which he can be a hero.

But he fails. The uninvited guest breaks through the barrier; and in the restaurant scene, technically one of the most brilliant scenes in American drama, Willy's resistance crumbles. In the men's room the reality of his failure overwhelms him and breaks his power to create any illusion of innocence. It is at this point that Willy, for the first time in the play, actually remembers what happened in Boston. We must believe this, because any other reading of the play would turn Willy into a cheap hypocrite. When Bernard asks him in Charley's office, "What happened in Boston, Willy?" Willy responds, "Nothing. What do you mean, 'what happened?' What's that got to do with anything?" He is angry because he is threatened, and he senses unconsciously that Bernard is probing for the truth. In the same scene Bernard says, "But sometimes, Willy, it's better for a man just to walk away."

> WILLY: Walk away?
> BERNARD: That's right.
> WILLY: But if you can't walk away?

Willy can't walk away from the truth, but he can't live with it either. Walking away would make him just like everyone else—like Howard, Happy, and Charley, who tell the social lies that are necessary to keep the world going. Living with it would destroy his innocence, and so his only recourse has been to repress it from consciousness by creating a different world, until the events of the day on which the play actually takes place bring the full truth flooding back. And when the truth comes back, we see the result—the shattered man planting seeds in his garden by flashlight, talking to his brother, Ben. Without his dream, Willy is lost. He struggles with the idea of suicide, but without Biff's love, even suicide would do him no good. "Why?" he asks Ben, "why can't I give him something and not have him hate me?"

Then the wonderful thing happens. Biff tries to explain himself to his father and in the process he breaks down:

> **WILLY,** *astonished*: What're you doing? What're you doing? *To Linda*: Why is he crying?
> **BIFF,** *crying, broken*: Will you let me go, for Christ's sake? Will you take that phony dream and burn it before something happens? . . .
> **WILLY,** *after a long pause, astonished, elevated*: Isn't that—isn't that remarkable? Biff—he likes me!
> **LINDA:** He loves you, Willy!

This is both the thematic and emotional climax of the play. In "Tragedy and the Common Man," Miller writes, "I think the tragic feeling is evoked in us when we are in the presence of a character who is ready to lay down his life, if need be, to secure one thing—his sense of personal dignity."[5] Willy will lay down his life at the end of the play for Biff. With the knowledge that Biff loves him, he will die to preserve the illusion of his worth. Arthur Ganz observes astutely, "It is the salvation of *Death of a Salesman* as a work of art that Willy never achieves easy self-knowledge or the automatic innocence that Miller associated with it."[6] He has lived for an illusion and he will die for an illusion. Ironically, it is the person for whom he died who understands that he should not have died at all. Charley's lament in the requiem is touching, but it is not the point of the play. Happy understands nothing; his life will recapitulate Willy's in a minor key. Biff's summary is the right one: "He never knew who he was. . . . He had the wrong dreams. All, all wrong." But what even Biff does not understand is *why* Willy has to hold onto his dream. Miller's stage directions in the climactic passage where Biff breaks down help us to a richer knowledge than Biff's. Miller describes Willy as "astonished" and "elevated." I have never seen a Willy Loman so "elevated" as Dustin Hoffman when he discovers Biff's love. Hoffman's Willy from this point to the end of the play is positively radiant. He dies for love, he dies for a dream that allows him to give love back with some dignity. Biff is right: "he had the wrong dreams"; but wrong as they are, without them he is only brown leaves floating on the water, as Jay Gatsby is without Daisy. Bigsby reminds us that "the basic theme of America's major dramatists is the effort to survive in times inimical to man."[7] Willy's death is the result of his effort to survive. His other option, that of self-knowledge, would cost him a price he cannot pay.

Of Miller's other major protagonists the one closest to Willy is Eddie Carbone, the longshoreman hero of *A View from the Bridge*. This play, like *Death of a Salesman*, turns on a premise that some members of its audiences neither understand nor want to take the time to follow through: that Eddie is no more conscious of his incestuous desire for his niece, Catherine, than Willy is of the effect of the Boston incident upon Biff's life. Eddie has a clear sense of his rightful status as a human being, which includes both his respect in the neighborhood and his role as father figure to Catherine. Eddie cannot allow himself to believe that his love for Catherine is unnatural, because such love is horrifying to his own sense of values:

> **BEATRICE:** You want somethin' else, Eddie, and you can never have her!
> **CATHERINE**, *in horror*: B! . . .
> **BEATRICE**, *crying out, weeping*: The truth is not as bad as blood, Eddie! I'm telling you the truth—tell her good-bye forever!
> **EDDIE**, *crying out in agony*: That's what you think of me—that I would have such a thought?

I don't think Eddie is lying. He honestly believes that his love for Catherine is pure, but to keep it pure he is forced, like Willy, to sublimate the truth by creating a series of illusions that will keep the truth hidden. Thus, as Bigsby perceptively notes, "He doesn't betray Rodolpho in order to gain Catherine for himself but to preserve her purity."[8] He first tries to discredit Rodolpho by having him branded as a bum and a homosexual. In the process he threatens the dignity of Marco, Rodolpho's older brother; and as the first act ends, Marco picks up the chair that Eddie has been unable to lift, thus threatening Eddie's position of supremacy in the household and setting the stage for the final confrontation in Act II.

Once an illusion has become deeply entrenched within a person, he must then create other illusions to reinforce the original one. Eddie, failing to dislodge Rodolpho on the grounds of homosexuality, now commits the act that precipitates the final tragedy: he informs on Marco and Rodolpho. He has now violated his own ethos, the ethos of the neighborhood, in which he believes passionately. The story of Vinny Bolzano is not told early in the play for nothing. So Eddie now has to force himself to believe that he did not turn the two men in, and it is a belief that he will die, if necessary, to maintain. "I want my name, Marco," he cries in anguish, as he moves toward him with the knife on which he himself will become impaled. He is prepared to kill or be killed rather than confess to anything that will destroy what he considers his rightful image of himself. Alfieri, the lawyer who serves a choral function in the play, mourns Eddie's passing in the concluding speech:

> Most of the time now we settle for half and I like it better. But the truth is holy, and even as I know how wrong he was, and his death useless, I tremble, for I confess that something perversely pure calls to me from his memory—not purely good, but himself purely, for he allowed himself to be wholly known and for that I think I will love him more than all my sensible clients. And yet, it is better to settle for half, it must be! And so I mourn him—I admit it—with a certain . . . alarm.

Like Willy Loman, Eddie Carbone cannot settle for half. He cannot face the truth of his own failure, his own guilt, and so we mourn him, as Alfieri does, "with a certain alarm," because civilization is based on settling for half. It is critical that we understand what "settling for half" means. It does not mean a moral compromise or a surrender of ethical standards. It means, I think, the kind of concession the individual must make to society if there is to be any civilization at all. It means the acceptance of guilt and the capacity to go on living with that acceptance. It means learning to live *after* the fall, learning to live with the reality of our own sinfulness, our own weakness. In Bigsby's words, "To accept imperfection in individuals and in society is not to capitulate before despair. Rather it is the first stage in the reconstruction of meaning and purpose. But there is a price to pay for such a revaluation. It means granting the death of innocence . . . "[9] Willy can't pay that price, nor can Eddie Carbone; nor can most of the central characters of Miller's first major play, *All My Sons* (1947).

All My Sons, a much clumsier and more traditionally structured play than the other two, shows Miller working with the reality-illusion theme in much the same way, except that he splits protagonists and concentrates the action as much on Kate Keller as he does on Joe. Both have an aspect of reality that they cannot face. Joe, like Willy and Eddie, is a man who is living a lie. Like them, he desperately needs the love and respect of his children. But unlike them, he is aware of his illusion, a life-lie which he has deliberately created in order to save his skin and his self-

135

respect. Joe Keller has sent an innocent man to jail to pay for his crimes and has so successfully hushed up matters that even Ann Deever believes in her father's guilt. Joe apparently can live with his own guilt as long as society and his family do not judge him guilty. But like Ibsen's Haakon Werle, he must pay conscience money; so he offers Deever a job when he gets out of prison and supports the marriage between Ann and his son Chris. But George Deever, like Gregers Werle, comes bolting onto the scene in rather melodramatic fashion to promptly rid each character of his illusions, and again like Gregers, he turns a happy household into a tomb. But our attitude toward the two is not the same. Ibsen's purpose in *The Wild Duck* is to show that misguided idealism can bring about tragedy; Miller's in *All My Sons* is to show that we *are* our brothers' keepers and that life without responsibility is not worth living. Joe Keller is not the tragic victim of George Deever's meddling; he has really been dead since the day he allowed the faulty engine blocks to be shipped. He has been able to keep up the illusion of innocence as long as Chris believes in him, but when George and Ann reveal the full truth to Chris, Joe can no longer pretend. Just as Willy cannot live without Biff's love, Joe cannot live without Chris's.

Joe Keller resembles Willy and Eddie in some respects; Kate Keller is like them in others, for she has sustained her life for three years on the illusion that her son Larry is still alive. Like Willy, she lives more in the past than the present, and she refuses to allow Ann and Chris to marry, because their marriage will destroy her illusion. Yet she is capable, unlike any of the others, of overcoming illusion. As the play ends she tells Chris, "Don't take it on yourself. Forget now. Live."

It is interesting to note that, in all the plays we have looked at thus far in this chapter, illusions are associated with the parental generation. Biff Loman, Catherine and Rodolpho, Ann and Chris (we might also remember O'Neill's Edmund Tyrone) will, for at least a while, be able to lead their lives free of illusion. Illusions, as we have seen in O'Neill also, are an inevitable part of aging. As time destroys our dreams and we are forced again and again to compromise with reality, we cling more desperately to vital lies to hold off those Indian hordes that circle round the soul. American family drama often pits an older generation clinging to its vital lies against a younger generation determined to break through those lies. This theme holds true not only in the plays of O'Neill, Miller, and Williams, but in more recent playwrights like David Rabe (*Sticks and Bones*) and Sam Shepard (*Buried Child*).

Can we survive without illusions? Most of Miller's early protagonists cannot, but John Proctor in *The Crucible* (1953), Quentin in *After the Fall*

(1963), and Von Berg in *Incident at Vichy* (1964) can. The subject of illusion in Miller is inseparable from the subject of guilt. We form illusions, the playwright suggests, primarily to protect the myth of our own innocence. One of the most poignant and ironic moments in Miller's drama is the scene in *The Crucible* where Elizabeth Proctor lies to protect her husband's innocence and in the process unwittingly destroys the validity of his testimony against the girls. John Proctor is unique among the protagonists in the plays of the first half of Miller's career, because he is the only one who can face the truth of his own guilt and not become immobilized by it. Proctor realizes, finally, that there are two kinds of guilt—guilt for one's private sins (his adultery with Abigail) and guilt for participation in society's sins (the witch trial). The great lesson that he learns is that he must not let his sense of personal guilt prevent him from trying to put a stop to public injustice. Personal sin does not disqualify a man from speaking the truth. Proctor learns that, as he says near the end, "You have made your magic now, for now I do think I see some shred of goodness in John Proctor. Not enough to weave a banner with, but white enough to keep it from such dogs."

What Miller deals with implicitly in *The Crucible* he takes up explicitly in *After the Fall* and *Incident at Vichy*, the two plays he worked on after his marriage to Marilyn Monroe and with which Elia Kazan chose to open the new Lincoln Center complex. Here Miller is wrestling with his own personal guilt over Marilyn's death, his feelings about his own actions and those of others during the House Un-American Activities Committee hearings, and the more general question of our implicit guilt for the holocaust. The central issue becomes: To what extent are human beings capable of good in a fallen world? We are all fallen. Quentin in *After the Fall* is partially to blame for the failure of his marriage with Louise, for Lou's death, and for Maggie's suicide. Our very instinct for life makes us secretly rejoice when another dies. Quentin says, "No man lives who would not rather be the sole survivor of this place than all its finest victims!" Leduc, the doctor, puts the issue even more clearly in *Incident at Vichy*, when he accuses Von Berg:

> Part of knowing who we are is knowing we are not someone else. And Jew is only the name we give to that stranger, that agony we cannot feel, that death we look at like a cold abstraction. Each man has his Jew; it is the other. And the Jews have their Jews. And now, now above all, you must see that you have yours—the man whose death leaves you relieved that you are not him, despite your decency. And that is why there is nothing and will be nothing—until you face your own complicity with this . . . your own humanity.

This speech brings us directly to the famous lines from *After the Fall* that I have used for the chapter's epigraph. As fallen men and women, we cannot go back to Eden. Our most fundamental illusion is the illusion of innocence. Willy Loman and Eddie Carbone die tragically rather than give up their belief in their own innocence. Quentin, who best represents what Miller learned during his long period of absence from the theater, accepts the reality of his own guilt: "the wish to kill is never killed, but with some gift of courage one may look into its face when it appears, and with a stroke of love—as to an idiot in the house—forgive it." Von Berg, the most heroic of Miller's protagonists, goes one step further; he gives up his life, not for an illusion, but to show Leduc that a human being at his best is capable of the very sacrifice that Leduc had a few moments earlier claimed to be impossible.

This leaves us, among Miller's major works, only *The Price* (1968) for consideration; and it does not fit easily into either of the categories we have been considering. Walter and Victor Franz are involved in a conflict that demands of each a confrontation with his own illusions. Walter, like many of Miller's earlier heroes, is guilty of having sacrificed others for his own advancement. But he seems to have rid himself of his illusions. He was once a combination of Joe Keller and Willy Loman, anxious for success and willing to pay the price to win the game; but the premise of the play is that Walter has changed and that his desire to help Victor is sincere. As Miller says in his production note:

> The actor playing Walter must not regard his attempts to win back Victor's friendship as mere manipulation. From entrance to exit Walter is attempting to put into action what he has learned about himself, and sympathy will be evoked from him in proportion to the openness, the depth of need, the intimations of suffering with which the role is played.

Walter, then, is to be viewed as a kind of successor to Quentin, one who has faced the reality of his guilt, his complicity in Victor's failure, and is attempting, as Quentin does, to rebuild his life on a more realistic footing. Yet it is very difficult for the audience to feel for Walter the sympathy that the playwright requires, because Victor—for all his wrongness—is the more lovable human being. Whether it is the play itself or my memory of the powerful performance by George C. Scott as Victor, I am strongly drawn to Victor, even though I realize he has wasted his life on the illusion of his father's poverty. He cannot accept Walter's offer, because it will mean the destruction of his pride in himself—what Miller calls "his sense of personal dignity"[10]—and though we realize that he is wrong and that he is unjust to Walter, maybe we mourn him as Alfieri mourns Eddie Carbone and as we mourn Willy—as a man who is wholly himself. Victor is not guilty in the sense that Joe Keller or Willy or Eddie is guilty, but he has destroyed his life for an illusion, the illusion that human beings are better than they are, and his final triumph is to turn that illusion into truth. He brings Gregory Solomon back to life, and just as he must remain true to the idealized memory of his father, he must remain true to his bargain with Solomon. And for this we love him, as we cannot love Walter.

2. Tennessee Williams

The major difference between the treatment of reality and illusion in Miller and Williams is that Miller is concerned primarily with the problem of guilt. Miller's characters lie to escape blame; Williams's characters lie because they can't help it. Miller stresses responsibility; Williams stresses circumstances. Williams's characters lie, dream, form illusions, and retreat into drink, drugs, and hallucination primarily to protect themselves from hurt. We must view them primarily as victims. In a *Life* interview Williams said, "For me the dominating premise has been the need for understanding and tenderness and fortitude among individuals trapped by circumstance."[11] Pity is the keynote in Williams's drama— pity for the different, the sensitive, the outsider, for those not understood by society. Arthur Ganz summarizes it well. Speaking of Laura in *The Glass Menagerie*, he says, "She is the sensitive, misunderstood exile, a recurrent character in Williams's work, one of the fugitive kind, who are too fragile to face a malignant reality and must have a special world in which they can take shelter."[12]

Tennessee Williams asks us to look beneath the surface and not to judge. Laura and Amanda Wingfield, Alma Winemiller, Blanche Dubois, Brick Pollit, and Larry Shannon are all figures the traditional world would be quick to condemn: their lives are dominated by illusions. But Williams asks us to understand them, to see *why* they have become what they are, and, finally, to love them. If we cannot, then the plays fall to pieces, which is exactly what happens in much of his weaker work. Bigsby summarizes the problem nicely. In the less successful pieces "his sympathy for the spiritually and materially dispossessed degrades into a coy celebration of the deviant, the emotionally incomplete, and the wilfully perverse."[13] When the delicate hero, the different hero, the outsider becomes the sick hero or the diseased hero, then Williams is asking for a kind of compassion the audience simply cannot give. Robert Hatch, reviewing one of Williams's plays for *The Nation*, said: "What ruins it for me is my inability to care whether anyone in the company sinks or swims. Let them die, let them breed, let them grow fat on the wealth—it is none of my business and I don't have to watch."[14] Ironically, the play to which he refers is *Cat on a Hot Tin Roof*, about which most viewers feel very differently, but his statement might well be valid for plays like *Sweet Bird of Youth* and many of the plays written during the terrible period in Williams's life after the death of his companion, Frankie Merlo, in 1962.

The Glass Menagerie (1945) has always been the most widely loved of Williams's plays, because it is his gentlest. Three sensitive people—Amanda Wingfield, her son, Tom, and her daughter, Laura—struggle to sustain an existence in a St. Louis slum during the depression. The reality of the world of the play is symbolized by the fire escape and the alley. As Williams notes in his opening stage directions, "The apartment faces an alley and is entered by a fire escape, a structure whose name is a touch of accidental poetic truth, for all of these huge buildings are always burning with the slow and implacable fires of human desperation." The world demands of us a certain toughness, a certain ruthlessness and brutality. Amanda, Tom, and Laura do not have those qualities, and so they will be hurt, bruised by the world. One is reminded of Brecht's Shen Te, but Brecht is interested in changing the world, and Williams wants us to love the victims, who, in this case, have no Shui Ta to call upon. They struggle. Amanda sells subscriptions to *The Homemaker's Companion*, Laura is sent to Rubicam's Business College to learn typing, and Tom works at Continental Shoemakers. But the reality of the outside world is too much for all of them. Each must re-create reality in order to survive. Amanda makes a heroic effort to make ends meet, but there is a delicacy about her that will not allow her to live without beauty in her life. And because there is no beauty in her present life, she retreats to the past, to the myth of the Old South, the genteel world of Blue Mountain, where on a certain Sunday afternoon she received seventeen gentlemen callers. One of the most touching moments in the play is the scene in which Amanda, dressed in the girlish frock of her teenage years, relives her past by entertaining Jim. The gentleman caller, it seems, is as much for her as he is for Laura. Amanda is one of Williams's most complex and most totally successful characters—at once heroic and cowardly, lovable and hateful, irritating and tender. She loves her children deeply but smothers them. She drives Tom crazy with her nagging and refuses to face the truth about Laura.

She does not permit the word "cripple" to be used in the house, and she constantly makes the mistake of assuming that Laura is the same kind of person she was as a girl. Yet her motives are never cheap or selfish.

If Amanda retreats into the past, Tom goes to the movies. When he finds the nagging of his mother and the grind of Continental Shoemakers intolerable, he vents his imagination by seeing pictures that take him into a world full of romance and glamour. He also writes poetry in the men's room at the factory, where he has earned the nickname "Shake-speare." Tom's world is different from that of his mother. While she dreams of a past to which she cannot return and which perhaps never existed, Tom dreams of a future when he will be free; for him there will be a chance of turning illusion into reality. Like O'Neill's Edmund, he is Williams's portrait of himself as a potential artist, even to the point of bearing his creator's real first name. In a sense the play really exists in Tom's mind. He calls it a memory play in his opening soliloquy, remind-ing us that one way of remaking the world is through art.

If Tom is the "author" of *The Glass Menagerie*, then Laura is its pro-tagonist, the character for whom the play is named and around whom the action centers. She is the *reason* for the play, which Tom writes out of his guilt at leaving her (much as Tennessee Williams wrote it as a tribute to his sister, Rose, for whose breakdown he felt much guilt and to whom he would be fiercely loyal all his life). Laura, as Williams tells us in the draft of an unpublished article, is a "delicate, haunted girl . . . the over-sensitive misfit in a world that spins with blind fury."[15] Unable to deal with the demands of real life, she retreats into her created world of the victrola and the tiny glass animals whose fragility resembles her own. It is a world Amanda refuses to acknowledge:

> TOM: She's terribly shy and lives in a world of her own and those things make her seem a little peculiar to people outside the house.
> AMANDA: Don't say peculiar.
> TOM: Face the facts. She is.
> AMANDA: In what way is she peculiar—may I ask?
> TOM: (*gently*) She lives in a world of her own—a world of little glass ornaments, Mother . . . She plays old phonograph records and—that's about all—

And so Amanda insists that Tom bring home a gentleman caller, and he does, thus precipitating the tragic climax of the play. Jim O'Connor, like Amanda, means well. And up to a point he does Laura a great amount of good. With patience and gentleness he leads her out of her dreamworld into the world of the everyday. In the famous unicorn sequence, Laura compares herself to the unicorn with the broken horn. "Now it is just like all the other horses," she tells him. "Maybe it's a blessing in disguise." For the first time in her life she feels a sense of confidence, a sense of her own human worth, because the boy on whom she had a high school crush has danced with her and treated her as someone important. But she cannot take the shock of his engagement; and she is, when he leaves, thrust back, this time more deeply into her inner world. Williams's stage directions emphasize the shock: "The holy candles in the altar of Laura's face have been snuffed out. There is a look of almost infinite desolation. . . . She rises unsteadily and crouches behind the victrola to wind it up." The long-range effect of the experience with Jim can only be guessed at. Tom closes the play with a long soliloquy, suggesting the passage of many years in his life. During his lines Amanda and Laura enact this scene in pantomime:

> Amanda appears to be making a comforting speech to Laura who is huddled upon the sofa. Now that we cannot hear the mother's speech, her silliness is gone and she has dignity and tragic beauty. Laura's dark hair hides her face until at the end of the speech she lifts it to smile at her mother. Amanda's gestures are slow and graceful, almost dancelike, as she comforts her daughter. At the end of her speech she glances a moment at the father's picture—then withdraws through the portieres. At the close of Tom's speech, Laura blows out the candles, ending the play.

The symbolism of the candles is central to the scene's meaning. The candles, we remember, were lit after supper and coincide with Laura's romantic hope for a life with Jim. Does the extinguishing of the candles at the play's end suggest a total withdrawal from reality by Laura or a more realistic and mature acceptance of herself as she is? The stage directions are ambiguous. Her smile to her mother does not suggest desolation, yet her blowing out of the candles must mean at least an end of all romantic hope. My own feeling is that Laura's smile is her way of telling her mother and us that she is all right in her dreamworld, that she *prefers* her dreamworld and understands that the world outside is not for her. For "nowadays the world is lit by lightning," says Tom, implying that there is no place for Laura in that world. And so perhaps it is better for the moths to stay away from the flame. Amanda and Laura have each been burned once, and another time might bring death.

Williams's next major play, and to many his masterpiece, *A Streetcar Named Desire* (1947), presents the conflict between illusion and reality in a somewhat different light, because of the introduction of the real world in the more sympathetic guise of Stanley Kowalski. Blanche Dubois is a familiar figure, a direct descendant of Amanda and Laura. She has the former's gentility and the latter's delicacy. We could pity Amanda and Laura because the outside world was so negatively presented. But Stanley we are not so sure about. For a good part of the play, our sympathies are more with Stanley and Stella than they are with Blanche. She seems, on the surface, a hypocritical intruder who is destroying her sister's marriage and trying to win Mitch with her "phoney airs." Stanley, for all his crudeness and vulgarity, has a raw vitality that is exciting. Foster Hirsch reminds us that "Williams, in fact, celebrates the sensual vigor and pride that Stanley so spectacularly incarnates."[16] The simple animal quality of Stanley and Stella's love for one another endears them to us, and Blanche's attempt to bring culture into the Kowalski household seems both hypocritical and, at times, downright silly. The real danger is, then, that Stanley will dominate the play, and that is exactly what happened in the original Broadway production and the first film, in large part because of the extraordinarily winsome performance of Marlon Brando.[17]

Both the director and the cast have the responsibility of creating a fine balance in the audience's sympathies between Stanley and Blanche, for unless we see Blanche as a tragic figure, trying desperately for one last chance to live, then the play loses its impact. Blanche and Stanley represent two ways of life, and the real point of the play is that the Stanleys are exterminating the Blanches from the face of the earth:

> Maybe we are a long way from being made in God's image, but Stella—my sister—there has been *some* progress since then! Such things as art—as poetry and music—such kinds of new light have come into the world since then! In some kinds of people some tenderer feelings have had some little beginning! That we have got to make *grow*! And *cling* to, and hold as our flag! In this dark march toward whatever it is we're approaching . . . don't—*don't hang back with the brutes!*

Blanche fights back against Stanley with the only resources she has—illusions. She puts paper lanterns on the light bulbs so that Mitch will not see her in the naked glare of the electric light. She tries desperately to sublimate her desires, she hides the truth about her past so that Mitch will accept her as a lady, and she very nearly succeeds. There is something inside of Mitch that needs Blanche as much as she needs him, but when Stanley tells him about her past life in Laurel, Mitch can't handle it. He tears the paper lantern off the light bulb:

143

BLANCHE: What did you do that for?
MITCH: So I can take a look at you good and plain!
BLANCHE: Of course you don't really mean to be insulting!
MITCH: No, just realistic.
BLANCHE: I don't want realism. I want magic! (*Mitch laughs.*) Yes, yes, magic! I try to give that to people. I misrepresent things to them. I don't tell truth, I tell what *ought* to be truth. And if that is sinful, then let me be damned for it!—*Don't turn the light on!*

He can't tell the difference between an external and an internal lie. Later in the same scene Blanche protests, "Never inside, I didn't lie in my heart." What she means is that her distortions of what we could call truth are only attempts to make outward reality conform to what it would have to be if life were to be bearable for her. She sees in Mitch a certain decency, a certain kindness that separates him from Stanley and the other poker players. She needs Mitch, and because she is not outwardly what Mitch would have her be, she changes reality by pretending to be what she needs to be in order to have him. In her heart she *is* what she pretends to be. There is no malice in her role as the genteel southern lady from Belle Reve (which means, of course, "beautiful dream"), no desire to hurt anyone else with her deception. All she can hope is that Mitch will understand. But Blanche's "magic" is too subtle for Mitch to grasp; he can only see the world that the naked light bulb reveals, and he leaves her to her death—that inexorable ride on the "streetcar named Desire" to one called Cemeteries, until she arrives at Elysian Fields, not her Elysian Fields, but Stanley and Stella's, which Stella will protect with her own vital lie. As the play ends and Blanche is taken away by the Doctor, Stella must believe that she has done the right thing by sending Blanche away and accepting Stanley's truth rather than Blanche's. In the world of *Streetcar Named Desire* there is no room for both.

By the time of *Cat on a Hot Tin Roof* (1955), Williams's next major Broadway success, his emphasis has shifted from the delicate female to the delicate male. In fact, *Cat*, with its father (Big Daddy), mother (Big Mama), and two brothers (Brick and Gooper), seems very much like a Miller play, and in some ways it follows the classic formula of Miller's family drama, where one of the sons challenges the illusions of the old generation. Brick sees the "mendacity" of the world that Big Daddy has created, the mendacity of Gooper and Mae and the minister, all buttering up to Big Daddy in the hopes of benefiting from his wealth. But Brick is not a Biff Loman or a Chris Keller, because Williams's primary interest is not in the world's lies, but in Brick's.

The great second-act confrontation between father and son thus

144

allows each character to reveal the illusions of the other. Big Daddy forces Brick to face the reason for his drinking—the death of his friend, Skipper, and he refuses to allow Brick to retreat into either alcoholic stupor or easy evasions. During the scene we feel both Brick's pain and his inability to deal with the issue. As Williams himself said, "I felt that the moral paralysis of Brick was a root thing in his tragedy,"[18] but Williams was careful both in the play and in statements about it not to be more specific. The issue, of course, is Skipper's homosexuality, Brick's attitude toward it, and the complex question of the playwright's attitude toward his own homosexuality. It was not until the famous *Playboy* interview of 1973 that Williams spoke openly and without defensiveness about his own homosexuality, but during the period of his greatest success as a playwright, both the Broadway code and prevalent public attitudes had made it impossible for Williams to deal openly with the question. Thus we see the playwright coming at it indirectly; but it is clearly there in both *Streetcar* and *Cat*, because Blanche and Brick have both betrayed, have both caused the deaths of homosexuals by failing to accept them. Blanche's tragedy is directly related to her young husband's death and Brick's tragedy to Skipper's. In *Cat* the question is not whether Brick is homosexual—given what we know about him, he probably is not—but Brick's disgust at Skipper's homosexuality and his rejection of Skipper as a friend because of that disgust. This is the truth that Brick drinks to escape; this is why he drinks from the play's beginning to its end, waiting for the "click" that will take him into a peaceful world where there are no moral questions. Brick wants to return to the simple world of the past where complex moral questions did not exist. He wants innocence, both his own and Skipper's, and he can't have that. Neither can America.

The character in the play who best understands how to live in a morally ambiguous world is the title character, Maggie, the "cat on a hot tin roof." When director Elia Kazan asked Williams to make alterations in the play for his Broadway production, Williams was most enthusiastic about enlarging the part of Maggie because "Maggie the Cat had become steadily more charming to me as I worked on her characterization."[19] Critic Signi Falk reminds us that "she is the one character in the play who seems unafraid to tell the truth, the only one who isn't living behind the protective covering of a lie."[20] Maggie, unlike Blanche Dubois and unlike Alma Winemiller in *Summer and Smoke*, is proud of her body and unafraid of using it. She has no Puritan qualms about sex, nor does she have any false southern gentility to repress her honest animal enjoyment of the bed, which is the central object onstage throughout the play.

When she lies at the end of the play about the child, it is all right. She has no illusions about the lie, and she has every intent of making the lie into truth at the first opportunity. Brick understands this: "No, truth is something desperate, an' she's got it. Believe me, it's something desperate, an' she's got it." We accept her desire for the land because of her childhood poverty, and we would certainly rather see Maggie and Brick than Gooper and Mae as heirs of the estate. She stands with Serafina della Rose in *The Rose Tattoo* (1950) and Maxime Faulk in *The Night of the Iguana* (1961) as what Harold Clurman calls "the embodiment of a credo, the affirmation of sex as the root feeling of a complete existence."[21] Maggie is rooted in the earth; what she wants is attainable, not in the pure form she would like it, but it is attainable, and she does not have to reinvent reality to get it.

For Williams's male protagonists reality becomes increasingly impossible to tolerate without some help from the imagination. In the last of his great plays, *The Night of the Iguana*, we find this revealing conversation between the protagonist, the Reverend T. Lawrence Shannon, and Hannah Jelkes:

> HANNAH: That word "fantastic" seems to be your favorite word, Mr. Shannon.
>
> SHANNON: Yeah, well you know we—live on two levels, Miss Jelkes, the realistic level and the fantastic level, and which is the real one really
> . . .
>
> HANNAH: I would say both, Mr. Shannon.
>
> SHANNON: But when you live on the fantastic level as I have lately but have got to operate on the realistic level, that's when you're spooked, that's the spook.

In this play the realistic level is meaningless. It is equated with Blake tours and silly, selfish old maids who want only to travel from Hilton Hotel to Hilton Hotel eating American food and seeing the sights that they feel they owe it to themselves to see. The "fantastic" level is the level of imagination. Reality drives people mad, unless they either kill their imaginations as Miss Fellowes and her fellow travelers have (pun intended), or they fulfill the needs of the imagination as Hannah and her grandfather, Nonno, have. It could even be said that the world of illusion is more true than the world of reality in the sense that the three really *live* characters in the play simply cannot exist in the real world. Shannon, Hannah, and Nonno are all artists, living in an illusory world of the imagination. Shannon is the most tragic of the three, because he is the least successful. He lives in two worlds at the same time, longing for human warmth, for love, for some release from the loneliness within him. He is attracted to Hannah, because he sees that they are soul mates. But Hannah's Puritan nature will not allow her to express love physically, and so Shannon must settle for the Widow Faulk. What Shannon really needs is a combination of the widow and Hannah, but reality does not supply that.

What happens to the sensitive individual in the world of reality? Like Shannon, he cracks up, and somebody has to be there to pick up the pieces. If Shannon had met Hannah Jelkes sooner, perhaps both of them might have been saved, Shannon from his "spook," and Hannah from her fear of physical love. But Williams had written that story in *Summer and Smoke*, without a happy ending. Williams's outsiders depend on the strength of their imaginations and "on the kindness of strangers." They struggle desperately not just to survive but to affirm their worth in a world that continually judges them as unfit and unworthy of love. Williams summarizes his drama poignantly in his *Memoirs* when he says, "Nowadays is, indeed, lit by lightning, a plague has stricken the moths, and Blanche has been 'put away' . . . "[22]

Part Three

Absurdism and After

12

Samuel Beckett and Eugène Ionesco

You're on earth . . . there's no cure for that.

—Samuel Beckett, *Endgame*

1. Samuel Beckett

Two tramps, Vladimir and Estragon, wait at an appointed place by a tree for a man who calls himself Godot. Their waiting is interrupted by Pozzo and his slave, Lucky, who are passing through. After Pozzo and Lucky leave, a boy comes to inform the two men that Mr. Godot cannot come but will surely come the next evening. On the following day Vladimir and Estragon continue their vigil. Estragon seems to have forgotten everything and has to be continually reminded by Vladimir of the existence of Godot, of Pozzo and Lucky. Pozzo and Lucky return, but Pozzo is blind, and Lucky, who had given a long, almost incomprehensible recitation previously, is dumb. The two visitors leave, and the tramps, alone once more, continue to wait for Godot. A boy comes, but it is not the same boy; rather it appears that he is the brother of the one who came previously. He too assures the tramps that Godot will come the next evening. And so the play ends with Vladimir and Estragon talking about leaving, but "they do not move" (final stage direction).

With this simple framework Samuel Beckett has created an archetypal dramatic myth, a play called *Waiting for Godot*, which has become, in the thirty-five years since its first production in Paris in January 1953, the single most influential play of our time. Because of its centrality, we must look at it in some detail.

Waiting for Godot is a myth about the human condition, clearly replacing those older myths in which a loving, personal God watches carefully over humanity. As the late Alan Schneider has said, *Waiting for Godot* "is no longer a play but a condition of life."[1] In Beckett's myth Vladimir and Estragon stand for humanity. As the blind Pozzo cries for help, Vladimir shouts, "But at this time, at this moment of time, all mankind is us, whether we like it or not." The situation, as we shall see, makes the rhetoric ironic; but the statement is nonetheless true. They are all mankind waiting for Godot. Who is Godot? He is whoever or whatever will redeem the lives of Vladimir and Estragon from meaninglessness:

> VLADIMIR: We'll hang ourselves tomorrow. (*Pause*) Unless Godot comes.
> ESTRAGON: And if he comes?
> VLADIMIR: We'll be saved.

The word "saved" is carefully chosen, for much of the play is conceived around the idea of salvation. Is Godot a reality? Is salvation through Godot a possibility? Vladimir wonders. He thinks of the story of the thief who is saved, obviously applying it to himself, but he doesn't like the odds. If he is saved, his friend Estragon will be damned. And besides, only one of the four evangelists mentions a thief being saved. He has prayed to Godot, and we discover at the end of the play that he is afraid to leave the appointed place because he believes that he and Gogo will be punished if they do leave. He questions the boy about Godot's appearance:

> VLADIMIR: Has he a beard, Mr. Godot?
> BOY: Yes Sir.
> VLADIMIR: Fair or . . . (*he hesitates*) . . . or black?
> BOY: I think it's white, Sir.
> *Silence*
> VLADIMIR: Christ have mercy upon us.

For Vladimir and Estragon, then, Godot represents that being, divine or human, white beard and all, who will save them, fill up the emptiness of their lives and give them purpose. Beckett's attitude toward such a view is, it would appear, profoundly ironic, and he explains why in his essay, *Proust*:

> Habit is the ballast that chains the dog to his vomit. Breathing is habit. Life is habit. Or rather life is a succession of habits, since the individual is a succession of individuals. . . . Habit then is a generic term for the countless treaties concluded between the countless subjects that constitute the individual and their countless correlative objects. The periods of transition that separate consecutive adaptations . . . represent the perilous zones in the life of the individual, dangerous, precarious, painful, mysterious, and fertile, when for a moment the *boredom of living* is replaced by the *suffering of being*.[2]

The periods of transition referred to in the essay are those periods in life when an individual is forced out of an old series of habits (routines) and has not yet adapted a new one. We are afraid of these periods, because in them we suffer, because in them we are forced to confront—alone—the ultimate reality of our being, our condition. That confrontation is frightening. So we invent all sorts of ways to avoid it. We create a Divine Being who will save us from emptiness and death, but *we will not know until after we are dead whether such a being exists or not*. So what shall we do while waiting? That is the real subject of the play. The French title, *En attendant Godot*, may be literally translated "While Waiting for Godot," and the "while" is of crucial importance, because life consists largely of finding things to do *while* waiting.

What do we do? Exactly what Vladimir and Estragon do—we develop habits and routines, we play games, we create diversions, we fill up the time so that we won't have to face the emptiness. That is the real issue—facing the emptiness. In a very important sense, the intellectual forebear of Beckett is Pascal, and the *Pensées* are as good a commentary on *Waiting for Godot* as anything I know. "The real tragedy of man," Pascal reminds us, "is that he cannot bear to remain at rest in his room." Beckett says, "Silence is pouring into this play like water into a sinking ship."[3] The metaphor is apt. Silence is precisely what Vladimir and Estragon are trying to avoid, not just the silence of the absence of speech, but in Michael Goldman's words, "a universal silence, a silence at the root of being."[4] They fight with one another, but neither will leave, because then he would be alone. Vladimir will not even let Estragon sleep, because the emptiness frightens him.

They talk. Some of the talk is pure vaudeville, pure burlesque, jokes to pass the time. They try to hang themselves, but that doesn't work. They argue. Estragon takes off his boots and puts them on. They play games with Lucky's hat—anything to avoid silence:

> ESTRAGON: In the meantime let us try and converse calmly since we are incapable of keeping silent.
> VLADIMIR: You're right, we're inexhaustible.

Later the same sort of dialogue occurs:

> ESTRAGON: I've tried everything.
> VLADIMIR: No, I mean the boots.
> ESTRAGON: Would that be a good thing?
> VLADIMIR: It'd pass the time. I assure you, it'd be an occupation.
> ESTRAGON: A relaxation.

VLADIMIR: A recreation.
ESTRAGON: We always find something, eh Didi, to give us the impression
 we exist?

Still later, after their name-calling contest, Vladimir exclaims, "How time
flies when one has fun!" But immediately after this, the two give out and
are saved from despair only by the second entrance of Pozzo and Lucky.
Vladimir's first reaction is "Reinforcements at last!" With Pozzo and
Lucky onstage, they will have something to amuse them, something to
help them, quite literally, get through the rest of the play.

There has been a great deal of discussion in the critical literature on
Godot about the degree to which Vladimir and Estragon are superior to
Pozzo and Lucky. Pozzo is a cruel, vindictive egotist, a symbol of some of
the baser aspects of capitalism. Lucky is an abject fool who has wasted
his gifts on Pozzo. Valdimir and Estragon can at least say, "We are not
saints, but we have kept our appointment." It is possible, as in the original New York production with E. G. Marshall and Bert Lahr, to play Didi
and Gogo for their charm. But it is also possible, as Alan Schneider did in
his 1970 Circle in the Square production, to make Vladimir and Estragon
more savage. In the second act, when Pozzo staggers onto the stage,
blind, crying desperately for help, they do nothing. Vladimir makes a
long rhetorical speech about how they are personally needed, but he
makes no move to help Pozzo. He and Estragon think of ways in which
they can make money off Pozzo, they play amusing word games at
Pozzo's expense. To them he is a diversion. If they help him, he'll be able
to go, and if he goes, they'll be alone. Estragon gives Lucky a few good
kicks in the crotch to pay him back for the first-act bite. In short,
Vladimir and Estragon are as cruel to Pozzo and Lucky in Act II, as Pozzo
is to Lucky and to them in Act I. Cruelty, it seems, is a way people have of
interrelating.

It is not until very close to the end of the play that there is a change.
For a brief moment Vladimir goes through one of those periods of transition referred to in the *Proust* essay. Estragon is asleep, and Didi
meditates:

> Astride of a grave and a difficult birth. Down in the hole, lingeringly, the
> grave-digger puts on the forceps. We have time to grow old. The air is full
> of our cries. (*He listens.*) But habit is a great deadener. (*He looks again at
> Estragon.*) At me too someone is looking, of me too someone is saying, He
> is sleeping, he knows nothing, let him sleep on. (*Pause.*) I can't go on!
> (*Pause.*) What have I said?

154

For a moment the "boredom of living" is replaced by the "suffering of being." Vladimir is experiencing a kind of Joycean epiphany, a moment of illumination when he both sees and feels the truth of his condition, but the light is too bright to live with, and he stops his meditation to begin pacing feverishly back and forth until interrupted by the boy who tells him that Godot, white beard and all, will come tomorrow. The play is filled with "perhaps-ness." Perhaps Godot will come, perhaps he will not. Perhaps he exists, perhaps he does not. We do not know. In the meantime, while waiting for Godot, we forget to live.

In Beckett's second play, *Endgame* (1957), there is no Godot to be found. If ever he did exist he has been relegated to the scrap heap of memory along with Nagg and Nell. All that is left is games. As Beckett himself said, writing of the 1967 Berlin production, "*Endgame* is only play. Nothing less."[5] The title *Endgame* suggests, as does the chess term on which it is based, finality—the end of a losing battle. Hamm says, "Old endgame lost of old, play and lose and have done with losing." "Something is taking its course," says Clov, repeatedly. The earth is sterile, the sun gone, the painkiller used up. Everything exists only in the past. Nagg and Nell, Hamm's aged parents, make their appearances, retell their stories, and slide into oblivion. Nell has sustained her life on the memory of the April afternoon on Lake Como when Nagg first told the story of the tailor. She dies, deep in memory. Nagg stays alive long enough to curse his son. Clov sets the house in order and prepares to depart; Hamm is left alone, at least as far as he knows, to play out the final scene with dignity:

> Clov!
> (*Long pause.*)
> No? Good.
> (*He takes out the handkerchief.*)
> Since that's the way we're playing it . . .
> (*He unfolds handkerchief*)
> Let's play it that way . . .
> (*he unfolds*)
> . . . and speak no more about it . . .

It is important to see the emphasis on "playing." Hamm, as his name suggests, is a ham actor, and, as June Schlueter observes, "he is a playwright and director as well."[6] He likes to dramatize, to play out scenes for all they are worth. He milks the story of the man who comes "crawling toward me, on his belly . . . " on Christmas eve, begging "bread for his brat." He can give the child corn, he admits, but what good will that do? The color will come back into the child's cheeks, but, says Hamm's protagonist to the man, "Use your head, can't you, use your head, you're on earth, there's no cure for that."

This is the central premise of Beckett's drama, and it is different from that of anyone we have considered in this book. Of course, Beckett did not invent the death of God. As Esslin so eloquently points out in the introduction to *The Theatre of the Absurd*, Nietzsche did that, and many twentieth-century writers have echoed his despair. What Beckett does, through his minimalist approach to theater, is, for the first time, I think, to admit to no world other than that on the stage. Vladimir and Estragon do not leave, because there is nowhere else. They enter, they play out the play. The world outside the play simply does not exist. Clov claims that he will leave, but he cannot go any more than the characters from *Godot* can. Shortly before the close of *Endgame*, he spies a small boy, and Hamm's reaction is, "If he exists he'll die there or he'll come here." Those are the only alternatives. If Clov is the small boy that Hamm restored to health by feeding him corn from his granary, as might well be the case, then after Hamm's death, Clov may become the next Hamm, and the small boy outside the next Clov. "He'll die or he'll come here."

Beckett's view of the human condition is uncompromisingly pessimistic, and it is also uncompromisingly honest. There is about Beckett, says his friend and critic Martin Esslin, an extraordinary integrity, a refusal to see the world except in terms of the abandonment of all illusions. There is, in Estragon's words, "Nothing to be done." That is the fundamental premise of Beckett's drama, that anything less than an honest facing of the awfulness of the human condition is unacceptable. And so Beckett goes on writing, in this, his eighty-second year, not because he believes his writing will change anything, but because as an artist he has no choice but to depict life as he sees it. Writing gives Beckett pleasure, as acting gives Hamm pleasure. We cannot help talking, and even as Beckett's plays become shorter and shorter, a certain pattern remains. There is a speaker and a listener. Speaking is essential. Someone to listen is essential, someone to cry our anguish to.

In *Happy Days* (1961) the speaker is Winnie and the listener is Willie. He is not always listening, but he is always there, unlike God. Winnie opens the first act with prayer, thus endowing the world with a meaning that it doesn't have. Even in the second act, when she has abandoned prayer, she begins, "Hail, holy light. . . . Someone is looking at me still. (*Pause.*) Caring for me still. (*Pause.*) That is what I find so wonderful." Up to her neck in sand, unable to move, to see anything of herself except her mouth and tongue, hardly able to hear, she still clings to the hope that life is meaningful. Her vitality is absolutely extraordinary. Like Vladimir and Estragon, she passes the time with small tasks, examining the objects in her black bag one by one, taking small joys from her toothbrush, her music box, her magnifying glass, her breasts, her parasol. In the second act, when she can no longer use her arms, she can still talk, still remember the past, tell stories. These are her last resorts. Her cheerfulness is as remarkable as it is without foundation, except for the presence of Willie:

> Not that I flatter myself you hear much, no Willie, God forbid. (*Pause.*) Days perhaps when you hear nothing. (*Pause.*) But days too when you answer. (*Pause.*) So that I may say at all times, when you do not answer and perhaps hear nothing, "Something of this is being heard, I am not merely talking to myself, that is in the wilderness, a thing I could never bear to do—for any length of time."

For all the emphasis on silence in Beckett's plays, his characters continue to talk. In *Not I* (1973) the characters consist of a mouth and an auditor. The Mouth seems to be that of a woman of seventy who, almost mute all her life, is suddenly seized, on an April morning in a field, with both the capacity and the compulsion to talk, to tell her story: "something that would tell . . . how it was . . . how she . . . what . . . had been . . . yes . . . something that would tell . . . how it had been . . . how she had lived." *Not I* is a kind of continuation of *Happy Days*, in which Winnie becomes the Mouth and Willie the Auditor, except that the Auditor is a stranger who apparently knows nothing of the woman's history. He keeps inquiring if the Mouth is telling her own story, but she, to use Beckett's terms, vehemently refuses to relinquish the third person, maintaining the role of artist or storyteller rather than that of autobiographer. Like Winnie, the woman whom the Mouth is describing seems to have retained some kind of belief in a traditional God, "brought up as she had been to believe . . . with the other waifs . . . in a merciful . . . (*brief laugh*) . . . God . . . (*good laugh*)." Just as Winnie refers to "the old style" of speech in which there were days and one "died," so the Mouth seems to associate the thoughts of the woman with a way of viewing life that is now patently absurd. The old language, the old nomenclature, is useless. Words such as *God, sin, mercy, punishment*—words that appear frequently in Beckett—are meaningless, but they continue to be used by

157

the characters who look back with feelings of both hope and fear to the time when the words were charged with meaning.

In the more recent plays, such as *Ghost Trio* (1975) and *But the Clouds* (1976), written for television, and *Rockaby*, written for a Beckett festival in the United States during the spring of 1981, these kinds of words disappear. The plays' central figures, unlike Winnie and the Mouth, are mute, and a strange inversion takes place, in which the actor becomes the listener and an outside voice or narrator becomes the speaker. In *Ghost Trio* a man plays a tape that contains both the music of the "ghost trio" of the title and the voice of the narrator. The man thinks he hears the sound of a remembered loved one, and he goes to the door, to the window, to the bed, three times, each time in vain, and all that he can see is his own face in the mirror over the bed. Outside it is raining, and the long hall gives way through mist to deeper darkness. On his third trip to the door, he sees a small boy,-smiling, dressed in slicker and rain hat. In *But the Clouds* a similar man goes to a private place where he contemplates his beloved, whose face appears to him from time to time, and who either vanishes, lingers, or speaks to him briefly, murmuring " . . . but the clouds." Most of the time she does not appear at all. In *Rockaby*, a woman dressed in black (brilliantly played by Billie Whitelaw) sits in a spotlight rocking, while listening to her recorded voice. Each time the voice stops she begs for more, this action repeated four times until, at the end of the final sequence, the woman rocks into death.

All these plays are brief, ten to fifteen minutes in duration, intensely lyrical in language, and poignant both in their sadness and their compassion. At first elusive, they evoke a rhythm to which the viewer is allowed to surrender. They cannot really be read, because Beckett has combined sound and visual effects in such a way that the appeal is primarily through the eye and the ear to the unconscious. More poetry than prose, they express the utter loneliness of human beings, the longing for peace, the yearning for reunion with a lost loved one associated with the past. The woman in *Rockaby* seems to have spent her life searching for that someone, first actively searching for "another living soul, one other living soul, going to and fro, all eyes like herself," then gradually retiring from the search to her window where she waited to see if there was "one blind up no more" where another like herself waited and watched. Despairing of that, she finally comes down to the porch to take her place in her mother's rocker, where her mother had rocked herself to death, and where she listens to her own voice rhythmically rocking her, just as Whitman's old crone rocks the cradle into death.

2. Eugène Ionesco

Despite the rise of Beckett's reputation during the last twenty years and the decline of Ionesco's, the two names are still inseparably linked, not only because each came to Paris and made French his native language and because each has been obsessed with the revitalization of traditional theater, but because the two men between them made the most important theatrical revolution of our time, a revolution whose effects we are still feeling. I spent the spring of 1985 in Paris, and it seemed wonderfully appropriate to me that there was a new production of *Godot* at the Théâtre d'Atelier and that *The Bald Soprano* and *The Lesson* were still running at La Huchette.

Like Beckett, Ionesco is concerned with games people play, particularly the games which bourgeois civilization has invented as a replacement for genuine living. The theater of Ionesco is from beginning to end an attack on what Martin Esslin describes as "the deadliness of present-day mechanical, bourgeois civilization, the loss of real, *felt* values, and the resulting degradation of life."[7] Examples can be given almost without limit from the early plays. *The Bald Soprano* (1949) is, almost in its entirety, an exaggerated depiction of the hollowness of bourgeois life through the use of caricature. Too much has been made of the obscurity of the play, and that is because people don't stop to listen to themselves talk. What is frightening about *The Bald Soprano* is how closely it resembles the banal conversations that go on in middle-class homes night after night. Granted, our own cocktail party or dinner conversation has more coherence, more of a surface of politeness, but that simply enables us to keep up the illusion that we are saying something worthwhile. Ionesco's exaggeration in the play is quite literally explosive, at once both farcical and terrible, both entertaining and at the same time extremely disquieting. The characters hide their boredom and their dislike for one another behind the clichés of polite speech and the routines of conventional behavior. So mechanical have their lives become that they are incapable of learning anything. Our illusions may be exploded by the violence of the ending, but the characters remain unchanged. The play simply begins again with the two couples exchanging roles; the process, presumably, is continuous.

Ionesco's favorite satiric target in the early plays is the official language of social, political, and literary institutions. Language becomes the means by which those in power intimidate and deceive the rest of us. If you like, language becomes the means by which those in power create illusions to control those out of power. In *The Lesson* (1950) the Professor uses deliberate distortions of logic and all kinds of esoteric jargon to intimidate and humiliate his pupil. The play, if read, for example, with George Orwell's famous essay "Politics and the English Language," reveals itself as an astute and frightening parable about both academic and political power. The Professor symbolizes not only the fossilization and pedantry of the academic profession, which metaphorically "kills" the Pupil, but also the methods of totalitarian brainwashing. The same type of character appears again and again in Ionesco—the Orator in *The Chairs* (1951), Mother Peep in *The Killer* (1957), and the Logician in *Rhinoceros*. Austin Quigley's analysis of the Orator's function is most convincing. The Orator, Quigley suggests, is the "figure of an old-fashioned author/artist come to deliver a message to an audience—exactly the kind of artist figure and artistic function that Ionesco's stagecraft is designed to transcend. For Ionesco, such a figure has nothing new to say and therefore nothing of consequence to art to say."[8] If we, like the Old Man and the Old Woman, hand over our deepest inner thoughts and feelings to such an artist for expression, the result will be nothing. Our messages will be lost.

Neither Mother Peep nor the Logician can say anything either, but that doesn't stop them from talking. Mother Peep is the ultimate political rabble-rouser, using language that apparently promises the people all sorts of changes while actually pledging them nothing:

> We won't persecute, but we'll punish and deal out justice. We won't colonize, we'll occupy the countries we liberate. We won't exploit men, we'll make them productive. We'll call compulsory work voluntary. War shall change its name to peace and everything will be altered, thanks to me and my geese.

The Logician is interested only in the abstract question of how to form a syllogism correctly. He teaches the Old Gentleman logic, and then goes on to prove that there is no way to prove logically whether there was one rhinoceros or two. He is the dominant figure in the first act, and it is of some significance that logic or abstract reasoning is of no help whatsoever in stopping the onset of the disease of rhinoceritis. Everyone, of course, is impressed with the brilliance of the Logician's reasoning, but they fail to notice that the questions of whether the rhinoceros is bicorned or unicorned, African or Asian are totally irrelevant to the issue at hand. All of these figures—the Professor, the Orator, Mother Peep, the Logician—are totally self-centered seekers after power and admiration, who use the subtleties of speech to gain their own ends.

In Ionesco's world, language has become so degraded, so twisted, so pedantic that it is incapable of carrying genuine emotion or feeling. What is needed, Ionesco cries, is the return to a poetic concept of life:

> When I wake up, on a morning of grace, from my nocturnal sleep as well as from the mental sleep of routine, and I suddenly become aware of my existence and of the universal presence, so that everything appears strange, and at the same time familiar to me, when the astonishment of being invades me—these sentiments, this intuition belongs to all men, of all times. We can find this state of mind expressed in almost the same words by all poets, mystics, philosophers, who feel it in exactly the same way I do.[9]

This kind of language is similar to Beckett's in the *Proust* essay with its emphasis on escape from routine, but it is much more romantic than Beckett's. One is reminded of Thoreau's passage from Chapter II of Walden on mental and spiritual awakening or of the rhapsodic conclusion to Emerson's "Nature." Ionesco, like the Romantic poets, is a radical individualist calling for the inner regeneration of each person from within, the reawakening of dormant feelings. One of his favorite words is *astonishment*: "I am always surprised. I go through life perpetually astonished at everything that happens around me."[10] Ionesco uses this romantic quality of wonder or astonishment as his primary contrast to the mechanization, the death in life, of middle-class routine. In *The Bald Soprano* nobody is alive, and that is precisely why the Smiths and the Martins are interchangeable. In *The Lesson* the Pupil is alive at the beginning of the play, and we witness the gradual destruction of her joy, her vitality, her freshness through the Professor's manipulation. In *The Chairs* we meet two of Ionesco's most vital characters—the Old Man and the Old Woman, who hope to communicate a lifetime of experience to a group of important people they have called together for the occasion. There is a double tragedy here: first, the point that has already been made, their folly in entrusting the task to a professional orator; and second, the primary tragedy of the empty chairs, suggesting a mindless, heartless mechanized audience who would neither hear nor understand even if the experience were communicated to them.

At the heart of Ionesco's attempt to dramatize the need for a return to a poetic concept of life are his three major full-length plays—*The Killer*, *Rhinoceros*, and *Exit the King*. The plays need to be studied both separately and together, separately because each is a unified, complete work of art, but together because each has as its protagonist the most memorable character in Ionesco's work—Berenger, Ionesco's Everyman, the common, ordinary man forced by circumstances to face a series of crises. Even in *Exit the King*, where he bears the title King Berenger I, he is still the common, ordinary person confronting the ultimate reality of death.

We first meet Berenger in *The Killer*, written in 1957 and produced in 1959, and still, in my opinion, his most powerful play. The English title, as others have pointed out, does not convey the full meaning of the French *Tueur sans gage* ("Killer Without Payment"), because at the heart of the play is the premise that the Killer kills for no reason at all. His presence is both irrational and inevitable. He is, on one level, death itself, which, no matter how hard we try, we cannot eradicate. The first act, which takes place in the radiant city, underscores this point. Berenger, who has stumbled into the radiant city by accident, is *astonished* by the achievement of the Architect. It is the objective correlative to his own inner dreams of beauty and wonder. The technological skills of modern civilization have destroyed poverty, ugliness, filth. The grayness of life has been conquered. Berenger rhapsodizes about his past joy and its return because of the radiant city:

> I was deeply aware of the unique joy of being alive . . . Suddenly the joy became more intense, breaking all bounds! And then, oh what indescribable bliss took hold of me! The light grew more and more brilliant, and still lost none of its softness, it was so dense you could almost breathe it. . . . And suddenly, or rather gradually . . . no it was all at once, I don't know, I only know that everything went grey and pale and neutral again . . . But *you* . . . you've given me back the forgotten light . . .

His sense of joy restored, Berenger immediately falls in love with the Architect's secretary, Mademoiselle Dany, who is in the process of leaving her job. Suddenly Berenger realizes that something is wrong. He and the Architect are the only people on the street. Where are all the inhabitants of the radiant city? Either moving out or locked in their houses, it seems, because of the Killer. For nothing human beings can do, not even our highest technological achievements can destroy death. The Killer strikes again, and this time his victim is Mademoiselle Dany. Berenger is desolate, desperate to do something, and he rushes home where he finds his consumptive friend, Edouard, waiting in his apartment. He tells Edouard about his discovery, and Edouard informs him that everyone in the city knows about the Killer. Berenger is stunned again. He is a human being, he is alive, he wants to do something—but no one cares. Everything conspires to stop him from taking action. He discovers that Edouard has in his briefcase all the Killer's tools of his trade, including the photograph of the colonel that he uses to lure his victims to the edge of the fountain, where he drowns them. Edouard creates a series of ridiculous stories about how the items got into his briefcase, and finally the two rush off to take the evidence to the police; but Edouard conveniently leaves the briefcase behind.

In the final act Berenger is again stopped from taking action. Edouard must be sent home for the briefcase, and Berenger must fight his way through an immense traffic jam, during which he discovers that the police have no interest in finding the Killer. Their job is to direct traffic. Up to this point the play may be read primarily as a social commentary on the nature of modern society. Berenger, the one man who is alive, the only person in the play who is real (in Ionesco's sense of the word), is thwarted at every point in his efforts both by human indifference (Edouard) and by institutional bureaucracy (the Architect, the police). Then comes the ending, almost a one-act play in itself, as Berenger is suddenly left alone onstage to confront the Killer. He argues with him, presents reasons to him, pleads with him, begs him to stop killing. He uses every weapon he can think of, but the Killer only chuckles insanely, and finally Berenger, worn down by his inability to make an impression, falls to his knees and surrenders to the Killer's knife as the curtain falls.

If the Killer represents in part the bestial or destructive side of humanity that cannot be eliminated, he also, as I suggested earlier, represents death. Berenger's confrontation with the Killer is an existential confrontation with his own mortality. The playwright's work always exists on two levels—the social and the existential. *The Killer* is a protest against social indifference and bureaucratic mechanization. It is an allegory about our illusion that we can destroy the killer among us through scientific progress. It is also a play about death, about our fear of death and our inability to live because of that fear. Berenger, like his creator, oscillates between states of ecstasy and despair, between great joy and terrible loneliness. Both states are preferable to the nonbeing of bourgeois conformity, but the euphoric state of ecstasy, Ionesco's desired reality, cannot be maintained because too much conspires to destroy it. Thoreau cannot live at Walden always. The morning state of the soul cannot be sustained. Our problem as human beings—Ionesco suggests—is to combat the darkness without giving up the genuine act of living, without using habit, routine, or some ghastly replacement for life, such as Fascism, as a crutch. To confront society without the loss of self, to confront death honestly and courageously—these are the virtues Ionesco most extols. In his next two major plays, *Rhinoceros* (1959) and *Exit the King* (1962), he will dramatize why it is so difficult for human beings to face these confrontations without illusions.

In *Rhinoceros* we find Berenger once more in an almost unbearably ambivalent situation. As in *The Killer*, he is set off from society. In the new play he is not so strong a figure, but more the pathetic little man, trapped by a mindless bureaucracy. He is obviously out of place at the office with its petty rivalries, and he escapes both his social insecurities and his existential fears by drinking:

> BERENGER: I don't like the taste of alcohol much. And yet if I don't drink, I'm done for; it's as if I'm frightened, and so I drink not to be frightened any longer.
>
> JEAN: Frightened of what?
>
> BERENGER: I don't know exactly. It's a sort of anguish difficult to describe. I feel out of place in life, among people, and so I take to drink. That calms me down and relaxes me so I can forget.
>
> JEAN: You try to escape from yourself!
>
> BERENGER: I'm so tired, I've been tired for years. . . .

His feeling of oppression is similar to Berenger's gray feeling in *The Killer*. He knows that he isn't alive, but he doesn't know what to do about it. He takes much longer to be stirred into life than his counterpart in *The Killer*. The radiant city reawakens life in the first Berenger, but it is not until the end of Act II, Scene II, when Jean turns into a rhinoceros before his eyes, that the second Berenger is jolted into life. He argues with Jean about political and social beliefs, and we see Berenger emerging now as the individualist, standing up against the demands of conformity and the brutalizing nature of totalitarian tactics (Ionesco claimed that the image of Nazi troops entering his native Romania reminded him of rhinoceroses). In Act III Berenger reaches his full stature as he argues with Dudard:

> I feel responsible for everything that happens. I feel involved, I just can't be indifferent. . . . If only it had happened somewhere else, in some other country, and we'd just read about it in the papers, one could discuss it quietly, examine the questions from all points of view and come to an objective conclusion. We could organize debates with professors and writers and lawyers, and blue-stockings and artists and people. And the ordinary man in the street, as well—it would be very interesting and instructive. But when you're involved yourself, when you suddenly find yourself up against the brutal facts you can't help feeling directly concerned—the shock is too violent for you to stay cool and detached.

Just as in *The Killer* Berenger seems to be the only one concerned, the only one alarmed about the spread of the disease. "You leave the authorities to act as they think best," says Dudard. "I'm not sure if morally you have the right to butt in." We've seen what happens, in *The Lesson*, *The Chairs*, and *The Killer*, when matters are left to the authorities, but Dudard's view seems to be the prevalent one, both when Ionesco wrote the play and in the conservative eighties. Dudard calls Berenger a Don Quixote—and he is right, for the two have much in common. Both see themselves as the only sane people in a crazy world, and because of it the world brands them as crazy. In such a world it is impossible to live without some support, and Berenger's support vanishes rapidly. First Dudard leaves, and then Daisy, who really seems to want to stay, decides to become a rhinoceros because she needs the love of the group. "After all," she rationalizes neatly, "perhaps it's we who need saving. Perhaps we're the abnormal ones . . . Those are the real people. They look happy. They're content to be what they are."

The ending of *Rhinoceros*, the most celebrated and controversial in Ionesco, deserves close attention. There are two prevalent views, both of which are overly simplistic: (1) that Berenger is a hero representing the individual who stands up against the pressure to conform, and (2) that Berenger really wants to conform and that his supposed heroism is nothing more than sour grapes. Since he can't be a rhinoceros, he might as well fight. The trouble with these positions is that they are based on a reading of something less than the whole play. Berenger has both these people in him. Early in Act I he says to Jean, "Solitude seems to oppress me. And so does the company of other people." Berenger has at many points expressed his individuality, his sense of responsibility. Thus his final decision not to capitulate is more than sour grapes. He *really is* different from other people, and that is precisely why he cannot become a rhinoceros. He is immune to the disease. But at the same time, being the only healthy person in a sick world is hardly ideal, because one is quarantined from the human race. The part of Berenger that wants love and companionship wants to be a rhino. He is not contradictory, only human.

In *Rhinoceros*, then, Berenger faces the paradox that, unless he accepts the illusions of society, he must exist without companionship. Thomas Stockmann can say that the strongest man is he who stands alone, but he has not yet learned the anguish of loneliness. Ionesco's realist—like the crusaders of Ibsen and Shaw—stands apart from society, but he has not the inner resources and strength of his earlier counterparts. The earlier heroes feel that they are working for something greater than themselves, and that hope, that force, sustains them in their quest. In Ionesco's universe no cosmic or religious meaning is given to Berenger's refusal to capitulate. He is serving neither God nor Shaw's Life Force, nor Chekhov's future. His only reality is his own existence, and that word brings us to the third of the Berenger plays.

Exit the King, like *The Killer*, has a slightly misleading title in English. The French title, *Le roi se meurt*, suggests the central theme of the play more forcefully. Literally translated as "The King Is Dying," it forces upon the reader or viewer the feeling of death's overwhelming power. Even kings die. Even Berenger, who has been convinced of his own immortality. In fact, as the play opens and he finds himself with a scant two hours to live, he has never given serious thought to his death. Thus the central action of the play is Berenger's education, his disillusionment, and his gradual willingness to accept and to understand his own mortality. Ionesco's primary technique is to contrast the two wives—Queen Marguerite, his first wife, and Queen Marie, his second. Marguerite is the real protagonist of the play, for she is the one who controls the action, in fact, quite literally. She assumes the role of teacher—first telling the king that he is going to die and then helping him to prepare for death. Marie is the primary symbol of illusion in the play, for she has spent her entire life keeping the king occupied in pleasure. Marguerite accuses her:

> It's your fault if he's not prepared. It's your fault if it takes him by surprise. You let him go his own way. You've even led him astray. Oh yes! Life was very sweet. With your fun and games, your dances, your processions, your official dinners, your winning ways and your firework displays, your silver spoons and your honeymoons!

Marie has loved the king, but she has loved him as if physical love could endure forever. Neither Marie nor the king can accept his coming death. He insists that he is in good health: "I'll die when I want to. I'm the king. I'm the one to decide." Illusions die hard. He limps about the stage, unable to bear the weight of his crown and scepter; but he still will not resign himself. The doctor urges him: "It's happened all at once and you're no longer your own master . . . Try and have the courage to look facts in the face!" Berenger then reverts to childhood, crying and pouting, like a schoolboy who has failed an exam and wants another try. It isn't fair, he protests. Next he begins to think of the future and hopes to gain immortality in a whole series of ways which seem absurd and yet closely resemble the practices of our own society: he wants his body preserved, he demands that schoolchildren study only his reign, he wants his likeness in all the churches. He wants—in short—to be remembered for all time.

Marie continues to feed him with illusions. She tells him that he is merely in exile and that in death " . . . you'll go back to where you came from when you were born." It is the familiar illusion of Godot. But the king has changed. His self-centeredness starts to vanish, and with the threat of imminent death staring him in the face, he begins to *live* for the first time. He begins to feel the preciousness of life itself, to appreciate the miracle of each of the small things in life: "Did you ever realize that every day you woke up? To wake up every day. . . . Every morning one comes into the world." In a marvelous exchange with the nursemaid, Juliette, he rhapsodizes, as the Berenger of *The Killer* has, about the wonder of everything: "You never realize you're breathing. You must think about it! Remember! I'm sure it never crosses your mind. It's a miracle." A bit later he says in a less poetic vein, "Till now I'd never noticed how beautiful carrots were." From this point on he fades gradually for the remainder of the play. One by one, each of the characters vanishes—first Marie, representing the life of the senses; next the Guard, representing his authority to command; next Juliette and the Doctor, those who can tend to the saving of his physical body. He is left alone with Marguerite, who may stand for his mind—the only character who is not essentially external to Berenger. Only she can teach him total resignation.

These three plays, along with the early one-act plays, represent Ionesco at his best; the work of the last fifteen years represents something of a falling off largely because, unlike Beckett, Ionesco has tended to repeat himself rather than to change either his technique or the emphasis of his subject matter. The most important plays of the seventies, in terms of the reality-illusion theme, are *Killing Game* (*Jeu de massacre*), written in 1970 but not performed in the United States until 1975, and *Man with Bags* (*L'Homme aux valises*), adapted by Israel Horovitz and first performed in this country in 1977.

Killing Game develops the theme of death from *The Killer* and *Exit the King*. This time death, instead of an ugly dwarf, is personified as a hooded black monk, who never speaks but, instead, stands silently watching as the inhabitants of the unknown town are slowly wiped out by a mysterious plague, against which there is no defense and for which there is no adequate explanation. Sharing elements of Defoe's *Journal of the Plague Year* and Camus's *The Plague*, Ionesco's play depicts the inhabitants of the town largely as fools, growing increasingly cruel to one another in their ludicrous attempts to seal off their houses from the disease, and groping for explanations in worn-out political, religious, and medical clichés. One of the ironies of the play is that those who face

167

the plague most honestly, like the Fourth Doctor in the council chamber scene, are among the first to be struck. The rich believe that the plague is caused by the poor, the religious see it as a punishment, the careful see it as the result of carelessness. But Ionesco's swift, kaleidoscopic sequence of scenes makes it abundantly clear that no explanation is possible.

The play's most important scene is its next-to-last one, in which an Old Man and an Old Woman, each of whom seems to speak for a part of Ionesco, are talking about their life together. The Old Woman is the romantic side of the playwright—childlike, full of wonder, joy, astonishment. Like his forebear Berenger, the Old Man admits that he too once had the same feelings:

> In the beginning the world filled me with astonishment. I too looked around. "What is all this?" Then I asked, "Who am I?" and I was even more astonished to discover myself. . . . But already in the earlier astonishment there had been a feeling of being threatened, this world and myself disturbed me and filled me with terror. . . . It is fascinating so long as the question mark exists. Then when one stops questioning, one gets tired. Only the threat remains, the gnawing anxiety. . . . Life is no longer a miracle, merely a nightmare. I don't know how you've been able *to keep your miracle intact* [italics mine].

To keep the miracle intact—that is the secret at the root of all Ionesco's plays. But his characters, like Ionesco himself, simply can't. Obviously some, like the Smiths and the Martins, the Logicians and Mother Peeps of the world, never knew what the mystery was in the first place. But those who *do* know can't simply choose to hold onto it. It is like the passage from childhood to adulthood, and like a child who does not want to grow up, Ionesco himself is buffeted by anxieties and fears of death, by the fear of not having lived. In "Scattered Images of Childhood" he says:

> I have always tried to live, but I have passed life by. I think this is what most men feel. To forget oneself one must not only forget one's own death, but forget that those one loves will die and the world will come to an end. The thought of the end fills me with anguish and fury. I have never been really happy except when drunk.[11]

Thus we have the strange duality in Ionesco's world—symbolized by the Old Man and the Old Woman—of childlike joy and existential anguish side by side, part of the same being, inextricably joined.

Berenger in old age, if you like. To keep the miracle intact in the face of death, in the face of pain and suffering, is the quality of life for which Ionesco's most sympathetic characters strive.

Man with Bags is a more difficult and complex play, less repetitive of earlier themes and characters than *Killing Game*. It is built around the central symbol of the journey, given embodiment in the title figure, a man with bags who is traveling somewhere but who seems constantly lost. In a widely quoted essay on Kafka, Ionesco said, "Absurd is that which is devoid of purpose. . . . Cut off from his religious, metaphysical, and transcendental roots, man is lost; his actions become senseless, absurd, useless."[12] The sentence describes accurately the condition of the central character of this play, who is known in the printed text simply as the First Man. Nameless, he struggles through the play holding desperately to his two suitcases, which seem to him more important than life itself, and he keeps speaking of a third suitcase he has lost, which, if found, would supply the clue to his identity. His papers are in it. Yet there is no third suitcase in the play. Is it imaginary? Did he lose it? Did it ever exist? Ionesco doesn't tell us.

Perhaps the parallels between the First Man and the playwright himself offer us the best clue to the play's meaning. The First Man spends most of the play in a country where he was born but from which he moved away. He has returned to the country to find his parents, to visit old friends, to discover who he is; but he is treated throughout the play as a suspicious foreigner, and he struggles to get from the French embassy papers allowing him to get back to France. The similarities to Ionesco's Romanian birth, his French citizenship, and his return to Romania to visit seem pretty evident. The confusion of the First Man's identity because of his dual nationality becomes one of Ionesco's most important symbols in the play. The most important, of course, is that of the bags, about which we feel profoundly ambivalent. On the one hand, we wish the First Man would just chuck the bags and begin to live. He's so busy worrying about losing the bags that he hasn't time to respond to the world around him. On the other hand, telling him to get rid of the bags may be like telling Vladimir and Estragon to stop waiting for Godot. Why don't they just leave, my students ask me? Because they can't, I answer. Nor can Ionesco's First Man throw away his bags. They are his identity, they are all he has. And he must learn to struggle through the bewildering maze of contradictions, red tape, and imbecilities called "life" the best he can. Because Ionesco's world is an absurd one, in an existential sense, the journey has no ultimate goal, no heavenly city like that at the end of *Pilgrim's Progress*. He must journey, because the journey is all there is.

Which finally brings us back to Beckett and to the pairing of these two figures in this chapter. Ruby Cohn reminds us that after *Godot* "it was theatrically viable to perform a deeply serious and playful play. . . . Blatant farce could jostle tragedy; obscenity could pun on the sacred."[13] Couldn't one say exactly the same thing about the impact of Ionesco? He too has opened doors for younger playwrights, and his characters too have an almost mythic status. While no single play of his has the status of *Godot*, he too has taught us to look at ourselves and the reality of our lives in a new way, to view theater in a new way, to experience language in a new way. He is one of those who can help us to keep the miracle intact.

13

Edward Albee

*We all peel labels, sweetie; and when you get through
the skin, all three layers, through the muscle, slosh
aside the organs . . . and get down to the bone . . . you
know what you do then? . . . when you get down to
bone, you haven't got all the way, yet. There's
something inside the bone . . . the marrow . . . and
that's what you gotta get at.*

—George in *Who's Afraid of Virginia Woolf?*

In a 1980 interview with the New York *Post* the late Alan Schneider, speaking of Edward Albee's career, said: "I've had this theory for several years . . . that most serious playwrights of the 20th century use one of two themes. One is you can't live without illusions. O'Neill falls into this category. . . . The other theme—and this is Ibsen, Arthur Miller, and Albee—is that you can't live without the truth."[1] While it has been, in part, the purpose of this study to demonstrate that such views as Schneider's are too simple, it is also encouraging to see that a director as important as Schneider acknowledges the centrality of the reality-illusion theme in modern drama as a whole and in the work of Edward Albee. Albee's plays, like those of Ionesco, whom Albee both admired and imitated, are primarily about social and existential illusions. His earlier plays, from *The Zoo Story* (1958) to *Who's Afraid of Virginia Woolf?* (1962), expose the illusions of the American middle class, particularly its middle-aged representatives. His late plays, from *All Over* (1971) to *The Lady from Dubuque* (1980), deal primarily with death as the final reality and our need to confront it without illusion. The middle plays—*Tiny Alice* (1964), *A Delicate Balance* (1966), and *Box* and *Quotations from Chairman Mao Tse-Tung* (1968) (generally known as *Box-Mao-Box*)—tend to combine social and existential elements, thus serving as transitions from the earlier plays to the more recent.

Albee starts out as an angry young man, a cross between Osborne and Ionesco. His target, as the preface to *The American Dream* makes clear, is the set of values that has dominated American life in the fifties:

The play is an examination of the American Scene, an attack on the substitution of artificial for real values in our society, a condemnation of complacency, cruelty, emasculation and vacuity; it is a stand against the fiction that everything in this slipping land of ours is peachy-keen.

Is the play offensive? I certainly hope so; it was my intention to offend—as well as amuse and entertain.

The Zoo Story and *The Death of Bessie Smith* launch their attacks within the framework of fourth-wall realism. *The Sandbox* and *The American Dream* are more experimental in technique, drawing primarily on absurdist dialogue that Albee seems to have learned from *The Bald Soprano*, *The Lesson*, and *Waiting for Godot*. But whatever the technique, all four plays depict the destruction of outsiders (Jerry, Bessie Smith, Grandma) by representatives of the status quo (Peter, the nurses, Mommy, Daddy, Mrs. Barker).

The Zoo Story presents the archetypal Albee situation. The setting is Central Park, a kind of neutral ground between the protected East Side, where Peter lives with his pipe, his parakeets, his daughters, and his wife, and the ragged, dirty West Side, where Jerry lives with the colored queen, the Puerto Rican family, the landlady, and the dog. The details are carefully chosen for each character. This is important to understand from the beginning, for even here Albee is not a pure realist. While his characters have names, they are essentially archetypes, standing for classes, life-styles, states of mind. They carry the characteristic details of whole groups. *The Zoo Story* is about the conflict between Peter's world and Jerry's, and the thrust of the plot comes from Jerry's attempt to make Peter recognize him as a human being, as a reality. Jerry concludes his classic story of "Jerry and the Dog," "I have learned that neither kindness nor cruelty by themselves, independent of each other, creates any effect beyond themselves; and I have learned that the two combined, together, at the same time, are the teaching emotion."

The play represents Peter's first experience in that peculiar combination of kindness and cruelty that teaches; and Albee is careful to use the audience's identification with Peter as a dramatic tool, implicating the audience in Jerry's death by having Peter hold the knife upon which Jerry impales himself. Like Peter, we want Jerry to go away, but an obscure sense of honor associated with the bench and the right to one's own place compels us to stay, because leaving, for both Peter and the audience, is a kind of admission that Jerry is there and can have the world. The only way that Jerry's death could have been avoided is through Peter's genuine recognition of him earlier in the play. Albee himself says in an interview with Michael Rutenberg, "Had Peter understood, had he not refused to understand, then I doubt the death would have been necessary. Jerry tries all through the play to teach and fails, and finally makes a last effort at teaching, and, I think, succeeds."[2]

Thus Albee's first play is one about breakthrough, about the radical means, the tragic means that a character like Jerry must use to bring Peter—Albee's first symbol of middle America—to a breakthrough from illusion (or fiction, as Albee calls it) to reality. In the other three plays no such breakthrough occurs. The man in the gray flannel suit shores up his defenses and goes on. In *The Death of Bessie Smith* (1960), the outsider, who is symbolically female, black, and an artist, is destroyed by the mores of southern white society, which manages quite successfully to deny that a problem exists by using the convenient device of attacking rather than defending. "Did you know she was dead?" the Intern asks Jack, and the Nurse echoes, "This man brought a dead woman here?" Rather than accepting the blame, they turn on Jack, and the Uncle Tom orderly accepts the verdict, "I never heard of such a thing . . . bringing a dead woman here like that." Jack becomes the convenient scapegoat for the death of Bessie Smith, and life goes on.

In *The Sandbox* (1960) and *The American Dream* (1961) Albee constructs the symbol that will dominate his work in some form or other for the rest of his career—his version of the American family. There is Grandma, the older generation, "pioneer stock" as she indicates; Mommy and Daddy, the middle generation, with Mommy the clearly dominant figure; and the Young Man, the rising generation, good-looking, muscular, but without soul, without heart. The two plays are variations on the same theme, and since *The American Dream* is the more fully developed version I will deal with it in greater detail.

At the center of the play is the conflict between Grandma and Mommy; they are protagonist and antagonist in an almost traditional sense. Mommy wants satisfaction. She is vicious, sensual without being loving, and totally materialistic. Having married Daddy for his money, she let him "bump his uglies" because he somehow paid for the right. Wanting a child, because, after all, American moms ought to have children, she adopts a "bumble" from the Bye-Bye Adoption Agency, but when the child threatens to be a human being with thoughts and feelings of its own, she has it totally emasculated. Albee's symbolism is clear and brutal—the bumble's eyes, penis, hands, and tongue are removed—the four sources of creativity in a human being. Then, naturally, the bumble turns out to be a lump of clay, and Mommy and Daddy complain bitterly. What is it that they want? The answer is—the American Dream, embodied by the soulless, mindless young man who appears toward the end of the play. He will satisfy Mommy's sexual desires without making any demands on her emotionally, he will leave poor old emasculated Daddy in peace, and he will solve Mrs. Barker's problem of fulfilling her professional duties by supplying the family with a new and ever-so-satisfactory bumble. So the play ends with Grandma's comment, "So let's leave things as they are right now . . . while everybody's got what he wants . . . or everybody's got what he thinks he wants."

It is particularly significant that this "happy ending" can only be secured by the elimination of Grandma who, as the real protagonist of the play, has the role of the Greek *eiron*, or the exposer. Like Jerry in *The Zoo Story*, she is the outsider, the sufferer whose death ought to teach the others something. Of course, in this play it doesn't. She speaks the truth in barbed and witty asides, in direct assault, in humorous cuts, but the more she speaks the truth, the more Mommy wants to get rid of her. Throughout the play Grandma is threatened with the van, a symbol both for the "old folks home," to which people like Grandma are banished because they are nuisances, and for death, which seems to occur near the end of the play when Grandma "leaves" and becomes an "offstage character." Because Grandma is "dead," she is no longer available to teach the characters anything, and they are, as a result, left with their illusions intact. We as audience, however, should not be. This is the real issue for Albee. Writing about *Virginia Woolf* in 1971, Albee commented, " . . . they saw people they knew, not themselves."[3] The same could be said of audiences of *The Sandbox* and *The American Dream*, who refused to admit they were like Mommy or Daddy or Mrs. Barker. The Mommies in the audience, being more subtle than the stage version, could dismiss the absurdist dialogue as ridiculous and extreme and thereby refuse to recognize the character beneath the surface. But Albee kept trying and completed for the 1961–62 Broadway season his most celebrated play, *Who's Afraid of Virginia Woolf?*

Virginia Woolf continues the theme of *The American Dream*, with Mommy and Daddy transmuted into Martha and George, and the American Dream into a combination of Nick and the imaginary son that George and Martha have created. A touch of Grandma remains in Martha's father, the college president who never appears onstage but has certain "pioneer" virtues associated with the older generation. Like its predecessors, *Virginia Woolf* is a play about the decline of American civilization. It is no accident that George and Martha bear the names of the first president of the United States and his wife, that George is a history teacher and Nick a biologist. As Martha and Nick complete the preliminary moves for the game of "Hump the Hostess," George pulls a book from the shelf and begins to read: "And the west, encumbered by crippling alliances and burdened with a morality too rigid to accommodate itself to the swing of events, must . . . eventually . . . fall." Closely juxtaposed to George's reading of this passage from Oswald Spengler's *The Decline of the West* is his confession to Honey: "When people can't abide things as they are, when they can't abide things as they are, when they can't abide the present, they do one of two things . . . either they turn to a contemplation of the past, as I have done, or they set about to alter the future."

The generational structure is important. Martha's father represents the past, George and Martha the present, and Nick and Honey the future. George attempts to deal with reality by ignoring it. He refuses to confront Martha's seduction of Nick; rather, he deliberately picks a book from the shelf, which only infuriates Martha and drives her more vigorously into Nick's arms. Nick, as the future, is the soulless young man of *The American Dream* in somewhat subtler form. He will move up the ranks by "ploughing pertinent wives," and as a biologist he will manipulate chromosomes so that everyone will become like him. Martha, like Mommy, finds the idea quite appealing in theory, but in reality it doesn't work out so well. Thus, the decline of America is represented by the generational structure of the play, in which each generation becomes more sterile than the one before, and the hope of the future is summed up in the impotent Nick and the empty-headed Honey, who is reduced to curling up in the bathroom sucking on brandy bottles.

Paralleling Nick as a symbol of the younger generation is Sonny Boy, George and Martha's imaginary son, blond-haired, blue-eyed, and twenty-one, that ultimate illusion who works in the play both on a personal level and on a social level. On the personal level, the son has been created by George and Martha as a kind of game, as a means of communicating. The combination of their sterility, George's professional failure, Martha's profligacy, and her father's hatred of her has led to an intolerable situation. George has escaped it in part by retreating into the past, but Martha cannot share this escape. They are intelligent people, intellectuals who enjoy playing word games, creative people who enjoy using their imaginations. So they create Sonny Boy. He is an illusion and they *know* he is an illusion. This is different from anything we have seen before. Even Henry IV, the most self-conscious fabricator of illusions in Pirandello, creates his role *after* he wakes up to find that he has been unconsciously playing it.

The game of "Bringing Up Baby" begins, perhaps as a joke, perhaps as a form of intimate playing, and it grows. We must remember that George and Martha have been at the game a long time and that the time on the

175

stage represents quite literally the final hours of a very long process. They have become so accustomed to the game that gradually Martha has ceased to distinguish between reality and illusion. She has, at times, thought of the son as real. So she breaks the compact and tells Honey about the son. This, combined with her blatant sexual advances with Nick, prompts George to destroy the illusion. It is important to understand that Albee's original title for the play was *The Exorcism*, the title he finally used for the third act. To exorcise is quite literally to cast out an evil spirit, and if the exorcism of the son is a freeing of Martha and George from the power of an evil spirit, then the ending can be read as a hopeful one, as both Albee and his director, Alan Schneider, believed it should be. "Did you . . . did you . . . have to?" Martha asks George plaintively at the very end. "Yes," he answers. "It was . . . ? You had to?" "Yes." "I don't know." "It was . . . time." "Was it?" "Yes."

If we look at the imaginary son in relation to the parallel characters in *The Sandbox* and *The American Dream*, then the implications of the destruction of the illusion become even more important. George, Martha, Nick, and Honey represent America, trapped between a sterile present and an inhuman, mechanized future. Now in middle age and having created nothing, George and Martha create the son, who is the American Dream of Success. He is our image of what we think we're supposed to be, if we're successful. Trapped in our illusion, we think we have created "the Great Society," but all around us evidence exists to the contrary. So finally we have the courage to face the truth and we try to exorcise the illusion, but the Mommies and Daddies, less creative and imaginative than George and Martha, have come to believe in the illusion, and they scream bloody murder about what the egghead intellectuals are doing. Thus, ironically, when George, the intellectual historian, does come out of his ivory tower to deal effectively with the reality of the present, he faces the wrath of the conservative middle class, which feels threatened by his truth telling.

Thus, all of Albee's work from *The Zoo Story* to *Virginia Woolf* is about the illusions Americans adopt, consciously or unconsciously, to hide the truth about themselves from themselves, which brings us to the quotation at the head of the chapter. At the core of Albee's work is his gift for peeling labels. *Virginia Woolf* is artfully structured around four games, each of which allows one or two characters to peel the labels from the disguises, the costumes worn by the others. In "Humiliate the Host" Martha is the exposer, or label peeler, and George the victim. In "Get the Guests" Martha and George combine to expose Nick and Honey. In "Hump the Hostess" Nick's myth of virility is exposed by his failure in bed, and in the climactic game, "Bringing Up Baby," George takes control of the play by destroying Martha's most comforting illusion—that of the son. For Albee, as Bigsby has thoughtfully observed, illusions cannot be equated with "Ibsen's term, 'life-lies.'" For Ibsen vital lies might be necessary for life itself. In Albee, Bigsby states, "They are, finally, destructive of life."[4]

Tiny Alice is a much more difficult play to talk about. It is also a game play, but instead of four victims, there is only one—Julian, who seems to have been chosen by the players—Lawyer, Butler, and Miss Alice—as the victim to be exposed. Cardinal, the fifth player, is for most of the play unaware of the nature of the game, but between the end of the second act and the beginning of the third, Lawyer and Butler inform him of what is really going on so that he will not spoil the results and lose his money. The difficulty with *Tiny Alice* is that the audience is never let into the secret, and while Miss Alice, Lawyer, Butler, and Cardinal seem to understand what is going on, we don't. This is acceptable up to a point. We don't know what is going on in *Virginia Woolf* either, but like Nick, who says in the play's final moments, "JESUS CHRIST I THINK I UNDERSTAND THIS," we piece together enough to be able to participate in the final catharsis. In *Tiny Alice* the character through whom we should experience the catharsis is Julian, and though we clearly pity him for the way he is used and manipulated by the forces in the play, our full participation in the drama is spoiled by a central ambiguity: we simply don't know what is happening to Julian in the play's closing scene. Two major views are possible.

The first is that God is an illusion and that faith in God is our ultimate vital lie. This would link Albee with Beckett and Ionesco and suggest parallels between the ending of this play and Berenger's agonized pleas to the Killer in Ionesco's play. What Julian comes to recognize is that, in Ann Paolucci's words, "his desire for glory and sanctification is empty and that religious sacrifice is an illusion. . . . Julian comes to understand at last that his so-called faith was in a God created in his own image. . . . That God is rejected in the soliloquy, and Alice—Nothing—is accepted in His place."[5] Thus Julian welcomes death as the final and ultimate reality, and it is death which finally engulfs him at the end.

The other view is summarized nicely by Michael Rutenberg:

> Julian, in his final moment of life, has been able to accomplish what he always believed was possible: communion with an abstraction; and if this abstraction called Tiny Alice is really his God . . . then what happens at the end of the play is the transfiguration and union of a Christian martyr with his God.[6]

Either view makes sense, but neither can be unequivocally defended, because of the ambiguity of the final scene.[7] Within the framework of both positions we can see how Albee is satirizing the worldly institutions of church and state that manipulate faith for their own ends, for whether the ending is to be taken as spiritual union or ultimate irony, Julian is to be admired for his refusal to accept the "play god," the "god created by man." That he must be shot in order to lubricate the machinery, to allow the creaky institutions to grind on, to allow Lawyer, Butler, and Miss Alice, with their clerical allies, to set up again in some new location, should not surprise us. That is consistent with the position of the earlier social plays. What is new in *Tiny Alice* is the religious and philosophical dimension, the central symbol of the model in which Tiny Alice supposedly dwells and to which the actors give their allegiance in the ceremony of Alice in the third act. Albee has moved from Ionesco to Genet, constructing a dark ritual in which characters act out parts they are seemingly destined to play, stripping off masks at unexpected points, as Alice does in Act I, scene 3, or playing roles in the manner of Claire and Solange of *The Maids*, as do Butler and Lawyer in Act II, scene 2. While all the role playing is fascinating and while the use of the model as a symbol for another dimension in which Julian is expected to believe is ingenious, there is a capriciousness about the sudden switches that leaves the reader at the end feeling more manipulated than moved or enlightened. The result is that Albee's theatrical trickery backfires on him, leaving us to admire individual strokes rather than the play as a whole.

A Delicate Balance (1966) marks another kind of change in Albee's work. Stylistically less innovative than *Tiny Alice*, it returns to the familiar living room of *The American Dream* and *Virginia Woolf*, and once again we find the American family as the cast. This time we have Agnes and Tobias as Mommy and Daddy, and once again they have no son, having lost one, Teddy, a number of years before the play opens. They have a daughter, Julia, who is about to return home for her fourth divorce, and Agnes has an alcoholic sister, Claire, who lives with them. They also have best friends, Harry and Edna, whose sudden arrival precipitates the crisis of the play. Harry and Edna, it seems, have been seized by a terror, the terror of death perhaps, a feeling of emptiness so strong that they have come to their "best friends" for solace, for love, at the very moment that Julia comes home for parental care after her failed marriage. The crisis, which begins Friday evening, ends early Sunday morning when Harry and Edna decide to go home, and the family is left with its delicate balance at least temporarily intact.

The change, as I see it, is in Albee's attitude toward his characters. *A Delicate Balance*, he has said, "is about the fact that as time keeps happening, options grow less. Freedom of choice vanishes. One is left with an illusion of choice."[8] Albee's use of the word "illusion" is interesting. Up until this point, he has been primarily a label peeler, lacerating America for its illusions, stripping away masks, leaving characters such as Peter, Martha, George, and Julian naked, with no choice but to die or begin again without illusions. Now we have a cast for whom it is too late, and that too-lateness will pervade the world of his plays for another decade. That sense of too-lateness is powerfully conveyed in Tobias's desperate speech to Harry in the play's final scene:

> The fact that I like you well enough but not enough . . . that best friend in the world should be something else—more—well, that's my poverty. So, bring your wife, and bring your terror, bring your plague.
>
> BRING YOUR PLAGUE. I DON'T WANT YOU HERE! YOU ASKED? NO! I DON'T. BUT BY CHRIST YOU'RE GOING TO STAY HERE.

People can no longer change. Julia cannot stay married, Claire cannot stop drinking, Tobias cannot love Harry in the way that a best friend ought, Edna and Harry cannot stave off the terror, and Agnes is limited to the role of maintaining order in her household, through aesthetics, through grace and manners, through decency. As she says, "There *is* a balance to be maintained, after all, though the rest of you teeter, unconcerned, or uncaring, *assuming* you're on level ground."

When Harry and Edna come, with their terror, their plague, the precarious balance teeters. Edna and Harry take over Julia's room, and deprived of her place, her refuge, she loses control, snatching up a revolver and screaming hysterically. Tobias is forced to sleep with Agnes, which in turn upsets his balance, and he spends most of the night downstairs in meditation. Claire goes off the wagon, and Agnes muses that one day she will go mad and leave them all to muddle through without her. It is not until Sunday morning when Edna and Harry depart that Agnes can say, "When the daylight comes again . . . comes order with it." The imagery of darkness and disease pervades this play as it does *Virginia Woolf*. At night the terrors are most severe, and just as the imaginary son is exorcised at dawn and George and Martha ascend the stairs to begin their new life without illusion after Honey and Nick depart, so do Tobias and Agnes, Claire and Julia have a chance to regain some peace. "Come now; we can begin the day," says Agnes as the curtain falls. But "begin the day" does not mean get rid of their old lives. It means that since they are not capable of real change, they can only sleep at night and keep the terror, the plague, at a distance where it will not harm them. They are not like the "true healers" of Camus's *The Plague*, immune to the disease. If they let the disease in, the risk is that they will be consumed by it, and so they go on, as do the characters in so many of Albee's later plays, keeping to their routines, talking, playing games, living within their limits. *A Delicate Balance*, Bigsby astutely observes, is Albee's version of Eliot's *The Cocktail Party*,[9] with Agnes and Tobias, like Lavinia and Edward left at the end to "make the best of a bad job." But there is no Celia in the play. The closest Albee had come to Celia was in Julian, but as we have seen, Eliot's clear faith is absent from *Tiny Alice*.

Albee's focus is shifting toward death. In *A Delicate Balance* it is hinted at. "What I cannot stand is the selfishness!" says Agnes. "Those of you who want to die . . . and take your whole lives doing it." That will be the central concern in *Box-Mao-Box* and *All Over*.

The voice from *Box* establishes the motif. The function of art is to create beauty and order ("Beautiful, beautiful, box."). The artist may have one of two purposes: (1) to create a vision of what can be attained, or (2) to create a picture of what has been lost:

> When the beauty of it reminds us of *loss*, instead of the attainable. When it tells us what we cannot have . . . well, then . . . it no longer relates . . . *does* it? That is the thing about music. That is why we cannot listen anymore. (*Pause*) Because we cry. (*Three-second silence*) And *if* he says, or *she* . . . why are you doing that?, and your only response is: art hurts.

The function of the artist in modern society is to *hurt*. As the voice reminds us at the end of the play, "When art hurts. That is what to remember. (*Two-second silence*) What to look for. Then the corruption . . . then the corruption is complete."

Albee realized in the process of composing *Box* and *Quotations from Mao Tse-Tung* that the two were really parts of a single play and that *Mao* would make more sense if *Box* was given both before and during the longer play as a kind of choral commentary on the speeches of the characters. Thus the new play evolved as *Box-Mao-Box* with the characters from *Mao* both literally and figuratively enclosed by the box which is the stage set for both plays.

There are four figures in the inner play: an old woman who recites a doggerel rhyme called "Over the Hill to the Poorhouse," a long-winded lady who speaks endlessly of her husband's death and her own near encounters with death, a minister who listens to the long-winded lady but says nothing, and the title character. Mao speaks his quotations carefully, reasonably, "like a teacher," Albee reminds us in the stage directions, but no one hears them. Among the characters there is no communication. The issue is not only American recognition of Red China, but American oblivion of the millions of people for whom Mao's little red book is a kind of Bible. America is sending its grandmothers to the poorhouse, its ministers are smoking their pipes and nodding, and her rich people are so insulated from reality that when they see it (death), they cannot distinguish the real thing from a movie scene:

> Oh, I remember the time the taxi went berserk and killed those people . . . all that glass . . . And I remember thinking: it's a movie! They're shooting some scenes right here on the street. (*Pause*) They weren't, of course. It was real death, and the fire, and the . . . people crying, and the crowds and the smoke. Oh, it was real enough, but it took me time to know it. The mind does that.

As in *Virginia Woolf* the play operates on both a social and personal level. Just as America is oblivious as a nation (remember, this is 1968) to the carnage it is causing in the world, so the long-winded lady seems unable to deal with the reality of her husband's death or her own. It is important to remember that Albee was forty in 1968 and that both *Box-Mao-Box* and *All Over*, his next play, are direct results of his awareness at thirty-eight or thirty-nine of his own mortality. In *All Over* the following dialogue occurs:

> WIFE: How *old* were you when you became aware of death?
> BEST FRIEND: Well . . . what it meant, you mean. The age we all become philosophers—fifteen?
> WIFE: No, no, when you were aware of it for yourself, when you knew you were at the top of the roller coaster ride, when you knew half of it was probably over, and you were on your way to it.
> BEST FRIEND: Oh. (*Pause*) Thirty-eight?

The question, then, that Albee begins to explore in *Box-Mao-Box* and then dramatizes more fully in *All Over* is: How does our awareness of our own mortality affect the way we live? What happens once the illusion of our immortality is gone? The answer Albee hopes for is that we begin to live more fully. "You see," he said in a *New York Times* interview when the play opened in 1971, "I write plays about how people waste their lives.

The people in this play have not *lived* their lives; that's what they're screaming and crying about."[10] And scream and cry they do, for two acts, while the man for whose sake they are together is dying behind a screen onstage. While we never see the man himself, the playwright keeps us fully aware of death by having the doctor and the nurse make repeated trips to his bed. The play is really a series of arias in which the characters—none of whom is named—describe their lives. The Wife sums it up best for them all near the play's end:

> All we've done . . . is think about ourselves. (*Pause*) There's no help for the dying. I suppose. Oh my; the burden. (*Pause*) What will become of *me* . . . and *me* . . . and *me*? Well, we're the ones have got to go on. (*Pause*) Selfless love? I don't think so; we love to *be* loved, and when it's taken away . . . then why *not* rage . . . or pule.

The word *pule* is well chosen; it is a good Elizabethan word meaning "to cry plaintively." And that is what she begins to do, first quietly and then in a literal explosion of "all that has been pent up for thirty years" (Albee's stage direction). "Why are you crying?" asks the Daughter. The Wife responds: "Because . . . I'm . . . UNHAPPY!" The full impact of these lines can only be understood in juxtaposition to the Doctor's "All over," which ends the play. The title words, never used until this point, refer both to the dead man and to the rest of the cast. The Wife, the Mistress, the Son, the Daughter, the Best Friend—Albee's American family once again, assembled for Daddy's death—have never lived. Their lives have been "all over" for a long time. Yet the Wife's closing cry is a cry for life. Each of them has covered up the emptiness of his or her own life, but brought together by death, each is made more aware of that emptiness and given the chance to begin again.

The word *begin* brings us to *Seascape* (1975), Albee's next play and the winner of the Pulitzer Prize for that year. In 1971, responding to his own midlife crisis, Albee had written, "I'm so much more aware of things around me now . . . I'm more aware of colors, of seasons, of textures."[11] He puts much of this awareness into *Seascape*, which, as was his custom, he carried in his head for a number of years before putting it on paper. Nancy and Charlie, the human couple in the play, are what is left of Albee's American family after the children have gone. They have reached the stage in their lives where they must begin again or die. Nancy wants to live, to experience life fully, to be always at the edge of the sea, which serves as a dual symbol in the play of that from which we must evolve (sea-escape) and that for which we yearn, the edge of land.

Charlie, like Tobias and most of the other Albee males, doesn't want to do anything. He is tired and feels like he has earned a rest. Nancy sounds the primary motif in the play by asking him, "But is that what we've come all this way for?" The question is Shavian and carries echoes, and rightly so, of the Life Force. Brendan Gill in *The New Yorker* put it nicely: " . . . no matter what age in no matter what time and place, acts of discovery remain to be undertaken. With luck, such acts will be found to have meaning; better still, there is the possibility they will bear fruit."[12]

Enter Leslie and Sarah, two lizards who are moving up in the evolutionary scale, having found that they don't belong in the sea. As Sarah says, "It was a question of making do down there or trying something else." If we take the play as an extended metaphor about life, which, in effect, all Albee's plays are, then we can argue that Leslie and Sarah are just different versions of Charlie and Nancy. We don't take their lizardness literally. Leslie and Sarah have been sent to Charlie and Nancy as a means of bringing Charlie back to life. He needs a mission, and his mission will be to help Sarah and Leslie evolve. The last line of the play is Leslie's "All right. Begin." Each is a means of life to the other. Perhaps Leslie and Sarah represent the potential for development in the human species *if* we use the experience of our failures, as Henry Hewes suggests, "to feed our experience into the evolution of a new and better species."[13]

Much of the confusion in *Seascape* stems from the fact that Charlie talks so much early in the play about wanting to go back down under the sea, as he had done as a child, a theme that is reinforced by Leslie and Sarah's feeling that they are better off as sea creatures. After all, human life offers them little but trouble, between the roar of jet planes, male ego, and emotional anguish. But Nancy reminds the lizards *and* the audience: "You'll have to come back . . . sooner or later. You don't have any choice. Don't you know that? You'll have to come back up." Shades of Shaw. It's right out of *Back to Methuselah*; we must evolve or perish, a curiously old-fashioned notion in 1975, but one that seems ironically appropriate in light of our ever-increasing arsenal of destructive technology. When I saw a production of *Seascape* in 1985, what struck me even more forcefully was that the two females, Nancy and Sarah, were so much more *human* than the males. Both men, with their distrust and their sensitive egos, are funny; and perhaps one feeling that Albee wanted to leave us with is that the first step, if we are going to be able to begin again, must be a change in the male psyche.

After a period of directing his own plays, in much the same manner as Samuel Beckett, whom he so much admires, Albee returned to his role as playwright in 1979 with *The Lady from Dubuque*, which opened on

Broadway in January 1980 under the direction of Alan Schneider, who had not done an Albee play since *Box-Mao-Box* in 1968. The play was a financial disaster, closing after only twelve performances to almost universally poor critical notices, but the play was not as bad as its initial reception indicated, and it was produced again during the summer of 1980 by the Hartford Stage Company, which had done so well with Albee's plays in 1976 and 1977, reviving *All Over* and presenting the stage premiere of the radio play *Listening*.

The Lady from Dubuque may well mark the final stage in the evolution of Albee's treatment of death. Albee's mistake in *The Lady from Dubuque* is not thematic, but technical. He unnecessarily mystifies something that is both clear and significant. In a *New York Times* interview with Robert Berkvist a few days before the official opening, Albee called the play "perfectly straightforward and clear." He goes on:

> Did you ever read Elizabeth Kubler-Ross's book on death and dying? She points out that the dying person lets loose his moorings from what passes for reality for the rest of us, and accepts a different kind of reality to die with. And that's what happens to Jo. The play is all about her moving into her own plane of reality so she can die.[14]

Once we understand this, the play makes perfect sense. Jo is dying of cancer and her husband is clinging desperately to her, trying to hold onto the physical reality of her presence. Their friends play games with Jo and Sam to keep death at a distance, to help them forget. "The games," says Albee, "are of comfort, not of pain."[15] But the games are illusion, nonetheless, a way of evading the reality of Jo's death. What she needs is someone to help her make the transition from our reality to whatever reality she needs to deal with death. Enter Elizabeth, "the lady from Dubuque," who claims to be Jo's mother, and who is, as Alan Schneider points out, "Jo's mother at a time when her own mother can't help her. . . . She's whatever Jo needs and what Sam can't give her."[16]

The title *The Lady from Dubuque* is derived from Harold Ross's statement that *The New Yorker* was not written for "the little old lady from Dubuque." Neither apparently was this play written for New Yorkers, and much of its problem lies in Albee's insistence on making bad jokes and much unnecessary mystification over who Elizabeth is. She functions in the play much as Albee and Schneider describe her role above, helping Jo transcend reality and move to another plane of being in preparation for death. She also, along with Oscar, her black sidekick, helps Sam understand that he can't hang onto Jo. Oscar reminds us, "What does

184

Sam know? Sam only knows what *Sam* needs . . . and what about what Jo needs? What does what Sam needs have to do with that?" What Sam cannot accept is Jo's need to leave him. "She diminishes," he cries. "The thing we must do about loss is, hold onto the object we're losing." But it is precisely that holding on that Jo does not need, and so Oscar and Elizabeth must forcibly break Sam's hold on Jo to allow her to die with dignity at the play's end.

Edward Albee has been an important force in American theater for almost thirty years, and neither *The Lady from Dubuque* nor the disastrous *Man with Three Arms* (1983) represents his achievements fairly. Like the late plays of Tennessee Williams, they are cries for compassion and understanding for an artist who can no longer work at the peak of his talent. They are a little sad and embarrassing. Albee will be remembered for his early plays, for that remarkable group of plays from *The Zoo Story* to *A Delicate Balance*, when he had the courage to speak out against complacency and hypocrisy in American life, in language so controversial that it prevented his masterpiece, *Who's Afraid of Virginia Woolf?*, from winning a richly deserved Pulitzer Prize. At a time when American theater was stagnating, he had the foresight to support the work of Beckett, Ionesco, and their British and American followers; and, by investing his profits in off-Broadway theater, to prepare the way for a new generation of American playwrights.

14

Harold Pinter

*The explicit form which is so often taken in twentieth
century drama is . . . cheating. The playwright assumes
that we have a great deal of information about all his
characters, who explain themselves to the audience. In
fact, what they are doing most of the time is
conforming to the author's own ideology. . . . When the
curtain goes up on one of my plays, you are faced with
a situation, a particular situation, two people sitting in
a room, which hasn't happened before and which is
just happening at this moment, and we know no more
about them than I know about you, sitting at this table.
The world is full of surprises. A door can open at any
moment and someone will come in. We'd love to know
who it is, we'd love to know exactly what he has on his
mind and why he comes in, but how often do we know
what someone has on his mind or who this somebody
is, . . . and what his relationship is to the others.*

—Interview with John Sherwood, 3 March 1960.[1]

The chapter epigraph is the right place to begin. Important changes in
art forms happen either when artists give us something we have not had
before or take away something we are accustomed to having. Pinter's
special contribution to the reality-illusion conflict stems from what he
has taken away and what that does to our perception of what is real.

The first thing we notice about a Pinter play is that we have very little
information about the characters. This is not because Pinter enjoys
mystifying us, but because Pinter believes that the omniscient playwright is as intolerable as the omniscient author. "You arrange and you
listen,"[2] he has said, stressing the *wright* in playwright. The craft of the
author is to select and arrange the incidents scenically and linguistically
without *knowing* the truth about his characters in any absolute sense.
"My characters tell me so much and no more, with reference to their
experience, their aspirations, their motives, their history. Between my
lack of biographical data about them and the ambiguity of what they say
there lies a territory which is not only worthy of exploration but *which it
is compulsory to explore*" [italics mine].[3]

This is Pinter's realism. He asks us, as audiences, to explore that territory. He does not hold back information; he presents what he knows. If his characters' speeches often seem evasive, it is because speech itself is a screen behind which we hide:

> There are two silences. One when no word is spoken. The other when perhaps a torrent of language is employed. This speech is speaking of a language locked beneath it. That is its continual reference. The speech we hear is an indication of that we don't hear. It is a necessary avoidance, a violent, sly, anguished or mocking smokescreen which keeps the other in its place. When true silence falls we are still left with echo but are nearer nakedness. One way of looking at speech is to say it is a constant stratagem to cover nakedness.[4]

For the Royal Court Theatre's production of *The Room* and *The Dumb Waiter* in 1960 Pinter wrote the following program note:

> The desire for verification is understandable but cannot always be satisfied. There are no hard distinctions between what is real and what is unreal, nor between what is true and what is false. The thing is not necessarily true or false; it can be both true and false. The assumption that to verify what has happened and what is happening presents few problems I take to be inaccurate. A character on the stage who can present no convincing argument or information as to his past experience, his present behaviour or his aspirations, nor give a comprehensive analysis of his motives is as legitimate and as worthy of attention as one who, alarmingly, can do all these things.[5]

I have quoted from Pinter at unusual length in the opening pages of this chapter not only because the playwright's critical statements are an excellent way into the plays, but because they seem to me the best explanation we have of what Pinter has taken out of his plays and why, for a very long time, it gave audiences so much difficulty.

When I apply Pinter's statements to the subject matter of this book, what I hear him saying to me is that there is no such thing as reality versus illusion because the two are inextricably mixed. All of the stories that characters tell in Pinter—Aston's story of his electric shock treatment in *The Caretaker*; Anna's, Deeley's, and Kate's stories of their pasts in *Old Times*; Spooner's and Hirst's stories about their time at Oxford and their early married years in *No Man's Land*; Max's story about Jessie in *The Homecoming*—are such mixtures of fact and invention, fabrication and genuine belief that we cannot sort out what is true and what is false. We cannot call something a vital lie, when we cannot really distinguish between lying and truth telling.

Austin Quigley puts the whole issue most clearly when he reminds us that *reality* in Pinter is not one "independent of the characters, but a reality that is constantly being negotiated by them."[6] Quigley argues cogently in *The Pinter Problem* that critics have misread Pinter because they have failed to understand "truth and reality as negotiable concepts."[7] Language in Pinter, Quigley goes on, is "interrelational" rather than "referential." If truth and reality are negotiable concepts, then language (particularly as Pinter describes it in the passage I quoted earlier) becomes a means of negotiation, not a series of references to outside symbolism or some higher truth. Language becomes a tool in the battle for survival, the struggle of each character to impose his or her view of reality upon the others.

We must remember that if reality is negotiable, then as human beings (as well as characters in plays) we are always in danger. Pinter's plays have been rightly called "comedies of menace." Two images—that of the room and that of the intruder—dominate his work from beginning to end, from *The Birthday Party* (1958) to *Betrayal* (1980). In early interviews Pinter stresses the theme over and over. "Obviously," he explains, "they are scared of what is outside the room. Outside the room is a world bearing upon them, which is frightening. . . . We are all in this, all in a room, and outside is a world . . . which is most inexplicable and frightening, curious and alarming."[8] Pinter's plays are about the fundamental menace to peace, safety, security that lies outside the rooms we have constructed to protect ourselves. But even as we say this we must remember that those who intrude are no less menaced than those who are in the room. Davies, the intruder of *The Caretaker*, is surely as much menaced as Aston, Anna as much as Deeley in *Old Times*, Spooner as much as Hirst in *No Man's Land*. The plays, frequently structured around three people, depict the struggle among the three to define reality in a way that must, by necessity, exclude not only at least one person's version of reality but that person as well.

At this point we ought to be able to proceed to an analysis of the major full-length plays and some of the more important shorter ones.

In *The Birthday Party* (1958) Stanley has retreated to Meg and Petey's boardinghouse at the seaside as a kind of sanctuary. Meg and Petey have assumed the role of parents for Stanley, with Meg pampering him as she would a baby. It has been pointed out that women in Pinter are usually mothers or whores. Their functions are archetypal. The mother figures spend most of their time cooking for their men, who usually require food or sex, but not usually both. Meg confuses her roles in *The Birthday Party*, treating Stanley both as her child and as a potential lover, finally precipitating Stanley's attempt to strangle her and rape Lulu at the climax of the second act. Stanley is caught in a position from which he cannot extricate himself. He would like to leave his room (womb), but he cannot handle the outside world. So he continues, however resentfully, to let Meg take care of him, knowing full well that the outside world will break in some day ("in a van" he tells Meg in Act I). She denies it vehemently. She doesn't want him to grow up. When the outside world does arrive, in the persons of Goldberg and McCann, it comes in a form so brutal and overwhelming that Stanley cannot stand up to it. The scene in the second act where the two intruders give Stanley the third degree is one of the most brilliant and telling in all of Pinter. It illustrates beautifully Quigley's point about language. The details do not matter. "Their function is to overcome Stanley by the quantity of accusation," Quigley says, "not by the truth-quality of any particular accusation."[9] It also reinforces Pinter's own point about verification. Why do the men ask Stanley these questions? Who are they? What was Stanley's previous connection with them? We don't know, and we don't need to know. *Times* critic Harold Hobson saw the matter very clearly:

> There is something in your past—it does not matter what—which will catch up with you. Though you go to the uttermost parts of the earth, and hide yourself in the most obscure lodgings in the least popular of towns, one day there is a possibility that two men will appear. They will be looking for you and you cannot get away. And someone will be looking for *them*, too. There is terror everywhere.[10]

The play is called *The Birthday Party* because it represents Stanley's induction into the adult world. He must leave the broken drum of childhood behind and be taken off to Monty to be "fixed" so that he can function outside the world of his room. But that very fixing is synonymous with destruction. Petey's last words to Stanley are, "Stan, don't let them tell you what to do." Then Meg enters and Petey cannot bear to tell her what has really happened to her "child." The play ends with her believing that he is still up in his room asleep.

One of the most enigmatic details in the play is Stanley's insistence that he was a concert pianist. It may be of help to us. "I gave a concert once," he tells Meg. "At lower Edmonton." It was, apparently, a great success. Then, Stanley goes on, "After that, you know what they did? They carved me up. Carved me up. It was all arranged." Certainly a parallel exists between Stanley's "carving up" and the arrival of Goldberg and

McCann. If the artist is going to make it in the world, he has to face this "carving up." "Don't you go away again, Stan," says Meg. "You stay here. You'll be better off." This is an important tension in the play. Stanley is destroyed by Goldberg and McCann because his life with Meg has rendered him unfit for the struggle in the outside world. He has no capacity to impose *his* view of reality on anyone outside the protected world of his adopted family.

The Caretaker (1960) develops the theme of menace in a more satisfying and, ultimately, in a more significant way. Pinter's plays are primarily about relationships, and the menace is more often than anything else a threat to a relationship. In *The Birthday Party* the threatened relationship is that between Stanley and Meg. One point of the play is that it needs to be. In *The Caretaker* Davies, the intruder, threatens the relationship between Aston and Mick; in fact, he threatens the very lifeblood of Aston's existence, and for that he is punished by being cast out into the world again.

At first glance Davies can hardly be called an intruder. It is, after all, Aston, the inhabitant of the room, who brings the old bum in as an act of charity. One senses throughout the play that Aston wants the companionship of Davies. He is lonely, and because of his particular condition he has great difficulty communicating. He attempts to compensate for his slowness of mind and speech by doing acts of kindness for the old man—finding him new shoes and clothing, acts that Davies repays with bitterness and resentment. It is Davies's attitude toward Aston that precipitates the crisis of the play. Puzzled by Aston, Davies turns more and more to the young brother, Mick, as a source of protection and employment. After all Mick *seems* saner than Aston, and his ideas for the development of the flat are much more exciting to the old man. It is one thing to be a caretaker, quite another to participate in an elaborate interior decorating project. Mick plays perfectly on Davies's pride and greed, establishing *his* reality in the old man's mind, finally manipulating him into a betrayal of the slow-witted older brother, which eventually costs Davies his place in the room.

The Caretaker is one of the clearest and most conventionally moral of Pinter's plays. The question being asked is, Am I my brother's keeper? and the answer is *yes*. The word *caretaker* itself is at the core of the play. Mick is responsible for Aston, Aston tries to be responsible for Davies, Davies would be allowed to stay if he were willing to be Aston's caretaker. Taking care of Aston is Mick's job, and Davies's failure to pass the human test causes his exile. The turning point is at the end of Act II and the beginning of Act III. Aston's long and brilliant monologue at the end of Act II, one of the most moving moments in all of Pinter, leaves the audience gasping, but Davies is indifferent to it. He understands nothing that Aston says. Early in Act III Davies exclaims to Mick that Aston's "got no feelings." The point is that Davies is the one with no feelings. Thus, when Mick turns on Davies at the end and exposes him, we feel, despite the cruelty of Mick's methods, a certain sense of poetic justice.

The story told by playwright Terence Rattigan is relevant at this point. Rattigan informed Pinter that he had figured out the meaning of *The Caretaker*: it was about the God of the Old Testament (Mick), the God of the New Testament (Aston), and Mankind (Davies). "Wrong," said Pinter, "It's about two brothers and a caretaker." The story is instructive. Because we are not supplied with identity cards and motives (Davies never does get down to Sidcup, we don't know what Mick does for a living, we're not sure if Aston's long story is true), we tend to come up with allegorical, mythic, or archetypal references for words and actions we cannot otherwise explain. But both Pinter's and Quigley's remarks caution us not to look for specific symbolic references. The play is, first of all, to be experienced literally, and on the literal level it is a story of three men trying to work out an arrangement about who shall have the rooms in question. The reality of what the rooms are is continually redefined during the course of the play. Allegorical readings may obscure rather than elucidate the play.

The same might be said about *The Homecoming* (1965), an extraordinarily powerful and theatrically compelling piece, which has given both readers and audiences great discomfort because it has no moral center. *The Caretaker* is primarily about brotherhood, about caring for one's brother; *The Homecoming* is a family play, but not in the American style of family plays. The cast consists of Max, the father; his three sons—Teddy, Lenny, and Joey; his brother, Sam; and Teddy's wife, Ruth. While the play is ostensibly Teddy's "homecoming," as the action develops it becomes increasingly clear that it is Ruth's homecoming. Ruth is an archetypal Pinter woman, the mother-whore supreme. Ruth can both cook for the men ("I've got the feeling you're a first rate cook") and satisfy their sexual needs; in fact this is the bargain she makes with Lenny toward the end of the play—her three-room flat, her wardrobe, her expenses in return for her services.

In two senses the play is about Ruth. She replaces Teddy in the family, sending him back to a kind of pasteurized and sterile America: "It's all rock. And sand. It stretches so far . . . everywhere you look. And there's lots of insects there." She, not Teddy, is one of the family. The sterile intellectual, who cannot even answer questions that fall within his province, will return to the campus and the swimming pool; and Ruth, who was "born quite near here" and who has never adapted to the American environment, will stay with the family where she belongs. She will also in the power structure replace the father. Literally, she will replace Jessie, the original mother-whore, but since Jessie's death Max has ruled the house with his stick and his mouth from his chair. At the end of the play Ruth has replaced Max in the chair with Max and Joey kneeling beside her and Lenny standing to one side, "watching."

Such a view may summarize adequately the central pattern of the play, but it doesn't do justice to particular twists in the action that seem to run counter to the scheme. One such twist is Teddy's commentary on his work:

> You wouldn't understand my works . . . It's nothing to do with the question of intelligence. It's a way of being able to look at the world. It's a question of how far you can operate on things and not in things. I mean it's a question of your capacity to ally the two, to relate the two, to balance the two. To see, to be able to *see!* I'm the one who can see. . . . I can observe it. I can see what you do. It's the same as I do. But you're lost in it. You won't get me being . . . I won't be lost in it.

I have called Teddy the sterile intellectual, and so he seems to be from the point of view of the family. But we have a more complex situation than that. A comment by Martin Esslin on another play, *The Lover*, may help us here. He says, "The ambivalence of our social selves, the coexistence in all of us of the primeval, amoral, instinct-dominated sensual being on the one hand, and the tamed, regulated social conformist on the other, is one of the dominant themes of Pinter's writing."[11]

It is also one of the dominant themes in all modern drama and has been a central concern of this book. Most of the playwrights we have considered have taken the position that society, by repressing healthy human instinct, creates illusory worlds against which the psyche naturally rebels. The self, to find its true reality, must look deeper than society, break through to some more meaningful reality outside the social realm. But Pinter doesn't believe that. In Arthur Ganz's view, "His plays embody the destructive as well as the gratifying elements in the urge to self-fulfillment through dominance, luxury, action, possession, sensual gratification."[12] Pinter refuses to romanticize passion. Unlike his colleague, Peter Shaffer, who seems to glorify the childlike, the natural, the genius of the primitive in *Equus* and *Amadeus*, Pinter frequently has his characters withdraw from the search for "heightened self-realization"[13] to protect themselves from their own and other people's darker and more frightening qualities. This may be precisely Teddy's choice in *The Homecoming*. He will retire to the safety of the campus and the distance of America where he can, in this larger symbolic room, continue his role as artistic observer without involving himself directly in the more vital, yet profoundly disturbing, life of the family.

After *The Homecoming* there is a change. *Landscape* and *Silence* (1970), *Old Times* (1971), and *No Man's Land* (1975) seem to be built on a different dramatic technique and a different pattern. The characters live more and more in the past, have more and more difficulty communicating, and retreat frequently into personal memories and/or fantasies, which they articulate in long, often highly lyrical speeches. The purpose of these speeches is often to impose *their* views of reality on the other characters, or at least on *one* other character whom they wish to influence or control.

In *Landscape* and *Silence* Pinter uses for the first time a technique similar to that of Beckett's *Play*, in which there is a combination of extreme compression with the almost total separation of the characters into personal worlds. The stage directions to *Landscape* indicate that the scene is the kitchen of a country house. "Beth sits in an armchair, which stands away from the table to its left. Duff sits in a chair at the right corner of the table. Duff refers normally to Beth, but does not appear to hear her voice. Beth never looks at Duff, and does not appear to hear his voice. Both characters are relaxed, in no sense rigid." The fact that the characters are relaxed would indicate that this sort of situation is common. We might argue that Beth's speech is purely interior monologue, not meant to represent speech at all, and that Duff is speaking at least part of his speech to her while she is dreaming in the armchair of the day she spent at the beach with her lover (who might even have been Duff himself). Neither seems to know the other's thoughts. The title *Landscape* suggests that each character is creating his/her own painting of his/her own interior landscape. In a passage quoted earlier Pinter calls speech "a stratagem to cover nakedness." This passage is reproduced on the back of the Grove Press edition of *Landscape* and *Silence*. My own reading of the plays would suggest that the quotation is inappropriate here. Pinter made the statement in 1962, and it applies well to the way language is used in *The Birthday Party*, *The Caretaker*, and *The Homecoming*. Davies and Mick, Goldberg and Lenny, for example, make long speeches. They pour out torrents of words, tell bizarre, fascinating stories most of which are probably not true. This is all part of that "necessary avoidance" Pinter speaks of in the passage, part of the way these characters seek to control reality. In *Landscape* both characters are closer to nakedness, because they are more nearly confessing their real thoughts and feelings. Duff asks:

> Do you like me to talk to you?
> *Pause*
> Do you like me to tell you about the things I've been doing?
> *Pause*
> About all the things I've been thinking?

There is a difference between language as thought and language as spoken dialogue. We often hide our real thoughts behind the banalities of everyday speech, and no one is better than Pinter at reproducing those banalities with a sharp edge, but in *Landscape* the language is more heightened and poetic, suggesting a greater revelation of the inner self. In fact, we may argue that it is precisely because the other doesn't hear that each character is able to reveal more.

The same thing is true in *Silence*. Stage directions indicate very simply, "Three areas. A chair in each area." The chairs are occupied by Ellen, Rumsey, and Bates. It appears that Ellen has been in love with both men and has had sexual relations with both at different times during the past. Again, reality exists only in the individual consciousness of each character. Pinter breaks the pattern by allowing Ellen to interact with both Rumsey and Bates in certain portions of the play, but the language of the interaction is terse and noncommittal. In part, the play is about the difference between what relationships really are and what people hope and imagine they will be. The characters carry these relationships in their minds, building them up with their imaginations, only to be let down by actual events. We see the three characters before, during, and long after the periods of their relationships, and in those portions of the play which take place in the old age of the three characters, even memory has begun to fail—or is it that Ellen does not want to share her intimate memories with her drinking companion and so lies, saying, "I have nothing to tell her about the sexual part of my youth. I'm old, I tell her, my youth was somewhere else, anyway I don't remember."

As the play moves to its close, the speeches become shorter and shorter, mere fragments of earlier scenes, tiny cuttings of memory adrift in the characters' minds with nothing to anchor them. In the final moments each fragment is separated from the next by a silence, not merely a pause, but a silence, which must to a theater audience seem much longer than the speech itself. The stage directions indicate twenty-five such silences on the last seven pages, ten of them on the last two pages. "When true silence falls, we are still left with echo but are nearer nakedness," says Pinter. At this point reading becomes totally inadequate. We must see the play and watch the expressions on the actors' faces, sense what they are feeling, during those silences.

Old Times develops in a full-length play some of the techniques that Pinter had experimented with in the two short plays. Again we have the separation of the characters. The play begins with "Deeley slumped in armchair, still. Kate curled on a sofa, still. Anna standing at the window, looking out." The play ends with Deeley in the armchair, and Anna and Kate on the two divans. The overall style of the play is not nearly so radical as that of the one-act plays, however. The characters talk to one another and appear to listen. On the surface the play is even realistic: Anna, an old friend of Kate's, has come to visit Kate and Deeley after an absence of a good many years. In the course of the evening the three reminisce about old times. What makes the play peculiar is that each character has a different version of what actually happened during that period when Kate gradually transferred her affection from Anna to Deeley and decided to marry him. Which of the versions is correct? Are any? They can't all be true because they contradict one another. According to Deeley, Kate was the only person in the theater when he saw *Odd Man Out*; in Anna's version the two girls went to see the film together. Anna denies having met Deeley; according to Deeley he gazed at her thighs at the Wayfarer's Tavern. In turn, Anna tells a story about a man (presumably Deeley) crying in Kate's lap, a happening that he does not recall. At the very end of the play Kate tells a story that seems almost to deny Anna's existence. "He asked me once, at about that time, who had slept in that bed before him. I told him no one. No one at all."

Remembering Quigley's caution that language in Pinter is interrelational rather than referential is particularly useful in dealing with this play. The issue is not one of lying versus truth telling. Anna says, "There are some things one remembers even though they may never have happened. There are things I remember which may never have happened but as I recall them so they take place." Memory is as much a part of reality as the events themselves. If a play such as this one is based on three characters sharing their memories, imposing, if you like, their memories on one another, then the play becomes a power struggle to see whose version will be accepted, whose version can be made to control the future lives of the people involved. What actually happened in the past is meaningless; what is happening onstage in the present is what matters, and what is happening seems to be a battle between Anna and Deeley for possession of Kate. Both love Kate, all their stories are about Kate, all their actions are directed toward Kate.

In this light, *Old Times* could be viewed as Kate's crisis. Having once lived with Anna in an intimate (possibly sexual) relationship, Kate gave up Anna for Deeley and settled in a quiet part of the country remote from the life in London associated with Anna. Her marriage with Deeley is not doing well. Symbolically, Kate could be considering a return to Anna, and so Anna appears at this moment, like Hilda Wangel, because Kate needs her. It is also possible, as Arthur Ganz does, to view Kate and Anna as two sides of the self. Anna is "an aspect of Kate—her vital, sensual self, from which she has retreated in her domestic heterosexual relationship with Deeley."[14] Thus Kate, after a long period of withdrawal under Deeley's domination, may be trying to reassert herself and recover the "Anna" aspect which has lain dormant for so long.

We might think of *Old Times* as Pinter's "midlife crisis" play. The playwright had just passed his fortieth birthday when he wrote it; Deeley, Anna, and Kate (played by Pinter's wife, actress Vivien Merchant) are all in their forties. They are, characteristically, looking back on the first half of their lives and trying to find a way of beginning the second half. The real crisis might be Deeley's rather than Kate's. From his point of view the issue is *his* renewal, which must come through Kate or Anna. The fact that he turns to each of them at the end of the play (repeating the action that Anna has described earlier), sobs in Kate's lap, and ends in the armchair suggests that he finds no answer to his problem in either woman. Quigley asserts: "In striving to adjust to one another, Pinter's characters are negotiating not only truth and reality but their very freedom to engage their preferred identities in the environments that surround them."[15] The statement applies particularly well to *Old Times*. The frustration of the characters, the same frustration that we will see in *Betrayal*, stems from the fact that no one can engage in his or her preferred identity without excluding an aspect of reality, of the self or others, that simply *cannot* be excluded. The issue of inclusion and exclusion becomes absolutely central in the last two major plays, *No Man's Land* and *Betrayal*.

In *No Man's Land* Pinter moves from middle age into old age. The central figures are now in their sixties. The play, Pinter's first for the National Theatre under Peter Hall, is an acting tour de force for John Gielgud (Spooner) and Ralph Richardson (Hirst). It is like David Storey's *Home* (1970) without the women. The play echoes all of Pinter's earlier work in different ways. Spooner's condition as the outcast derelict reminds us of Davies in *The Caretaker*. The sinister servants, Briggs and Foster, are Goldberg and McCann or, in another way, Mick and Aston. The family structure reminds one of *The Homecoming*. In its emphasis on the past and the need to recall the past, the play is more like its immediate predecessors.

The originality of the play lies in Hirst. We've seen Spooner before, the outcast ingratiating himself to become accepted in the family, to be kept in "the room," but Hirst is new. What seems to be happening in the play is a kind of cricket match between Hirst and Spooner, in which each has his innings, each his chance to win the game. Spooner's problem is that he overplays his power game in each of his innings and frightens his opponent out of the match, thereby winning the innings but losing the game. In both acts, Spooner becomes overly aggressive, attacking Hirst for his portrait of his pastoral past in the first act and viciously attacking him for his sexual mores in the second act. In each act Spooner follows up these powerful innings with a request to be kept on in Hirst's employ as a friend and/or secretary.

During the course of the innings, both men tell remarkably inventive stories that emphasize England's idyllic past, golden days at Oxford, afternoons in the country, bucolic literary sessions and poetic readings. Nowhere in Pinter are the stories more absurd; nowhere does the audience come so close to rebelling against the whole fabric of the play. Spooner is a phony, Hirst is a phony. Who is Charles Wetherby? Did either man go to Oxford? Is either a poet? In *No Man's Land* we are frozen forever in a tissue of lies and deceit, a tissue of games, roles, fabrications controlled by the servants, in which all the manners of polite society are observed but underneath which Hirst lives a kind of death in life, "which never changes, which never grows older, but which remains forever, icy and silent." Maybe, we think at first, Spooner could change that, but Spooner at heart is no better than Briggs and Foster. He too can bite. And if he is to be expelled, which it seems almost certain at the end that he will be, then he, like Davies earlier, deserves it.

And so, after all this, where are we? I think of Pinter's work as a field of glaciers in the North Sea, powerful, awesome, hidden in the depths of the icy waters, brilliant, merciless, the product of a keen eye and one of the finest ears for the nuances of English speech in modern times. But if you're climbing the icy walls there is no place for a foothold. There is no place to stick a teleological pickax or an ontological ice hammer. In this, Pinter shares a certain brutal honesty and pessimism about the human situation with the other authors in the last part of this study, but his world is even less inviting than that of Beckett and Ionesco. Perhaps "no man's land" itself is a good image for that world, a neutral zone between two battlefields that belongs to no one, a zone into which combatants come to struggle for control. In *Betrayal* we see that world more clearly than in any other Pinter play, because the playwright has made it easier for us.

There are three characters—Robert, his wife, Emma, and his best

197

friend, Jerry. Jerry has betrayed his friendship with Robert by having an affair with Emma. Emma has betrayed her marriage and, in turn, her relationship with Jerry by lying to him about how much Robert knows. Robert appears to have betrayed his relationship with Emma by having had several affairs, but we are not certain. Pinter tells the story in such a way—at least partly chronologically in reverse—that we, as audience, are much more aware of *how* the characters are operating than we have ever been before. We see the hidden codes behind their words and actions and can therefore interpret meanings that are not available to the characters being manipulated by the codes. We know what the game is, what the rules are, and, finally, why the game doesn't lead anywhere. Quigley, in his new study, summarizes it astutely:

> The inclusions and exclusions, the revealing and concealing that give these episodic relationships their novelty and value cannot be indefinitely controlled, and the choice repeatedly confronted is how long to try to salvage and when to decide to dispense with relationships that are initially sustained by, and eventually betrayed by, their basis in special occasions.[16]

The key word here is "controlled." In *Betrayal* each character tries to control the situation by getting as much information as possible from the other two characters while giving away the least amount possible. Each tries to find out what the others know without coming right out and asking. Thus Pinter constructs an elaborate "code" language, especially for the two men, by means of which they can talk about the latest Spinks or Casey novel or about playing squash or the difference between boy and girl babies while actually giving and receiving information and at the same time conveying deeper layers of meaning to the audience, which is, almost for the first time in Pinter, in on the game. In the world of *Betrayal* romanticism is an escape, not a possibility. The intense hope with which Jerry begins his affair with Emma (significantly in the play's final scene) seems to parallel Robert's reading of Yeats on Torcello and Jerry's retreat to the Lake Country with Wordsworth. These escapes, Pinter affirms, are both temporary and inadequate because they demand the exclusion of too much. We may hate the modern world, the latest Spinks or Casey novel, and yearn to create for ourselves a private, romantic world in which the betrayals of reality do not exist, but we cannot. We must come back from the Lake Country, from Torcello, from the apartment in another part of town, to the world of marriages, children, friendships, and business, in which relationships must be continually negotiated and renegotiated. This is Pinter's reality.

One for the Road, Pinter's most recent play, brings us full circle, reminding us both of how Pinter has changed and of his consistency. Like *Betrayal* it is crystal clear. "It describes a state of affairs," Pinter tells us in an introductory essay, "in which there are victims of torture. You have the torturer, you have the victims."[17] In its explicitness *One for the Road* demonstrates how Pinter's style has evolved from the highly metaphorical pieces of the early years, such as *The Birthday Party* and *The Dumb Waiter*; but as Pinter himself points out in the interview from which I have just quoted, his new play, like the early plays, is "essentially about the abuse of authority."[18] Pinter's reality from beginning to end is one in which hidden figures—the man upstairs in *The Dumb Waiter*, Monty in *The Birthday Party*, and the God-fearing, patriotic government figures in *One for the Road*—control people's lives. Reality is menacing, and the sad truth is that, for us as for Harold Pinter, it is even more menacing in 1988 than it was when Pinter began his career in 1958. Of all the thoughts this playwright leaves us with, this one is the most sobering.

15

Theater as Reality/ Reality as Theater

The real theme of the play is the theme of illusion . . .

—Genet on *The Balcony*

They will not experience a story, but watch a theatrical event . . .

—Handke on *Kaspar*

Of course it was Pirandello who started it, but something has happened during the period since Beckett and Ionesco arrived on the scene to make it grow in a direction far different from anything Pirandello imagined—this business of writing plays about plays, novels about novels. Borges, Barth, and Pynchon in fiction, who have called their productions "fictions" rather than stories; Weiss, Genet, Handke, and Stoppard in the theater. Do we still call them plays? No, "theatrical events," says Peter Handke, yet "play" is a good word, because so much of what we will be examining in this chapter involves a self-consciousness about playing. June Schlueter in her fine 1979 study calls this phenomenon "metafictional characters in modern drama."[1] I like to call it "theater as reality/ reality as the theater."

"Me—to play," says Hamm in *Endgame*. Self-consciousness about playing, awareness of the play as play, is the signal element in the plays to be examined in this chapter. In Peter Weiss's *Marat/Sade* (1965) we in the audience are seeing a play written by Weiss about "the Persecution and Assassination of Jean Paul Marat, as Performed by the Inmates of the Asylum at Charenton."[2] When, for example, we see the "character" Marat, we are not seeing the historical Jean Paul Marat as interpreted by Peter Weiss, the playwright. We are seeing the historical Marat as interpreted by the Marquis de Sade, a character in Weiss's play, and played by an inmate who suffers from paranoia. To put it another way we have a Marat who is simultaneously a twentieth-century Marxist (Weiss's spokesman), an eighteenth-century rabble-rouser (the figure of the French Revolution), a paranoic (the inmate), and a character in a play (he reads the lines Sade sets down before him). To put it still another way, we have *layered* theater. As Michael Goldman has pointed out in *The Actor's Freedom*, the actor who plays the part of Marat (or any of the other inmates) has three levels of preparation—the naturalistic or Stanislavskian, the Brechtian, and the Artaudian. He must actually learn how a madman behaves. In fact, Peter Brook, the director of the famous Royal Shakespeare Company production of *Marat/Sade*, actually took his cast to an asylum so that they could study the behavior of the insane. He also gave them extensive training in Artaud's theories and methods.

Thomas R. Whitaker summarizes this multiplicity of levels nicely by calling it "consciousness of consciousness. As our late romanticism gives another twist to the baroque, every point of view tends to include an insistence that it is only a point of view."3

Thus, *Marat/Sade* expands and multiplies the consciousness of both actor and audience. To play a role in *Marat/Sade* the actor must operate on several levels at the same time. He cannot simply *be* Marat in the Stanislavskian sense, nor can he play Marat in the Brechtian sense. He must at once be the madman, illustrate Sade's script, and play Weiss's Marxist with a sincerity and a passion that transcend the limits Sade would place on him. He must overcome his own script. As actor, Marat is playing to at least three audiences. When he speaks, he speaks to his own followers and enemies (the inmates); to the director of the asylum, Monsieur Coulmier, and his wife and daughter, who are present for the occasion along with other visiting ladies and gentlemen from the bourgeois culture that Marat is condemning; and, of course, he speaks directly to us. In this way, we as audience are offered multiple choices of how we relate to the action. We can relate to Marat directly, we can relate to him through the admonitions and comments of Sade, we can relate to him through the story or through Coulmier and the establishment.

For Weiss, then, as Whitaker says, every point of view is only a point of view. But we have the sensation, after repeated viewings of *Marat/Sade*, that if we get enough points of view we will be closer to reality in some sense. The way the play works allows us to experience it differently each time we see it. We can listen to different people, watch different things; the layered-ness may confuse, even frighten us at first. But so does life. The point of Weiss's theatricality is not simply to play the reality-is-illusion-is-reality-is-illusion game. That will come with Genet. Weiss is grounded in a different kind of worldview, and he uses his multiple levels of theater in a more strictly Artaudian sense than Genet to expand the world of the audience, to literally blow the audience out of its comfortable bourgeois chairs into a new consciousness of itself as participants in the powerful feelings it has repressed out of fear. Thus, as Ruby Cohn has pointed out, the impact of *Marat/Sade* in the theater is based on the reality of *both* inner *and* outer action in the play and the relevance of both "to the reality in which we live."[4]

The central metaphor of the play is that of *insanity*. On the surface the play revolves around the famous Marat-Sade debates, with Marat representing the Marxist, revolutionary point of view, and Sade a radical individualism. The debates are important, but they must be viewed as taking place theatrically within the framework of another set of dualities: insanity-sanity and freedom-repression. The insane people who are locked in the asylum play the parts of the followers of Marat. As the action develops, they keep singing, "Marat we're poor . . . we want our revolution NOW." Metaphorically, the insane and the poor may be equated. The inmates of the asylum of Charenton want their freedom in 1808 in the same way that the poor people of Paris wanted theirs in 1793. The same people are equated in Weiss's view with the soldiers who were asked to fight in Vietnam in 1964. The people who cannot abide the standards and values of the normal world are either imprisoned or called insane. Listen to Artaud:

> And what is an authentic madman? It is a man who has preferred to go mad, in the sense in which society understands the term, rather than be false to a certain superior idea of human honor. That is why society has had all of those of whom it wanted to rid itself, against whom it wanted to defend itself because they had refused to become its accomplices in certain acts of supreme filthiness, condemned to be strangled in its asylums. For a madman is also a man to whom society did not want to listen and whom it wanted to prevent from uttering unbearable truths.[5]

Now listen to the great British psychologist, R. D. Laing:

> In the context of our present pervasive madness that we call normality, sanity, freedom, all our frames of reference are ambiguous and equivocal. . . . A man who prefers to be dead rather than Red is normal. A man who says he has lost his soul is mad. A man who says that men are machines may be a great scientist. A man who says he *is* a machine is "depersonalised" in psychiatric jargon.[6]

What *Marat/Sade* seems to be enacting, in the view of Artaud and Laing, is the eternal paradox that the truly sane are locked up and called insane, thereby becoming insane, not as a result of their innate psychological condition, but as much because of being locked up. The repression of their freedom causes them to be increasingly violent until they "illustrate" their insanity by behaving in the very manner that the "sane" people outside expect them to behave. This seems to be the point of Sade's play. If the inmates become violent and finally end the play by raping the nuns and tearing the place to pieces, it is not because they are insane. Sade admonishes Marat:

> Marat
> these cells of the inner self
> are worse than the deepest stone dungeon
> and as long as they are locked
> all your Revolution remains
> only a prison mutiny
> to be put down
> by corrupted fellow prisoners.

"And what's the point of a revolution / without general copulation," sing the citizens/inmates. "What kind of city is this?" asks Charlotte Corday, watching the children play with little toy guillotines. Sade is arguing for some transformation of the self at the deepest level, which would prevent the disease from reaching the point of outburst that it does in the revolution/play. But the play itself tells us nothing about how to cure our illness. The Brechtian rabble-rousing priest, Jaques Roux, screams the last words, "When will you learn to take sides?" He tries to force the patients back into some order, but caught up in their "mad and marchlike dance, many of them hop and spin in ecstasy." Coulmier "incites the nurses to extreme violence," the patients are struck down and then retaliate violently, and Sade ends the play by "laughing triumphantly." Coulmier doesn't get the point; he will banish further plays at the asylum because they are dangerous, because they rile up the patients too much. But what about us?

We are not going to start a revolution. We are not going to end the war, unlock the prison, release the inmates of asylums. It is unlikely that either Marat's rhetoric or Jaques Roux's rabble-rousing will cause us to change either our social and political affiliations or our economic status. A selection from Peter Brook's *The Empty Space* may help us here; he asks us to consider what happens to the inmates of an asylum during sessions of psychodrama:

> On certain days, for some of the inmates, there is an event, something unusual, something to look forward to, a session of drama. . . . I have no

views at all on the value of psychodrama as a treatment. Perhaps it has no lasting medical result at all. But in the immediate event there is an unmistakable result. Two hours after any session begins all the relations between the people are slightly modified, because of the experience in which they have been plunged together. As a result, something is more animated, something flows more freely, some embryonic contacts are being made between previously sealed off souls. When they leave the room, they are not quite the same as when they entered. . . . Neither pessimism nor optimism apply: simply, some participants are temporarily, slightly, more alive.[7]

Marat/Sade can affect us in the same way. Theater of this sort may rightly be called "magic," in the sense that it has the power to transform, to make the invisible visible, to make us experience staged reality in such a way that we come to experience our own daily reality differently. For two and a half hours I can cast away the concept of a responsible, ordered social self and immerse myself in that half-sacred, half-blasphemous series of acts taking place on the stage. I move with the actors in a ritual of song, dance, screaming, nightmare, rhetoric, pain, rejoicing, eroticism, violence, revolution, and death. All the time I know that it is not real; I know that the chaos and violence are carefully orchestrated. I also know that I need the intensity, the passion in my own life that is presented onstage, but I fear and repress those feelings that will allow the intensity to surface, and so I allow the actors to "play" these things for me or, in a sense, *with* me. I allow them to enact my need to transcend that smaller theater we have placed ourselves in, the theater of the everyday. We seat ourselves in rows, and the women rattle their packages from Bonwit's and Lord & Taylor's, and in the process we are changed, temporarily, like the inmates described by Brook. And the actors, too, are changed by their participation in the magic. Ruby Cohn reminds us that "Ian Richardson, who played Marat in Peter Brook's production of the play, claimed: 'We have had actual physical violence of a very serious sort breaking out.' "[8] An important reminder, indeed, about both the power and the danger of the process.

This, then, is what I mean by "theater as reality." I mean that we are more changed by the action of performance, to use Whitaker's phrase, than by the performed action. It is *the theatrical act itself* that renews us, not the story that the theatrical event portrays. This is the basic point of the theories of Antonin Artaud upon which both Weiss and the *Marat/Sade* director, Peter Brook, have drawn so heavily. As Martin Esslin points out, "For Artaud the theater was not just a religious art, an art form serving a religion, but a manifestation of the religious impulse itself."[9] Note that it is not the action or the story of the play which serves the religious impulse, but the theater itself. Shortly before his death, Artaud wrote the following poem:

> And I shall henceforth devote myself
> exclusively
> to the theater
> as I understand it
> a theater of blood
> a theater which at every performance will have
> achieved some gain
> *bodily*
> to him who plays as well as to him who comes to see the playing,
> moreover
> one doesn't play
> one acts.
> The theater is in reality the *genesis* of creation.
> It will be done.[10]

At the heart of the religious impulse is the idea of rebirth, renewal, or resurrection, not so much a life after death (though that is one form of it) as a qualitative change in this life that will supply to us the feeling of innate vitality. It is symbolized in the Greek tradition by Dionysus, and as we have seen "the ghost of joy," or the ghost of Dionysus, has haunted us all the way through this study. And Goldman reminds us in his recent essay on Beckett that the struggle between vitality and deadness is not only a central theme in modern drama, but that "every important modern play attempts to revitalize a stage it thinks of as dead."[11] The audience comes to the theater in pursuit of the ghost of Dionysus; the audience seeks rebirth through participation in the theatrical event. "The theater is in reality the *genesis* of creation," says Artaud. And what do we create? If the event itself is rich and vital enough, we create ourselves. We participate with Charlotte Corday, actively, fearfully, in the ritual murder of the god (Marat), and out of his blood we are born, renewed, changed momentarily, charged like the inmates who have participated with us with new energy. And then the magic is over, and we come out, knowing that the experience must be sought again and again. How small conventional theater is by comparison.

***

With Jean Genet we look at the other side: reality as theater. In Weiss the term *theater* is associated, as in Artaud, with *acting*, the acting out of myths, the acting out of the deeper impulses of the self to give them expression—"theater as reality," as I have called it. With Genet the term theater is associated with illusion. To explain this I would like to look at three plays: *The Maids* (1947), *The Balcony* (1956), and *The Blacks: A Clown Show* (1959). I am going to summarize the action of each play before I discuss it, because, particularly in the case of Genet, it is not at all obvious to the audience what is happening on the stage, and part of the power and mystery of each play is that sense that something different is actually happening from what the audience thinks it is seeing. In order to understand the plays we must first know what is happening.

In the first play two maids, Solange, the elder, and her sister, Claire, alternate playing the roles of their mistress, Madame, and the other maid. On this evening, Claire plays Madame and Solange plays Claire, while Madame is out of the house. This gives each of the maids an opportunity to act out her ambivalent love-hate attitude toward Madame, both by playing her and playing against her. An alarm clock rings, and the two maids suddenly revert to themselves, dropping their theatrical tones, and begin to put away the "props" they have used for their masquerade. They want to kill Madame but haven't the strength, so they have turned in her lover, Monsieur, to the police, for robbery. When Madame returns from the police station, they try to kill her by poisoning her tea, but she doesn't drink it. Instead, hearing that Monsieur has been released, she rushes off, leaving Claire and Solange to continue enacting the roles they had begun before she returned. This time, Claire, as Madame, drinks the tea, poisoning herself, while Solange as Claire exults in Madame's death and the joy and freedom of the two maids.

As Jean Paul Sartre has pointed out in his introduction to the play, "It is the element of fake, of sham, of artificiality, that attracts Genet to the theatre. He has turned dramatist because the falsehood of the stage is the most manifest and fascinating of all."[12] In Genet's play nothing is real; all is illusion. In fact, it was Genet's hope that the three roles of Solange, Claire, and Madame be played by adolescent boys. In this way, the audience would know immediately that an illusion was being perpetrated. It would also feel the double poignancy of Solange and Claire's exclusion from Madame's world, if it knew that the boys were acting out their own fantasy of both hating and wanting to be accepted by society. Genet's primary point is that the world that our social roles represent is as illusory as the theatrical world. When Solange and Claire play roles, they do so with the consciousness that both their daily roles and the roles that they play in their "theatricals" are illusory.

The difference between Genet's world and those of the other playwrights we have been exploring lies precisely here: in Genet's world

206

there is no escape from illusion; one can choose which illusions to play, how to play them, and what theatrical form with which to give them life. But there is no such thing as shedding illusions: reality is theater—in Ruby Cohn's words, "I am what I play."[13] This is the difference, for example, between Hedda Gabler's death and Claire's. Both are suicides, both in part caused by the inability of the character to break out of the social trap in which she is caught. Both wish to be *free*. Within the framework of Ibsen's view, Hedda achieves a kind of freedom in her death, a triumph over the Judge Bracks of the world who would limit that freedom. Claire's death is a theatrical act, a playing of her role *all the way*; it has no transcendent meaning. If Claire were not Claire, she would be Madame. If Claire were Madame, she would not be free either. It makes no difference; it just must be played well.

One thinks of Genet's interview in *Playboy*. When asked by the interviewer in 1964 if he was still a thief, he answered:

> I don't steal the same way the average person does. In any case, I don't steal the way I used to. I receive big royalties from my books and plays— at least they seem big to me—and the royalties are the result of my early thefts. I continue to steal, in the sense that I continue to be dishonest with regard to society, which pretends that I'm not.[14]

Genet never denies his own falseness. His role as a writer in society is a theatrical act as much as his role as a thief or a prisoner was. He plays it differently, realizing all the while that it is a role.

This is the point that director Peter Zadek made about *The Balcony* in 1957: "Genet's great importance in the theater is his theatricality. He does not 'use' the theater to imitate the externals of our world; he shows us that our world is as fake as grease paint itself, and that therefore the theater can be the perfect mirror held up to the *danse macabre* which is life as Genet sees it."[15]

In *The Balcony* Genet uses one of civilization's oldest institutions, the house of prostitution, to symbolize the human condition. The play's central figure, Madame Irma, has modernized and sophisticated her operation to the point where the actual sexuality is subordinate to the fantasies each of the customers plays en route to his climax. The function of "the Grand Balcony" is to set up and prepare "secret theatres" for each of her customers, the most important of whom are the Bishop, the Judge, and the General, men who have chosen their fantasies deliberately from the roles of their counterparts in the real world. In that "real" world a revolution threatens to overturn the country's establishment.

What Genet manages to do is to juxtapose, in grotesque and theatrically brilliant fashion, the images that the false Bishop, Judge, and General have created with society's need for illusion or, to be more specific, society's inability to function without *theatrical images of religious, political, and military leadership.*

The revolution cannot proceed without an image, and so Roger, its leader, persuades the girl, Chantal, a refugee from Madame Irma's establishment, to play the role. "At least the brothel has been of some use to me," she says. "It's taught me the art of pretense, of acting. I've had to play so many roles that I know almost all of them." When it looks as if Chantal will succeed, Madame Irma is persuaded to impersonate the Queen; and the Bishop, Judge, and General are pushed into the roles of their *real* counterparts in society. Chantal is shot, and when the people see that the images they have worshiped are still alive, the revolution fails and the Bishop concludes that "there will never be a movement powerful enough to destroy our imagery." The Bishop, Judge, and General, of course, much prefer their roles at Madame Irma's to their roles in society. The Bishop puts it beautifully: "For ours was a happy state. And absolutely safe. In peace, comfort, behind shutters, behind padded curtains. . . . You tore us brutally from that delicious, enviable, untroubled state." Thus Genet suggests that the theater is no different from the world outside in its use of roles, masks, costumes; it is simply safer, more comfortable, less threatening to those who participate. Madame Irma reminds the audience as the play ends of their roles in life:

> Prepare yours . . . judges, generals, bishops, chamberlains, rebels who allow the revolt to congeal. I'm going to prepare my costumes and studios for tomorrow. . . . You must go home, where everything—you can be quite sure—will be falser than here.

It sounds like Pirandello, but it isn't. Pirandello might agree with Genet that life is a series of roles, of masquerades played both publicly and privately. But we sense in Pirandello the idea of the unified self, that self we get to when the layers of the onion are peeled away, that core of being that he as an artist represents in his heroes—his Ponza and his Henry who are forced to play roles to protect that *authentic* selfhood. Genet does not believe in that self. Human beings in Genet are protean, ever adapting, ever playing new roles for whatever theater in which they may need to survive.

One reason the leftists were disappointed by both *The Balcony* and *The Blacks* is that the plays insisted that the revolutions behind and under the primary actions were as illusory as the images associated with contemporary life in its current political and social structures. Roger is no better than the Chief of Police. It is *our* illusion, says Genet, that the revolution might improve things; Roger has his need for imagery, too, and when the revolution is over, his choice of the Chief of Police as image allows the real Chief to descend to his Mausoleum forever, perpetuated now in life by those who will keep his image alive, which is, after all, *him*. And Genet keeps reminding us, *us*.

With *The Blacks* Genet takes his performance one step further; he adds one more layer. In *The Maids* it was two maids playing their mistress. In *The Balcony* it was three men pretending to be a Bishop, a Judge, and a General, who in turn are forced to impersonate real bishops, judges, and generals. In *The Blacks* we add the self-consciousness of performance.

The summary would go something like this. A group of black actors—twelve of them—enters. Seven, in evening dress, announce that they will perform for us. The other five, wearing white masks, will play the roles of the Court: the Missionary, the Judge, the Governor, the Queen, and the Valet. They will symbolize white society, the society against which the play is directed, but they will clearly be black actors playing caricatured roles prepared in a previously written script. The seven will act out the story of the murder of a white woman, played by one of the seven who is dressed in blouse and skirt and also wears a white mask. In turn, the court will act out its horror at the murder and its desire to revenge their murdered "sister." But at the end it is not the "blacks" who die but the "whites" who crumple in a heap on the stage, illustrating the end of their dominance over the blacks and their inability to continue imposing their view of color on other races.

Surrounding and complicating this action is another action. The actors are, it seems, members of a black revolutionary group, and one of their members, Newport News, dressed in sweater and jeans, spends most of the play offstage attending (presumably) the trial of a black leader who has betrayed the revolutionary group. He reports in from time to time on the progress of the outer action and, finally, near the end arrives to announce that the trial is over, the malefactor executed, and a new leader selected. The actors can now go because they are no longer needed. "As for you," he tells the cast, "you were only present for display."

In voice, the characters slip back and forth from the formal rhetoric called for by their stage roles (a rhetoric varying from parody of white political and religious jargon to impassioned speeches of black protest)

209

to the rather casual, colloquial speech that signals either their workaday selves or their roles as part of the revolutionary cadre. There are hundreds of shifts of tone, requiring careful signaling on the actors' parts both to one another and to the audience as to what role they may be playing. For example, Virtue and Village, the central characters in the story that the blacks enact, have real difficulty both with their roles in the story and with their feelings toward one another as two members of the acting troupe. Virtue even tries to stop the inner play because she sees Village's role in it as fundamentally threatening to her.

When it was so brilliantly performed in 1966 in the United States with Roscoe Lee Browne, James Earl Jones, Godfrey Cambridge, and Cicely Tyson in the major roles, the play caused the same sort of confusion among the liberals that *The Balcony* had caused in Paris. Blacks liked the play because it was antiwhite; it seemed like a prophetic work advocating black power before figures like Eldridge Cleaver and Huey Newton had arrived on the scene. It irritated Norman Mailer because it didn't come out on the side of the blacks strongly enough. But it was never Genet's purpose to write a leftist play. Like *The Balcony*, *The Blacks* is a play that comes full circle on itself. Bernard Frechtman, Genet's English translator, explains in the show bill for the American production, "At the end, when the elaborate structure seems to be completed, we discover that there has been no plot at all, that the magician has been diverting us with ceremony itself."[16]

Perhaps Frechtman overstates the point. It may be better to say that each of the plots is equally illusory. The black revolution, like the revolution in *The Balcony*, is no more "real" than the diversions the actors have put on for us. Revolution, Genet hints, may be just another kind of theater. Thus we are driven to the inescapable conclusion that both what we have been calling life or reality and what we have been calling theater are kinds of games, games that can be played well or badly, performed with style and grace or performed clumsily and barbarically. So, to restore to the theater some dimension of reality, Peter Handke, the Austrian dramatist who so thoroughly shook the German theater world in the late sixties and early seventies, eliminated the play and left the audience only with the event or performance. "They will not experience a story," he says in the preface to *Kaspar*, his most famous play, "but watch a theatrical event."

The best introduction to Handke's world is his series of short plays, written in 1966, which he called *Sprechstücke*, or "speak-ins." In an interview with Artur Joseph, he said in reference to *Offending the Audience*, the first of these pieces:

. . . I wanted to show that the dramaturgy of the old plays did not satisfy me any more (that, indeed, it bores me, in the sense that the conventional events on stage are far removed from me). I couldn't stand the pretence of reality any more. I felt as if the actors were under a glass bell. My point was to use words to encircle the audience so they'd want to free themselves by heckling; they might feel naked and get involved. . . . This dramaturgy is a hundred years old; it runs behind the reality of the day like a rusty bicycle.[17]

In *Offending the Audience* Handke's four speakers tell the spectators, "You have the standard idea of two worlds. You have the standard idea of the world of the theater. You don't need this standard now. You are not attending a piece for the theater. . . . You feel the discomfort of being watched and addressed, since you came prepared to watch and make yourselves comfortable in the shelter of the dark."

Throughout the "play" the speakers contrast what they are enacting with the old theater, the old plays. "Everything that was played expressed something real. The play was not played for the play's sake but for the sake of reality. You were to discover a played reality behind the play." The only reality, Handke suggests, is the here and now of the performance. In the old plays, the playwrights presented the illusion of time; in *Offending the Audience* he presents the immediate and uncomfortable reality of time. If Weiss's *Marat/Sade* presents theater as reality and Genet's plays present reality as theater, Handke takes the next logical step. He presents theater as illusion, and he says that a new form must be developed if the audience is going to experience any true awareness of its own reality. Handke takes Brecht's theory of *Verfremdung* and applies it more vigorously than Brecht himself. He distances the audience from both the theater and the actors in order to make *their* thoughts and feelings the central experience of the play.

Thus in his first full-length play, *Kaspar* (1968), he introduces the text with the telling comment: "The play *Kaspar* does not show how IT REALLY IS OR REALLY WAS with Kaspar Hauser. It shows what IS POSSIBLE with someone." In other words, let us dispense with the old notion of theater telling us about reality in the sense of story and see theater as a medium for the exploration of immediate experience, in this case, the experience of learning to speak. Kaspar is not the Kaspar Hauser who was found wandering the streets of Nuremberg in 1928 repeating the single sentence, "I want to be a horseman like my father once was." Handke's Kaspar is a kind of everyman learning to speak, a child being socialized by the impersonal modern world. From the beginning he is taught to associate language with order. If he learns to speak according to the rules laid down by the prompters, he will have power over his environment. The chairs, the table, the closet are objects of terror to him until he learns their names. When he learns to make sentences about them, then he can rearrange them, place them in order, make them serve his purposes.

The first act dramatizes the process by which Kaspar is painfully, torturously stripped of his own sentence and then carefully programmed by the prompters to be a good citizen. "I am healthy and strong. I am honest and frugal. I am conscientious. I am industrious, reticent and modest. I am always friendly. I make no great demands . . . ," he tells us at the end of the act, apparently unaware of the irony. He is the perfect social being, adaptable to any situation, but without character. Earlier one of the programmers had told him: "you are normal once your story is no longer distinguishable from any other story," and so he is, until the presence and activities of the other Kaspars drive him step-by-step during the second act to feel pain, anguish, doubt, and confusion. Just before the end he realizes what Handke wants us as audience to understand also—"Already with my first sentence I was trapped."

As in Ionesco's *The Chairs*, Handke dramatizes the way in which language is manipulated by those in power to create social automatons—speech robots who can speak only in the way that they have been programmed. Richard Gilman summarizes the playwright's aim as follows: "His plays demonstrate how we operate with words and are operated upon by them; what they reject is language thought of as containing meanings requiring no further investigation, language employed to communicate pre-existing truths about the world and our natures."[18]

The term "pre-existing truths" is crucial, because that is one of the subjects with which this book is centrally concerned. The world of Beckett and Ionesco, the world of Weiss, Genet, Handke, and Stoppard, the world of the younger dramatists working on the edges of consciousness during the last two decades is not a world that can be depicted in the dramatic language of traditional realism. Neither the stage techniques nor the linguistic structures associated with realism allow the playwright the room to present his own vision of the shifting, confusing, subjective world we call "reality." Hence the term *antitheater*, first used in connection with the work of Ionesco and now employed, as in Ronald Hayman's book on the subject, to mean the use of "negative force directed against previous art" in order to "provide a valid alternative to realism."[19]

All of these playwrights use radical techniques to force the audience to reconsider its own view of what is real, to break down barriers between the conscious and the unconscious, theater and reality, acting, performing, and living. Some, such as Tom Stoppard in *The Real Thing* (1982), have been able to fuse elements of traditional theater with experimental techniques to hold audiences that have rejected the more radical playwrights. Others have been more consistently experimental. What they have in common is a determination to expand the reality of their audiences, to awaken distrust in their readers and spectators about the kind of cultural pap they are fed daily by politicians, the movies, television, and popular magazines. Part of a wider literary phenomenon that has come to be known as postmodernism, they are more difficult for us to understand than their immediate predecessors; but we ought to remember that they are no more difficult for us in the 1980s than Ibsen and Strindberg were for their audiences a hundred years ago, and they are really, in their own way, doing the same thing: trying to give us *more* reality, not less.

16

Reality and the Hero

> *If Rank, Camus, and Buber are right, man cannot stand
> alone, but has to reach out for support. If transference
> is a natural function of heroism, a necessary projection
> in order to stand life, death and oneself, the question
> becomes: what is* creative projection? *What is* life-
> enhancing *illusion?*

—Ernest Becker, *The Denial of Death*[1]

In the second half of *The Denial of Death*, Ernest Becker argues with great clarity and forcefulness that human beings cannot live without illusions. The issue is not "whether" but "what kind." His ideas may help us to put the heroes of modern drama into some kind of perspective as we bring this study to a close. Becker allows the individual three basic choices:

1.   *The normal.* "The essence of normality is the *refusal of reality*,"[2] says Becker. Normality means not asking embarrassing, unanswerable questions about life, it means keeping one's mind on the day-to-day problems of living as society maps these problems out for us, it means tranquilizing ourselves with the trivial. It is fundamentally the establishment of a complex defense system to keep out of consciousness those questions fundamentally disturbing to the equilibrium.
2.   *The neurotic.* In this category Becker would place those who, unable to maintain the "lies" needed to remain normal, have created dreams, fantasies, and other escape mechanisms to protect themselves from the threat of reality, which would otherwise destroy them.
3.   *The hero.* The hero, according to Becker, is one who knows that the final reality of life cannot be faced without some help and therefore creates "a second world, a world of humanly created meaning, a new reality that he can live, dramatize, nourish himself in." For the hero, illusion means "creative play at its highest level."[3]

Much of the confusion in modern drama stems from the difference between the second and third groups. Often the distinctions between madness and genius, neurosis and creativity, are not clear. The Father in

Six Characters, argues Eric Bentley, is clearly "mad." So are Henry IV and Ponza. They are, in R. D. Laing's terms, schizophrenics who have adopted special strategies to protect themselves from the engulfment or implosion of the world. They are like pieces of glass that require special packaging to keep from being shattered. The heroines of Tennessee Williams, Laura Wingfield and Blanche Dubois, along with Mary Tyrone in Eugene O'Neill's *Long Day's Journey*, seem to fit into this second category. The amount of alcohol consumed on the stage in American plays testifies to the difficulty normal people have maintaining their "lies" and to the struggle the neurotics have escaping into a more comfortable, protected world. There are few "heroes," in the sense that Becker uses the term, in American drama.

From Ibsen to the present, the major playwrights of the Western tradition have insisted on the need for heroism in that larger sense. Most of them would, I believe, agree with Becker's assessment. What has changed most between 1870 and the present is not the cry for "a world of humanly created meaning" but the vision of what that created meaning can be. What actually is a life-enhancing illusion, and what form can that illusion take? Answers to these questions have changed dramatically during the hundred or so years from *A Doll House* to the present.

During the first phase of its development, up to the beginning of World War I, modern drama is dominated by what Brustein calls a "messianic" vision. There is the sense not that God is dead but that we have been worshiping the wrong God. The emphasis is on *seeing*. In Ibsen, Strindberg, Chekhov, and Shaw there is the hope, however weakly articulated, that if we *see* deeply enough, we will change our lives. I have emphasized the Hegelianism of these writers, their hope that progress can be brought about by the creation of new work syntheses, deeper unions of male and female, body and spirit, practical power and spiritual vision. During this period the emphasis is much more on the remaking than the repudiation of the Christian vision. Much of the thrust in Ibsen and Shaw and late Strindberg is on the need to return to the "true" Christianity of the Gospels, which according to Shaw has never been tried, a Christianity that might be "honest enough to follow its own commandments,"[4] as Becker phrases it. Throughout this period we find strong emphasis on the capacity of human beings to change, to grow, to evolve. Christy Mahon grows to manhood in *The Playboy*, Vivie Warren chooses a higher morality, Don Juan opts for heaven, Nora leaves the Doll House, Dr. Stockmann stands alone, Strindberg's Stranger struggles on the road to Damascus and finally commits himself to the Father Confessor, Nina changes from a sea gull into an actress. Even where the heroes fail, as in

Ghosts or *The Master Builder* or *Miss Julie*, the concept of growth is central, and the playwright's affirmation of the need for change and its possibility is strong. The heroes, within this framework, are usually at odds with society, with the "normal" world; and at the end of their respective plays, as Michael Goldman emphasizes, they must usually leave their worlds—Caesar and Joan, Christy and Nora—or die—Hedda and Julie and Solness. "People don't do such things," says Judge Brack, and that is the whole point of the heroic vision in the plays of this period. Armed with a deeper vision of reality, the heroes cannot go back to what people "do." The heroes seem to know what they are doing; it is the world that does not understand.

In the second phase of modern drama, that which corresponds to Brustein's social phase, the heroes seem less certain. This period begins around the time of World War I with the plays of Pirandello and Brecht on the Continent, late Shaw in England, and early O'Neill in the United States. It continues through the forties and fifties in England and America with the work of T. S. Eliot, Arthur Miller, and Tennessee Williams. This phase ends with the appearance of absurdism, which as Rodney Simard's new study reminds us, "clearly indicated the need for a new form of expression in a postmodern world."[5]

It is a period of confusion and bifurcation, moving the tradition of Western literature both further to the left in a Marxist direction and further to the right in an individualistic, almost anarchistic direction. The heroes of the first phase seem larger, almost godlike, compared to the protagonists of this phase, whose selves are fragmented and uncertain. We think first of Pirandello's figures—Ponza, Henry, the Father—all of them looking for some way to protect the self, to authenticate the self, against the increasing barbarity of an uncivilized civilization. It is during this period that the heroes, if we can call them that, seem most dependent on vital lies for survival. "Humankind," Eliot reminds us, "cannot bear very much reality."

Only the saints can face it squarely, and there are few enough of them. The heroes grow smaller and more needy—Brecht's Mother Courage, Galileo, Shen Te, Grusha—more ordinary and less *extra*ordinary. "I am not Prince Hamlet," cries Eliot's Prufrock, and the burgeoning modern world echoes his cry in O'Neill's people, trapped by forces too big for them to control. Robert Mayo can never get beyond the horizon. The Tyrone family hangs on grimly, and the best of them, Edmund, can only stammer. They are "fog people," an apt image to contrast them with Ibsen's late heroes, who are climbers, who move up the glacier out of the fog below. In Pirandello, Brecht, and O'Neill there is more a cry for compassion, and less hope that people can change. Brecht's Marxism is based on the idea that morality is created by environment rather than vice versa. During the twenties and thirties Marx and Freud emerge as the twin patron saints of Western literature, and both tend to see the individual as the victim of impersonal forces rather than the creator of worlds. Willy Loman and Blanche Dubois are classic examples of such victims, Willy destroyed by what the competitive, capitalistic system has taught him he must believe about himself, and Blanche by social and psychological forces she can deal with only by being a traditional southern "lady." Eliot sees hope in the Christian faith, but his voice is a rare religious island in a widening sea of humanism and environmental determinism.

During the final phase, corresponding to Brustein's existential stage, two things happen: on the one hand, heroes become more human, more recognizable as the ordinary person; on the other, playwrights become so obsessed with presenting life in images of theatricality, role playing, and game playing that considerations of humanness become almost irrelevant. In the first group I would place Beckett and Ionesco; in the second, Pinter and Genet and, to some extent, Albee.

Beckett and Ionesco are fundamentally humanistic in their orientation, deriving their existential points of view from their experiences during the French resistance in World War II and from their philosophical kinship with writers like Sartre, Camus, and Heidegger. What they seem most concerned with is human dignity and the way in which those who content themselves with the tranquilization of the self by the trivial destroy their humanness in the process. Whether it is the Smiths and the Martins in Ionesco or Beckett's irrepressible but blind Winnie, the non-heroes of these two playwrights cling to the normal in order to keep out silence and death, the two inescapable components of reality. The most heroic figures in the plays of Beckett and Ionesco are those who confront the mystery of death and the riddle of existence with the least fuss—Hamm at the conclusion of *Endgame*, the woman in *Rockaby*, Berenger stripped of his support at the ends of *Rhinoceros* and *Exit the King*. Beckett and Ionesco, in a kind of paradox, create heroes who deny the possibility of heroism in Becker's sense. Is there such a thing as "life-enhancing illusion," as Becker calls it? The absurdist may very well be saying "no" and calling for human beings to accept their existential situations as the only reality there is. Those who accept the truth with most dignity are the true heroes. Life is absurd. We cannot deny its absurdity by fixing some illusory meaning upon it (like Godot); but we can live it humanly in the face of its absurdity. Beckett and Ionesco, especially Beckett, seem to call for a bare and simple existence, stripped of vital lies; and the bare, stripped form of Beckett's drama, particularly his most recent plays, becomes the theatrical image for his ethic.

Writers like Pinter and Genet we cannot call existential or humanistic in the same sense. Beckett, for all his pessimism, seems finally to affirm human dignity. We are affected with a profound sadness for the human condition by *Waiting for Godot* and *Endgame*. We are all Vladimir and Estragon waiting for Godot, we are all Berenger confronting the Killer. In the world of Pinter and Genet we are not given that kind of dignity, and if we identify with their figures, we do so with some misgiving. What strikes us most about the characters in their plays is the brilliance of their role playing. Layer after layer is created, and the joy of the actor is in the acting, the thrill of the audience in discovering each new role under the one we *thought* was real. The theatrical shocks of McCann and Goldberg grilling Stanley, the ringing of the alarm clock in *The Maids*, the Bishop's disrobing in *The Balcony*, the reversals of Spooner and Hirst in *No Man's Land* are almost without parallel in the plays written before the late fifties. It is the direction toward which Pirandello was moving—an insistence on life as a kind of theatrical enterprise, which is both mirrored and unmasked in theater. We can't call the illusions of Pinter's or Genet's characters vital lies, because the games that are left after one level of play is unveiled are no different from those that had been played before. The winner in a Pinter play, Quigley reminds us, is the one who can impose his or her idea of reality on the others. It is so, if I can make you believe it's so.

Albee, very much like Pinter in some ways, tries to present a more humanistic answer in *Virginia Woolf* by having George and Martha abandon their game at the end of the play. Games are unhealthy, and it is better, Albee seems to affirm, to face reality without them. But Pinter and Genet might respond that, even if it's better, it's not possible. Pinter sees role playing, game playing, as innate, as necessary, as continuing. It is, in *Betrayal*, a way of life. Much of the sadness in the important plays of the last two decades lies in the fact that games are being played for which the players are unprepared. "What's the game?" Mick asks Davies in *The Caretaker*. Stoppard's Rosencrantz and Guildenstern spend an entire play trying to figure out what the game is in *Rosencrantz and Guildenstern Are Dead*. It's as if characters have wandered onto sets where plays are already going on and are asked to improvise roles without scripts. It is a nightmare, tragic if you don't know what the rules are, and comic if you happen to be in charge. The metaphor of reality as play or reality as game seems to be the dominant image of our time, and it is fundamentally a much more cynical image than those of other periods. Perhaps it is appropriate that the president of the United States during the 1980s has been an actor, an accomplished performer whose public rituals have had enormous popular support. But what is real? Is the performance all there is? Is there to be no breakthrough to a reality underneath? Is the idea of a breakthrough itself outmoded, a part of modernism that must be relegated to Undershaft's scrap heap of old ideas?

Perhaps. But even as the games are being played, the lines learned, the dimensions of the set explored, there wanders onto the stage a player whose coming has not been expected. He looks around slowly and motions to each of the other characters. One by one they depart, and each of us is left alone to play the final scene. "Nothing to be done," says Estragon. But the tower is to be climbed, Hilda reminds us, and the car starts in Willy Loman's garage. "People don't do such things," says Judge Brack, but Hedda does, and Kattrin dies to save the town. How do you play that final scene, that unexpected scene that takes us unprepared? That was the favorite subject of the Elizabethan and Jacobean playwrights, and in the shifting, illusory, multimirrored world of modern drama, it is still the obligatory scene, the final reality to be played.

Notes

Preface

1. Ernest Becker, *The Denial of Death* (New York: The Free Press, 1973), iv.
2. Becker, 4.
3. Becker, 51.
4. Becker, 55.
5. Becker, 55.
6. Michael Goldman, "The Ghost of Joy: Reflections on Romanticism and the Forms of Modern Drama," in *Romantic and Modern: Revaluations of Literary Tradition*, ed. George Bornstein (Pittsburgh: University of Pittsburgh Press, 1977), 60.
7. Ruby Cohn, "Growing (Up?) with Godot," in *Beckett at 80/Beckett in Context*, ed. Enoch Brater (New York: Oxford University Press, 1986), 13.
8. Austin Quigley, *The Modern Stage and Other Worlds* (New York: Methuen, 1985), xii.

Chapter 1: Reality, Illusion, and the More Abundant Life

1. Michael Goldman, "Vitality and Deadness in Beckett's Plays," in *Beckett at 80/Beckett in Context*, ed. Enoch Brater (New York: Oxford University Press, 1986), 67.
2. Goldman, "The Ghost of Joy," 62.
3. Michael Goldman, *The Actor's Freedom* (New York: Viking Press, 1975), 65.
4. Arthur Miller, *The Theater Essays of Arthur Miller*, ed. Robert A. Martin (New York: Viking Press, 1978), 7.
5. Goldman, *The Actor's Freedom*, 55.

Chapter 2: Henrik Ibsen

1. Brian Johnston, *The Ibsen Cycle* (Boston: Twayne Publishers, 1975), 10–11.
2. James McFarlane, ed., *The Oxford Ibsen*, vol. 4 (London: Oxford University Press, 1960), 10.
3. Passages from *Emperor and Galilean* are from *The Oxford Ibsen*; those from *Brand* are from Michael Myer's translation (London: Methuen, 1967). The remaining passages are from Rolf Fjelde, *Ibsen: The Complete Major Prose Plays* (New York: New American Library, 1978).

4. Arthur Ganz, *Realms of the Self: Variations on a Theme in Modern Drama* (New York: New York University Press, 1980), 153.

5. James McFarlane, ed., *Henrik Ibsen: A Critical Anthology* (Harmondsworth (England): Penguin Books, 1970), 78.

6. McFarlane, *Henrik Ibsen*, 78.

7. Ganz, *Realms of the Self*, 156.

8. Quoted in Michael Myer, *Henrik Ibsen* (New York: Doubleday, 1971), 541.

9. Fjelde, 493.

10. Keith May, *Ibsen and Shaw* (New York: St. Martin's Press, 1985), 76.

11. R. D. Laing, *The Politics of Experience* (New York: Pantheon Books, 1967), 101.

12. May, 89.

Chapter 3: August Strindberg

1. August Strindberg, *Letters of Strindberg to Harriet Bosse*, ed. and trans. Arvid Paulson (New York: Grosset and Dunlap, 1959), 87–88.

2. Michael Myer, *Strindberg* (New York: Random House, 1985), 72ff.

3. Quotations from *The Father, Miss Julie, Easter, A Dream Play*, and *The Ghost Sonata* are from *Six Plays of Strindberg*, trans. Elizabeth Sprigge (New York: Anchor Books, 1955). Passages from *To Damascus*, Part I, and *There Are Crimes and Crimes* are from Evert Sprinchorn, ed., *The Genius of the Scandinavian Theater* (New York: New American Library, 1964).

4. For a series of fascinating examples of how Strindberg uses Nietzsche, see Myer, *Strindberg*, 204–7.

5. Gunnar Brandell, "Toward a New Art Form," in *The Genius of the Scandinavian Theater*, ed. Evert Sprinchorn (New York: New American Library, 1964), 597.

6. Eric Bentley, "The Ironic Strindberg," in *The Genius of the Scandinavian Theater*, ed. Evert Sprinchorn (New York: New American Library, 1964), 601.

7. Gunnar Ollen, *August Strindberg* (New York: Frederick Ungar Publishing Company, 1972), 12.

8. Maurice Valency, *The Flower and the Castle* (New York: Universal Library, 1966), 328.

9. Strindberg, *Letters*, 129–30.

10. Strindberg, *Letters*, 48.

11. Quigley, *The Modern Stage*, 141.

Chapter 4: Anton Chekhov

1. David Magarshack, *Chekhov the Dramatist* (New York: Hill and Wang, 1960), 159ff.

2. Quoted in Ronald Hingley, *Chekhov* (London: Allen & Unwin, 1950), 234.

3. Harvey Pitcher, *The Chekhov Play: A New Interpretation* (London: Chatto and Windus, 1973).

4. Ganz, *Realms of the Self*, 40.

5. Quoted in Daniel Gilles, *Chekhov: Observer Without Illusion* (New York: Funk & Wagnalls, 1968), 368.

6. All passages from the plays are from the translation of Ann Dunnigan, *Chekhov: The Major Plays* (New York: New American Library, 1964).

7. Ganz, *Realms of the Self*, 40.

8. Richard Peace, *Chekhov: A Study of the Four Major Plays* (New Haven, Conn.: Yale University Press, 1983).

9. Both the texts of the letters to Suvorin relating to the Sakhalin trip and a fascinating account of the trip itself may be found in Ernest Simmons, *Chekhov: A Biography* (Chicago: University of Chicago Press, 1962), 203–35.

10. Anton Chekhov, *Letters of Anton Chekhov*, ed. Avrahn Yarmolinsky (New York: Viking Press, 1973), 209.

11. Chekhov, 226.

12. Ganz, *Realms of the Self*, 40.

13. Chekhov, 115.

14. Chekhov, 170.

15. Christopher Fry, "Comedy," in *Comedy: Meaning and Form*, ed. Robert W. Corrigan (San Francisco: Chandler Publishing Company, 1965), 15.

Chapter 5: George Bernard Shaw

1. Alfred Turco, Jr., *Shaw's Moral Vision: The Self and Salvation* (Ithaca, N.Y.: Cornell University Press, 1976). Warren Sylvester Smith, *Bishop of Everywhere: Bernard Shaw and the Life Force* (University Park, Pa.: Pennsylvania State University Press, 1982).

2. The most complete study of Shaw's philosophy is Smith's, mentioned above, but Arthur Ganz presents an excellent brief summation in *George Bernard Shaw* (New York: Grove Press, 1983), 38–53.

3. Warren Sylvester Smith, 71.

4. George Bernard Shaw, *The Quintessence of Ibsenism* (New York: Hill and Wang, undated), 40.

5. Northrop Frye's ideas may be found in the chapter "Comedy: The Mythos of Spring," in *Anatomy of Criticism* (Princeton, N.J.: Princeton University Press, 1962).

6. What I have called the higher reality may be embodied by either males or females, but renunciation of sexual love seems to accompany the journey to that wisdom. We see it in Vivie Warren, to some extent in Ellie Dunn, and in Joan of Arc, as well as in such male figures as Marchbanks, Don Juan, Undershaft, Shotover, and the Ancients of *Back to Methuselah*.

7. A detailed analysis of the relation between Shaw's ideas and those of

Teilhard de Chardin may be found in Warren Sylvester Smith, *Bishop of Everywhere*.

8. Ganz, *Realms of the Self*, 84.

9. Lewis Thomas, "On the Uncertainty of Science," *Harvard Magazine*, September–October 1980, 19–22.

Chapter 6: John Millington Synge

1. Maurice Bourgeois's position is expressed in *John Millington Synge and the Irish Theatre* (New York: Benjamin Blom, 1965), 220–21; Alan Price's in *Synge and Anglo-Irish Drama* (London: Methuen, 1961), 77. Donna Gerstenberger's summary of the issue is in *John Millington Synge* (New York: Twayne Publishers, 1964), 58; Weldon Thornton's in *J. M. Synge and the Western Mind* (Gerards Cross, Bucks: Colin Smythe, 1979), 127–41. Thornton refers directly to both Price's and Gerstenberger's arguments to build his own.

2. Ganz, *Realms of the Self*, 35: "And from the beginning of Synge's work the literal discomforts and insecurities of the life of a beggar or tramp become symbols of the painful spiritual exile of the artist, separated from the bourgeois world, seeking a realm of permanence and beauty." Martin and Mary are not artists of the same caliber as Nora Burke and Christy Mahon, but they are poets of a sort, creating their selves out of their own imaginations, even if they know those selves are fictions.

3. Gerstenberger, 55.

4. Thornton, 141. Thornton's entire fifth chapter, pages 127–41, is an extremely useful discussion of the reality-illusion theme in these two plays. He also handles the theme of language in *The Playboy* effectively.

Chapter 7: Luigi Pirandello

1. Roger Oliver, *Dreams of Passion: The Theater of Luigi Pirandello* (New York: New York University Press, 1979), x.

2. For the first four plays I have used the translations in *Naked Masks*, ed. Eric Bentley (New York: E. P. Dutton, 1958). For *Tonight We Improvise* I have used the version of Marta Abba in *Eleven Plays: An Introduction to Drama*, ed. Gerald Weales (New York: W. W. Norton, 1964).

3. Susan Bassnett-McGuire, *Luigi Pirandello* (New York: Grove Press, 1983), 75.

4. Oliver, 52.

5. Eric Bentley, *The Theater of War* (New York: Viking Press, 1973), 45–46.

6. Robert Brustein, *The Theatre of Revolt* (Boston: Little, Brown, 1964), 308.

7. Oliver, 68.

8. Bentley, *The Theater of War*, 52.

9. Ganz, *Realms of the Self*, 174.

10. Bentley, *The Theater of War*, 56–57.
11. Oliver, 77.
12. Oliver, 97.

Chapter 8: Bertolt Brecht

1. Quigley, *The Modern Stage*, 146.
2. Quotes from Brecht's plays are taken from the Eric Bentley editions of the individual plays, published by Grove Press, except for *In the Swamp* and *Saint Joan of the Stockyards* from *Seven Plays*, ed. Eric Bentley (New York: Grove Press, 1961).
3. Bertolt Brecht, *Brecht on Theatre*, ed. John Willet (New York: Hill and Wang, 1964), 37.
4. Quigley reproduces the table and comments interestingly on its implications in *The Modern Stage*, 148–49.
5. Brecht's passage and Martin Esslin's analysis of it are from *Brecht: A Choice of Evils*, 4th ed. (London: Methuen, 1984), 7.
6. Brecht, 23.
7. Frederic Ewen, *Bertolt Brecht: His Life, His Art, and His Times* (New York: Citadel Press, 1967), 175.
8. Brecht, 220.
9. Brecht, 229.
10. Ewen, 342.
11. Eric Bentley, *The Brecht Commentaries* (New York: Grove Press, 1981), 179.
12. Quigley, *The Modern Stage*, 146.
13. Ronald Hayman, *Brecht: A Biography* (New York: Oxford University Press, 1983), 4.

Chapter 9: T. S. Eliot

1. Michael Goldman, "Fear in the Way: The Design of Eliot's Drama," in *Eliot in His Time*, ed. A. Walton Litz (Princeton, N.J.: Princeton University Press, 1973), 164–65.
2. T. S. Eliot, *Selected Prose* (Harmondsworth (England): Penguin Books, 1953), 79.
3. Carol H. Smith, *T. S. Eliot's Dramatic Theory and Practice* (Princeton, N.J.: Princeton University Press, 1963), 238.
4. Carol H. Smith, 238.
5. For a fascinating discussion of Eliot's use of ghosts both here and in his other plays, see Goldman, "Fear in the Way," 155–80.

Chapter 10: Eugene O'Neill

1. Biographical information in this chapter is drawn from Louis Sheaffer's monumental books: *O'Neill: Son and Playwright* (London: J. M. Dent, 1968) and *O'Neill: Son and Artist* (Boston: Little, Brown, 1973).

2. Robert F. Whitman, "O'Neill's Search for a 'Language of the Theatre,'" in *O'Neill*, ed. John Gassner (Englewood Cliffs, N.J.: Prentice Hall, 1964), 144–45.

3. Whitman, 143.

4. Tom Driver, "On the Late Plays of Eugene O'Neill," in *O'Neill*, ed. John Gassner (Englewood Cliffs, N.J.: Prentice Hall, 1964), 121.

5. Reproduced in Oscar Cargill et al., eds., *O'Neill and His Plays: Four Decades of Criticism* (New York: New York University Press, 1961), 115.

6. Doris Falk, *Eugene O'Neill and the Tragic Tension* (New Brunswick, N.J.: Rutgers University Press, 1958), 67.

7. Letter reproduced in Cargill, 125–26.

8. From the manuscript "On Masks" in the Yale Collection. Quoted in C. W. E. Bigsby, *A Critical Introduction to Twentieth-Century American Drama*, vol. 1, 1900–1940 (Cambridge (England): Cambridge University Press, 1982), 67.

9. Eugene O'Neill, "On *The Great God Brown*," New York *Post*, 13 February 1926.

10. Jerzy Grotowski, *Towards a Poor Theatre* (New York: Simon & Schuster, 1968), 123.

11. Whitman, 160.

12. C. W. E. Bigsby, *A Critical Introduction to Twentieth-Century American Drama*, vol. 2 (Cambridge (England): Cambridge University Press, 1984), 208.

13. Bentley's analysis is most easily found in *The Theater of War*, 87–92; Bigsby's, in *Critical Introduction*, vol. 1, 89–90.

14. Bigsby, *Critical Introduction*, vol. 1, 90.

15. Edwin Engel, *The Haunted Heroes of Eugene O'Neill* (Cambridge, Mass.: Harvard University Press, 1953), 277.

16. Bigsby, *Critical Introduction*, vol. 1, 105.

17. Bigsby, *Critical Introduction*, vol. 1, 102.

Chapter 11: Arthur Miller and Tennessee Williams

1. Arthur Miller, *Collected Plays* (New York: Viking Press, 1957), 23.

2. Bigsby, *Critical Introduction*, vol. 2, 162.

3. Bigsby, *Critical Introduction*, vol. 2, 8.

4. Miller, *The Theater Essays*, 4.

5. Miller, *The Theater Essays*, 4.

6. Ganz, *Realms of the Self*, 135.

7. Bigsby, *Critical Introduction*, vol. 2, 208.

8. Bigsby, *Critical Introduction*, vol. 2, 205.

9. Bigsby, *Critical Introduction*, vol. 2, 227.

10. Miller, *The Theater Essays*, 4.

11. Tennessee Williams, interview, *Life*, 16 February 1948.

12. Ganz, *Realms of the Self*, 110.

13. Bigsby, *Critical Introduction*, vol. 2, 16.

14. Robert Hatch, review of *Cat on a Hot Tin Roof*, by Tennessee Williams, *Nation* 180 (9 April 1955): 341.

15. From the playwright's papers at the University of Texas, reproduced in Bigsby, *Critical Introduction*, vol. 2, 70.

16. Foster Hirsch, *A Portrait of the Artist: The Plays of Tennessee Williams* (Port Washington, N.Y.: Kennikat Press, 1979), 31.

17. For an excellent account of Brando's performance and its impact on the audience's perception of the characters, see Harold Clurman's review in *Lies Like Truth: Theatre Reviews and Essays* (New York: Macmillan, 1958), 72–80.

18. Tennessee Williams, "Note of Explanation," in *Cat on a Hot Tin Roof* (New York: New American Library, 1958), 125.

19. Williams, "Note of Explanation," 125.

20. Signi Falk, *Tennessee Williams* (New York: Twayne Publishers, 1961), 103.

21. Harold Clurman, review of *The Rose Tattoo*, by Tennessee Williams, *The New Republic* 124 (19 February 1951): 72.

22. Tennessee Williams, *Memoirs* (Garden City, N.Y.: Doubleday, 1975), 125.

Chapter 12: Samuel Beckett and Eugène Ionesco

1. Quoted by Ruby Cohn in "Growing (Up?) with Godot," 13.

2. Quoted in Martin Esslin, *The Theatre of the Absurd*, rev. ed. (Garden City, N.Y.: Doubleday Anchor Books, 1969), 38.

3. Quoted in Goldman, "Vitality and Deadness," 68.

4. Goldman, "Vitality and Deadness," 69.

5. Quoted in June Schlueter, *Metafictional Characters in Modern Drama* (New York: Columbia University Press, 1979), 63.

6. Schlueter, 63.

7. Esslin, *The Theatre of the Absurd*, 162.

8. Quigley, *The Modern Stage*, 194.

9. Esslin, *The Theatre of the Absurd*, 163. All quotations from the plays of Ionesco are from the standard English language versions published in the United States by Grove Press.

10. Tom Bishop, "Ionesco on Olympus," *Saturday Review*, 16 May 1970, 21.

11. Quoted by Edmund White in review of *The Hermit*, by Eugène Ionesco, *The New York Times Book Review*, 27 October 1974, 6.

12. Quoted in Esslin, *The Theatre of the Absurd*, 5.

13. Cohn, "Growing (Up?) with Godot," 23.

Chapter 13: Edward Albee

1. Alan Schneider, interview, New York *Post*, 31 January 1980.
2. Michael Rutenberg, *Edward Albee: Playwright in Protest* (New York: Drama Book Specialists, 1969), 239.
3. Edward Albee, interview with Guy Flatley, *The New York Times*, 18 April 1971, sec. 2, 10.
4. Bigsby, *Critical Introduction*, vol. 2, 267.
5. Ann Paolucci, *From Tension to Tonic: The Plays of Edward Albee* (Carbondale: Southern Illinois University Press, 1972), 96–97.
6. Rutenberg, 134.
7. Bigsby wisely does not take sides but does an excellent job of presenting a variety of possibilities and commentaries by Albee, by the director of the original production, John Gielgud, and by Irene Worth, who played Alice. See *Critical Introduction*, vol. 2, 284–86.
8. Edward Albee, interview, *Newsweek*, 29 May 1966.
9. Bigsby, *Critical Introduction*, vol. 2, 294.
10. Albee, *The New York Times*, 18 April 1971.
11. Albee, *The New York Times*, 18 April 1971.
12. Brendan Gill, review of *Seascape*, by Edward Albee, *The New Yorker*, 3 February 1975.
13. Henry Hewes, review of *Seascape*, by Edward Albee, *Saturday Review*, 8 March 1975.
14. Edward Albee, interview, *The New York Times*, 27 January 1980.
15. Albee, *The New York Times*, 27 January 1980.
16. Schneider, New York *Post*, 31 January 1980.

Chapter 14: Harold Pinter

1. Quoted in Martin Esslin, *Pinter: A Study of His Plays*, rev. ed. (New York: W. W. Norton, 1976), 38–39.
2. Esslin, *Pinter*, 45.
3. Esslin, *Pinter*, 44.
4. Harold Pinter, interview, London *Sunday Times*, 4 March 1962.
5. Reproduced in Esslin, *Pinter*, 40.
6. Austin Quigley, *The Pinter Problem* (Princeton, N.J.: Princeton University Press, 1975), 70.
7. Quigley, *The Pinter Problem*, 71.
8. Harold Pinter, interview with Kenneth Tynan, British Broadcasting Corporation, 28 October 1966.
9. Quigley, *The Pinter Problem*, 66.
10. Harold Hobson, review of *The Birthday Party*, by Harold Pinter, London *Sunday Times*, 25 May 1958.

11. Esslin, *Pinter*, 135.

12. Ganz, *Realms of the Self*, 214.

13. Ganz, *Realms of the Self*, 193.

14. Ganz, *Realms of the Self*, 210.

15. Quigley, *The Pinter Problem*, 276.

16. Quigley, *The Modern Stage*, 245. Quigley's detailed analysis of *Betrayal* in this book is extremely helpful and should be required reading for anyone interested in the play.

17. Harold Pinter, "A Play and Its Politics: A Conversation Between Harold Pinter and Nicholas Hern," introduction to *One for the Road* (New York: Grove Press, 1986), 8.

18. Pinter, "A Play and Its Politics," 8.

Chapter 15: Theater as Reality/Reality as Theater

1. June Schlueter, *Metafictional Characters in Modern Drama*.

2. The following translations have been used in this chapter: for *Marat/Sade*, the English version by Geoffrey Skelton and Adrian Mitchell (New York: Atheneum, 1965); for Genet, the Bernard Frechtman translations published by Grove Press; for Handke, *Kaspar and Other Plays*, Michael Roloff, trans. (New York: Farrar, Straus & Giroux, 1969).

3. Thomas R. Whitaker, *Fields of Play in Modern Drama* (Princeton, N.J.: Princeton University Press, 1977), 12.

4. Ruby Cohn, *Currents in Contemporary Drama* (Bloomington: Indiana University Press, 1969), 218.

5. Quoted in Martin Esslin, *Antonin Artaud* (Baltimore: Penguin Books, 1977), 106.

6. R. D. Laing, *The Divided Self* (Baltimore: Penguin Books, 1965), 11–12.

7. Peter Brook, *The Empty Space* (New York: Avon Books, 1968), 22.

8. Cohn, *Currents*, 222.

9. Esslin, *Artaud*, 86.

10. Quoted in Esslin, *Artaud*, 89.

11. Goldman, "Vitality and Deadness," 68.

12. Jean Paul Sartre, introduction to *The Maids*, by Jean Genet (New York: Grove Press, 1954), 8.

13. Cohn, *Currents*, 233.

14. Quoted in Richard N. Coe, ed., *The Theater of Jean Genet: A Casebook* (New York: Grove Press, 1970), 241.

15. Quoted in Coe, 94.

16. Quoted in Coe, 127.

17. Peter Handke, interview, *The Drama Review* 15:1 (1970), 57–59.

18. Richard Gilman, *The Making of Modern Drama* (New York: Farrar, Straus & Giroux, 1974), 270–71.

19. Ronald Hayman, *Theatre and Anti-Theatre* (New York: Oxford University Press, 1979), 241.

Chapter 16: Reality and the Hero

1. Becker, 158.
2. Becker, 178.
3. Becker, 189.
4. Becker, 204.
5. Rodney Simard, *Postmodern Drama: Contemporary Playwrights in America and Britain* (University Press of America, 1984), x.

Bibliography

Albee, Edward. Interview with Guy Flatley. *The New York Times*, 18 April 1971.
———. Interview. *The New York Times*, 27 January 1980.
———. Interview. *Newsweek*, 29 May 1966.
Bassnett-McGuire, Susan. *Luigi Pirandello*. New York: Grove Press, 1983.
Becker, Ernest. *The Denial of Death*. New York: The Free Press, 1973.
Bentley, Eric. *The Brecht Commentaries*. New York: Grove Press, 1981.
———. "The Ironic Strindberg." In *The Genius of the Scandinavian Theatre*, ed. Evert Sprinchorn, 599–603. New York: New American Library, 1964.
———. *The Playwright as Thinker*. Rev. ed. New York: Meridian Books, 1955.
———. *The Theater of War*. New York: Viking Press, 1973.
Bigsby, C. W. E. *A Critical Introduction to Twentieth-Century American Drama*. Vol. 1, 1900–1940. Cambridge (England): Cambridge University Press, 1982.
———. *A Critical Introduction to Twentieth-Century American Drama*. Vol. 2. Cambridge (England): Cambridge University Press, 1984.
Bishop, Tom. "Ionesco on Olympus." *Saturday Review*, 16 May 1970.
Bornstein, George, ed. *Romantic and Modern: Revaluations of Literary Tradition*. Pittsburgh: University of Pittsburgh Press, 1977.
Bourgeois, Maurice. *John Millington Synge and the Irish Theatre*. New York: Benjamin Blom, 1965.
Brandell, Gunnar. "Toward a New Art Form." In *The Genius of the Scandinavian Theatre*, ed. Evert Sprinchorn, 583–98. New York: New American Library, 1964.
Brater, Enoch, ed. *Beckett at 80/Beckett in Context*. New York: Oxford University Press, 1986.
Brecht, Bertolt. *Brecht on Theatre*. Ed. John Willet. New York: Hill and Wang, 1964.
Brook, Peter. *The Empty Space*. New York: Avon Books, 1968.
Brustein, Robert. *Theatre of Revolt*. Boston: Little, Brown, 1964.
Cargill, Oscar, et al., eds. *O'Neill and His Plays: Four Decades of Criticism*. New York: New York University Press, 1961.
Chekhov, Anton. *Letters of Anton Chekhov*. Ed. Avrahn Yarmolinsky. New York: Viking Press, 1973.
Clurman, Harold. Review of *The Rose Tattoo*, by Tennessee Williams. *The New Republic* 124 (19 February 1951): 72.
———. Review of *A Streetcar Named Desire*, by Tennessee Williams. In *Lies Like Truth: Theatre Reviews and Essays*. New York: Macmillan, 1958.

Bibliography

Coe, Richard N., ed. *The Theater of Jean Genet: A Casebook*. New York: Grove Press, 1970.

Cohn, Ruby. "Growing (Up?) with Godot." In *Beckett at 80/Beckett in Context*, ed. Enoch Brater, 13–24. New York: Oxford University Press, 1986.

———. *Currents in Contemporary Drama*. Bloomington: Indiana University Press, 1969.

Driver, Tom. "On the Late Plays of Eugene O'Neill." In *O'Neill*, ed. John Gassner, 110–23. Englewood Cliffs, N.J.: Prentice Hall, 1964.

Eliot, T. S. *Selected Prose*. Harmondsworth (England): Penguin Books, 1953.

Engel, Edwin. *The Haunted Heroes of Eugene O'Neill*. Cambridge, Mass.: Harvard University Press, 1953.

Esslin, Martin. *Antonin Artaud*. Baltimore: Penguin Books, 1977.

———. *Brecht: A Choice of Evils*. 4th ed. London: Methuen, 1984.

———. *Pinter: A Study of His Plays*. Rev. ed. New York: W. W. Norton, 1976.

———. *The Theatre of the Absurd*. Rev. ed. Garden City, N.Y.: Doubleday Anchor Books, 1969.

Ewen, Frederic. *Bertolt Brecht: His Life, His Art, and His Times*. New York: Citadel Press, 1967.

Falk, Doris. *Eugene O'Neill and the Tragic Tension*. New Brunswick, N.J.: Rutgers University Press, 1958.

Falk, Signi. *Tennessee Williams*. New York: Twayne Publishers, 1961.

Fjelde, Rolf. *Ibsen: The Complete Major Prose Plays*. New York: New American Library, 1978.

Fry, Christopher. "Comedy." In *Comedy: Meaning and Form*, ed. Robert W. Corrigan, 15–17. San Francisco: Chandler Publishing Company, 1965.

Frye, Northrop. *Anatomy of Criticism*. Princeton, N.J.: Princeton University Press, 1962.

Ganz, Arthur. *George Bernard Shaw*. New York: Grove Press, 1983.

———. *Realms of the Self: Variations on a Theme in Modern Drama*. New York: New York University Press, 1980.

Gassner, John, ed. *O'Neill*. Englewood Cliffs, N.J.: Prentice Hall, 1964.

Gerstenberger, Donna. *John Millington Synge*. New York: Twayne Publishers, 1964.

Gill, Brendan. Review of *Seascape*, by Edward Albee. *The New Yorker*, 3 February 1975.

Gilles, Daniel. *Chekhov: Observer Without Illusion*. New York: Funk & Wagnalls, 1968.

Gilman, Richard. *The Making of Modern Drama*. New York: Farrar, Straus & Giroux, 1974.

Goldman, Michael. *The Actor's Freedom*. New York: Viking Press, 1975.

———. "Fear in the Way: The Design of Eliot's Drama." In *Eliot in His Time*, ed. A. Walton Litz, 155–80. Princeton, N.J.: Princeton University Press, 1973.

———. "The Ghost of Joy: Reflections on Romanticism and the Forms of Modern Drama." In *Romantic and Modern: Revaluations of Literary Tradition*, ed. George Bornstein, 53–68. Pittsburgh: University of Pittsburgh Press, 1977.

231

Bibliography

————. "Vitality and Deadness in Beckett's Plays." In *Beckett at 80/Beckett in Context*, ed. Enoch Brater, 67–83. New York: Oxford University Press, 1986.

Grotowski, Jerzy. *Towards a Poor Theatre*. New York: Simon & Schuster, 1968.

Handke, Peter. Interview. *The Drama Review* 15:1 (1970), 57–59.

Hatch, Robert. Review of *Cat on a Hot Tin Roof*, by Tennessee Williams. *Nation* 180 (9 April 1955): 341.

Hayman, Ronald. *Brecht: A Biography*. New York: Oxford University Press, 1983.

————. *Theatre and Anti-Theatre*. New York: Oxford University Press, 1979.

Hewes, Henry. Review of *Seascape*, by Edward Albee. *Saturday Review*, 8 March 1975.

Hingley, Ronald. *Chekhov*. London: Allen & Unwin, 1950.

Hirsch, Foster. *A Portrait of the Artist: The Plays of Tennessee Williams*. Port Washington, N.Y.: Kennikat Press, 1979.

Hobson, Harold. Review of *The Birthday Party*, by Harold Pinter. London *Sunday Times*, 25 May 1958.

Johnston, Brian. *The Ibsen Cycle*. Boston: Twayne Publishers, 1975.

Laing, R. D. *The Divided Self*. Baltimore: Penguin Books, 1965.

————. *The Politics of Experience*. New York: Pantheon Books, 1967.

McFarlane, James, ed. *Henrik Ibsen: A Critical Anthology*. Harmondsworth (England): Penguin Books, 1970.

————. *The Oxford Ibsen*. Vol. 4. London: Oxford University Press, 1960.

Magarshack, David. *Chekhov the Dramatist*. New York: Hill and Wang, 1960.

May, Keith. *Ibsen and Shaw*. New York: St. Martin's Press, 1985.

Miller, Arthur. *Collected Plays*. New York: Viking Press, 1957.

————. *The Theater Essays of Arthur Miller*. Ed. Robert A. Martin. New York: Viking Press, 1978.

Myer, Michael. *Henrik Ibsen*. New York: Doubleday, 1971.

————. *Strindberg*. New York: Random House, 1985.

Oliver, Roger. *Dreams of Passion: The Theater of Luigi Pirandello*. New York: New York University Press, 1979.

Ollen, Gunnar. *August Strindberg*. New York: Frederick Ungar Publishing Company, 1972.

O'Neill, Eugene. "On *The Great God Brown*." New York *Post*, 13 February 1926.

Paolucci, Ann. *From Tension to Tonic: The Plays of Edward Albee*. Carbondale: Southern Illinois University Press, 1972.

Peace, Richard. *Chekhov: A Study of the Four Major Plays*. New Haven, Conn.: Yale University Press, 1983.

Pinter, Harold. Interview with Kenneth Tynan. British Broadcasting Corporation, 28 October 1966.

————. Interview. London *Sunday Times*, 4 March 1962.

————. "A Play and Its Politics: A Conversation Between Harold Pinter and Nicholas Hern." Introduction to *One for the Road*. New York: Grove Press, 1986.

Pitcher, Harvey. *The Chekhov Play: A New Interpretation*. London: Chatto and Windus, 1973.

Price, Alan. *Synge and Anglo-Irish Drama*. London: Methuen, 1961.

Quigley, Austin. *The Modern Stage and Other Worlds*. New York: Methuen, 1985.

Bibliography

————. *The Pinter Problem*. Princeton, N.J.: Princeton University Press, 1975.

Rutenberg, Michael. *Edward Albee: Playwright in Protest*. New York: Drama Book Specialists, 1969.

Sartre, Jean Paul. Introduction to *The Maids*, by Jean Genet. New York: Grove Press, 1954.

Schlueter, June. *Metafictional Characters in Modern Drama*. New York: Columbia University Press, 1979.

Schneider, Alan. Interview. New York *Post*, 31 January 1980.

————. *Entrances: An American Director's Journey*. New York: Viking Penguin, 1986.

Shaw, George Bernard. *The Quintessence of Ibsenism*. New York: Hill and Wang, undated.

Sheaffer, Louis. *O'Neill: Son and Artist*. Boston: Little, Brown, 1973.

————. *O'Neill: Son and Playwright*. London: J. M. Dent, 1968.

Simard, Rodney. *Postmodern Drama: Contemporary Playwrights in America and Britain*. University Press of America, 1984.

Simmons, Ernest. *Chekhov: A Biography*. Chicago: University of Chicago Press, 1962.

Smith, Carol H. *T. S. Eliot's Dramatic Theory and Practice*. Princeton, N.J.: Princeton University Press, 1963.

Smith, Warren Sylvester. *Bishop of Everywhere: Bernard Shaw and the Life Force*. University Park, Pa.: Pennsylvania State University Press, 1982.

Sprinchorn, Evert, ed. *The Genius of the Scandinavian Theater*. New York: New American Library, 1964.

Strindberg, August. *Letters of Strindberg to Harriet Bosse*. Ed. and trans. Arvid Paulson. New York: Grosset and Dunlap, 1959.

————. *Six Plays of Strindberg*. Trans. Elizabeth Sprigge. New York: Anchor Books, 1955.

Thomas, Lewis. "On the Uncertainty of Science." *Harvard Magazine,* September–October 1980, 19–22.

Thornton, Weldon. *J. M. Synge and the Western Mind.* Gerards Cross, Bucks: Colin Smythe, 1979.

Turco, Alfred, Jr. *Shaw's Moral Vision: The Self and Salvation.* Ithaca, N.Y.: Cornell University Press, 1976.

Valency, Maurice. *The Flower and the Castle.* New York: Universal Library, 1966.

Whitaker, Thomas R. *Fields of Play in Modern Drama.* Princeton, N.J.: Princeton University Press, 1977.

White, Edmund. Review of *The Hermit,* by Eugène Ionesco. *The New York Times Book Review,* 27 October 1974.

Whitman, Robert F. "O'Neill's Search for a 'Language of the Theatre.'" In *O'Neill,* ed. John Gassner, 142–64. Englewood Cliffs, N.J.: Prentice Hall, 1964.

Williams, Tennessee. Interview. *Life,* 16 February 1948.

————. *Memoirs.* Garden City, N.Y.: Doubleday, 1975.

————. "Note of Explanation." In *Cat on a Hot Tin Roof.* New York: New American Library, 1958.

Permissions

The following organizations have extended permission to quote material in this book:

The Society of Authors, on behalf of the Bernard Shaw Estate, for quotations from *Arms and the Man, Man and Superman, Caesar and Cleopatra, Major Barbara, Heartbreak House, Back to Methuselah,* and *Candida.*

Yale University Press, for quotations from Eugene O'Neill, *Long Day's Journey into Night.*

New Directions Publishing Corporation, for quotations from Tennessee Williams, *Streetcar Named Desire* (copyright 1947, Tennessee Williams); *Cat on a Hot Tin Roof* (copyright 1954, 1955, 1971, 1975, Tennessee Williams); *Night of the Iguana* (copyright 1961, Two Rivers Enterprises, Inc.).

Curtis Brown, Ltd., for quotations from *Six Plays of August Strindberg,* translated by Elizabeth Sprigge (copyright 1955, Elizabeth Sprigge).

NAL Penguin, Inc., New York, for quotations from *Chekhov: The Major Plays,* translated by Ann Dunnigan (copyright 1964, Ann Dunnigan); and Henrik Ibsen, *The Complete Major Prose Plays,* translated by Rolf Fjelde (copyright 1965, 1970, 1978, Rolf Fjelde).

E. P. Dutton, a division of NAL Penguin, Inc., for quotations from Luigi Pirandello, *Naked Masks: Five Plays,* edited by Eric Bentley (copyright 1922, 1952, E. P. Dutton; renewed 1950, in the names of Stefano, Fausto, and Lietta Pirandello; renewed 1980, Eric Bentley).

Harcourt Brace Jovanovich, Inc., for quotations from T. S. Eliot, *Murder in the Cathedral* (copyright 1935, Harcourt Brace Jovanovich, Inc.; renewed 1963, T. S. Eliot); *The Family Reunion* (copyright 1939, T. S. Eliot; renewed 1967, Esme Valerie Eliot); *The Cocktail Party* (copyright 1954, T. S. Eliot; renewed 1978, Esme Valerie Eliot); and *The Confidential Clerk* (copyright 1954, T. S. Eliot; renewed 1982, Esme Valerie Eliot).

Index

Index

237

Index

About the Author

Anthony S. Abbott is Professor of English at Davidson College. He received his bachelor's degree from Princeton University and his master's and doctorate from Harvard University. He is the author of *Shaw and Christianity* and books on *The Great Gatsby* and *The Invisible Man* in the Barron's Book Notes series.